Credits

Illustrators
Len Ebert
Carol Heyer
Susan Jaekel
Jane McCreary
Hetty Mitchell
D.J. Simison

Digital Illustrator
Marty Harris

Cartoon Illustrator
Steve Mark

Design
Leslie Anderson

Desktop Production
Leslie Anderson
Jack Ross

Consultants

Augusta DeSimone Clark
St. Mary's Hall
San Antonio, Texas

Michael Nettleton
Smoky Hill High School
Aurora, Colorado

Mirta Pagnucci
Oak Park River Forest High School
Oak Park, Illinois

Ann J. Sorrell
South Burlington High School
South Burlington, Vermont

Nathalie Gaillot
Language Specialist
Lyon, France

ISBN 978-0-82196-015-8

Printed in the United States of America
3 4 5 6 7 8 9 10 11   19 18 17 16 15 14 13 12

C'est à toi!

Second Edition

Authors

Karla Winther Fawbush

Toni Theisen

Dianne B. Hopen

Sarah Vaillancourt

Contributing Writers

Diana Moen

Linda Klohs

EMC Publishing

St. Paul • Indianapolis

To the Student

C'EST À TOI! (*It's Your Turn!*), as your book's title suggests, invites *you* to express yourself in French by interacting with your classmates. Either in pairs or in small groups, you'll be talking right away about subjects that interest both you and French-speaking teens: music, sports, leisure activities, food, etc. Don't hesitate to practice your French every chance you get both during and outside of class. You will make mistakes, but your ability to speak French and your confidence will improve with continued practice.

Bienvenue au monde francophone! (*Welcome to the French-speaking world!*) You are beginning an exciting journey of discovery. You will not only visit many of the countries where people speak French every day, but you will also learn how to communicate and interact with them. In addition, as you are exposed to new ways of thinking and living in other cultures, your horizons will widen to include different ways of seeing and evaluating the world around you. Learning how to speak French will not only open the door to the French-speaking world, it will give you a knowledge, insight and appreciation of French culture. Language and culture go hand in hand, and together they reflect the spirit of the francophone world. An appreciation of French culture helps you understand what we have in common with French speakers and how we differ. And learning about an important world culture and its language will help you appreciate your own culture and language even more.

People speak French well beyond the borders of France itself. More than 150 million people are native French speakers. On our continent, French speakers live in places like Louisiana, New England and Quebec. Besides in Europe, people also speak French in Africa and Asia, as well as in the Caribbean. Obviously, these diverse French speakers come from a wide variety of cultural backgrounds. Communicating with them will help you understand their way of life and give you a more global perspective. During your lifetime, you will hopefully be able to use your French as you visit at least one of these lands. But even if your travels abroad are limited to "living the language" in your classroom, you will be exposed to a new way of viewing the world.

Internationally, French is one of the primary languages, and people who speak and understand it are an asset in the world of work. Knowing French can expand your career options in areas such as international trade or law, investment, government service, technology and manufacturing. Multinational companies hire hundreds of thousands of Americans who have proficiency in at least one world language. Just knowing French will not assure you of the job you want, but, combined with another specialization, it will increase your employment opportunities. French may be the key that gives you the competitive edge in the global marketplace. Whatever your reasons for learning French, **bon voyage** as you begin to discover the culture and language of the French-speaking world, and **bonne chance** (*good luck*)!

Table of Contents

Unité 3 Au café 57

Unité 4 À l'école 99

Unité 5 En famille 135

Unité 6 Tu viens d'où? 175

Unité 7 On fait les magasins. 221

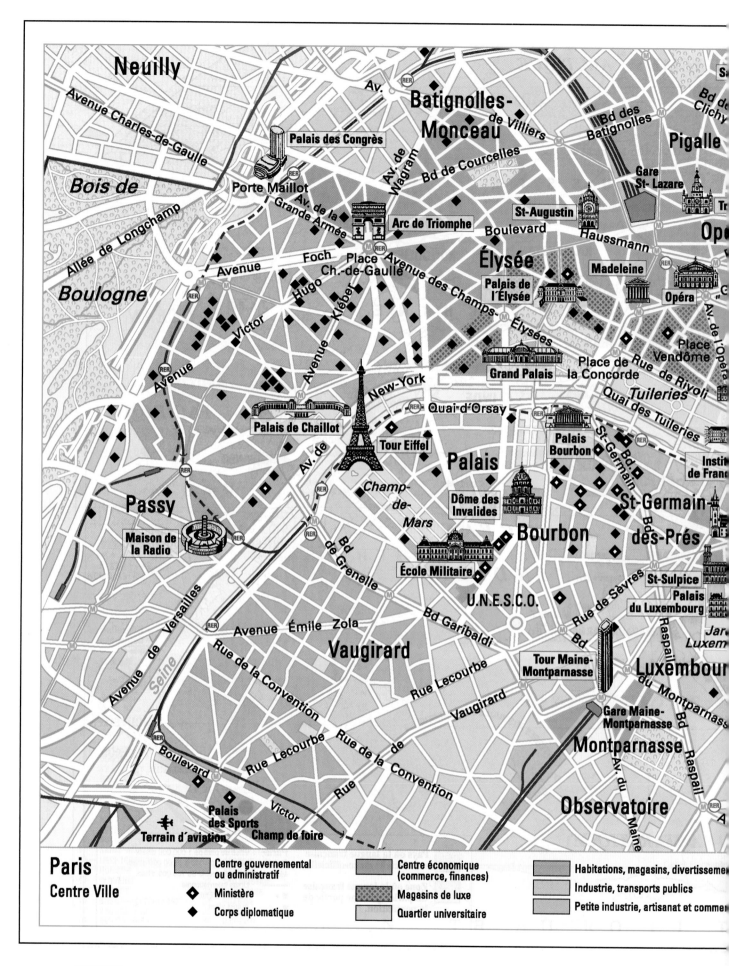

Paris
Centre Ville

Centre gouvernemental ou administratif

◇ Ministère

◆ Corps diplomatique

Centre économique (commerce, finances)

Magasins de luxe

Quartier universitaire

Habitations, magasins, divertissemen

Industrie, transports publics

Petite industrie, artisanat et commer

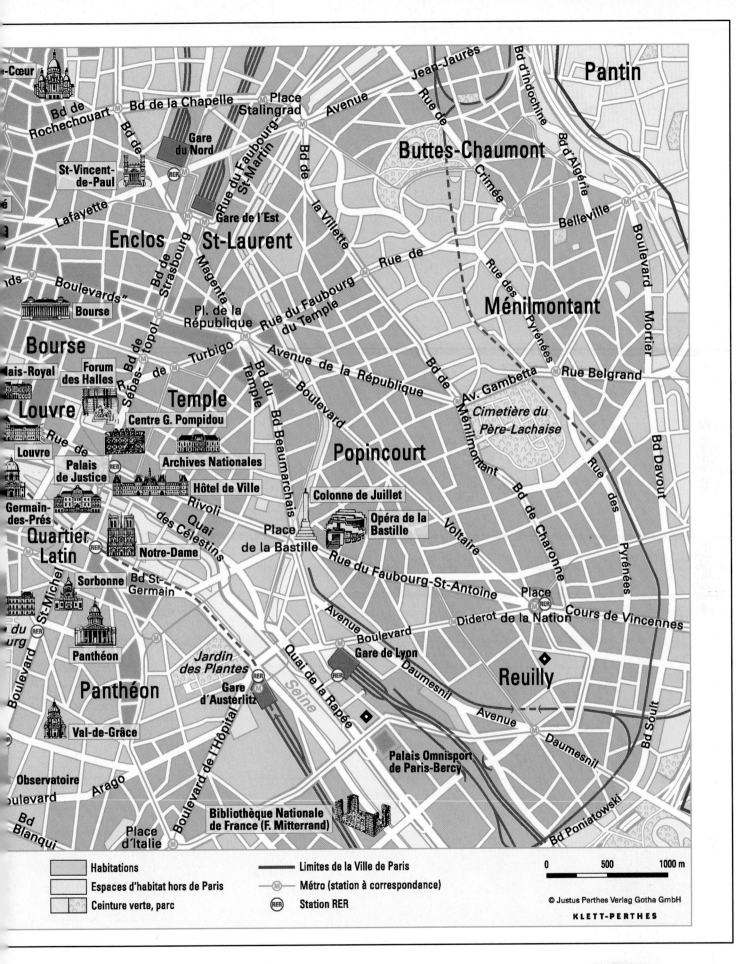

Pantin

Bd d'Indochine

Bd d'Algérie

Jean-Jaurès

Rue de

Buttes-Chaumont

Bd de la Chapelle
Place Stalingrad
Avenue

Bd de Rochechouart
-Cœur

St-Vincent-de-Paul

Gare du Nord

Crimée

Belleville

Boulevard Mortier

Lafayette

Bd de la Villette

Rue de

Bd de Strasbourg

Gare de l'Est

Ménilmontant

Enclos St-Laurent

Magenta

Rue des Pyrénées

Boulevards"

Bourse

Pl. de la République

Rue du Faubourg du Temple

Bourse

Bd de Sébastopol

Turbigo

Av. Gambetta

Rue Belgrand

ais-Royal
Forum des Halles

Temple

Avenue de la République

Cimetière du Père-Lachaise

Louvre

Rue de Sèb

Rue de

Centre G. Pompidou

Bd du Temple

Bd de Ménilmontant

Louvre

Archives Nationales

Bd Beaumarchais

Popincourt

Rue des

Palais de Justice

Hôtel de Ville

Boulevard

Germain-des-Prés

Rivoli

Colonne de Juillet

Voltaire

Bd de Charonne

Quai des Célestins

Opéra de la Bastille

Bd Davout

Quartier Latin

Notre-Dame

Place de la Bastille

Pyrénées

Sorbonne

Bd St-Germain

Rue du Faubourg-St-Antoine

Place de la Nation
Cours de Vincennes

St-Michel

Panthéon

Diderot

du urg

Avenue

Boulevard

Gare de Lyon

Reuilly

Panthéon

Jardin des Plantes

Boulevard

Daumesnil

Val-de-Grâce

Gare d'Austerlitz

Seine

Observatoire
oulevard

Arago

Quai de la Rapée

Boulevard de l'Hôpital

Avenue

Daumesnil

Bd Soult

Palais Omnisport de Paris-Bercy

Bd Blanqui

Place d'Italie

Bibliothèque Nationale de France (F. Mitterrand)

Bd Poniatowski

	Habitations		Limites de la Ville de Paris
	Espaces d'habitat hors de Paris	Ⓜ	Métro (station à correspondance)
	Ceinture verte, parc	RER	Station RER

0   500   1000 m

© Justus Perthes Verlag Gotha GmbH

KLETT-PERTHES

XIX

Unité

1

Salut! Ça va?

In this unit you will be able to:
- greet someone
- leave someone
- thank someone
- introduce yourself
- introduce someone else
- ask someone's name
- tell someone's name
- give telephone numbers
- restate information

www.emcp.com

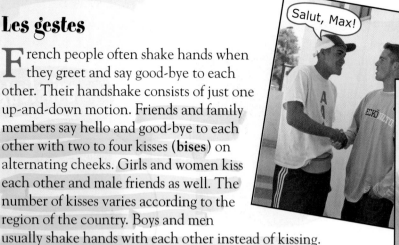

Les gestes

French people often shake hands when they greet and say good-bye to each other. Their handshake consists of just one up-and-down motion. Friends and family members say hello and good-bye to each other with two to four kisses (**bises**) on alternating cheeks. Girls and women kiss each other and male friends as well. The number of kisses varies according to the region of the country. Boys and men usually shake hands with each other instead of kissing.

Les salutations

French speakers change the way they talk depending on the situation. They will often use slang and casual speech when talking to friends and family. Teenagers will use more formal words with adults as a sign of respect. For example, a student would say hi to a friend with either **Salut** or **Bonjour**, but would generally say **Bonjour, Monsieur** (*Mr.*), **Bonjour, Madame** (*Mrs.*) or **Bonjour, Mademoiselle** (*Miss*) to a teacher. In writing, these titles are abbreviated as follows:

Monsieur = M.   **Madame = Mme**   **Mademoiselle = Mlle**

La cour

The school courtyard, **la cour**, is a very popular meeting place for French students between classes and before and after school. Teenagers talk with their friends and play games there.

Students meet in *la cour* before their classes begin. (Verneuil-sur-Seine)

1 ▸ Masculin ou féminin?

Write "M" if the speaker is talking to a male; write "F" if the speaker is talking to a female.

2 ▸ Répondez!

Answer the following questions.

1. What are three words for saying hello in French? Which one can you say only when talking on the phone?
2. What do boys do when they say hello to each other?
3. What do girls do when they say hello to friends?
4. Where can students meet between classes? Does your school have one?

3 ▸ Les présentations

Choisissez la bonne réponse. (Choose the correct answer.)

1. How does Abdou say hello to André?
   A. Pardon.
   B. Tiens.
   C. Salut.
2. How does André introduce Nadine to his friend?
   A. Je te présente Nadine.
   B. Je m'appelle Nadine.
   C. Bonjour, Nadine.
3. What does Abdou say when he doesn't hear Nadine's name?
   A. Eh....
   B. Tiens....
   C. Pardon....

4. What does Abdou say to Nadine to find out her name?
   A. Tu t'appelles comment?
   B. Je te présente Nadine.
   C. Je m'appelle Nadine.
5. How does Nadine give her name?
   A. Tu t'appelles comment?
   B. Je m'appelle Nadine.
   C. Je te présente Nadine.
6. What does Abdou say after meeting Nadine?
   A. Tiens, Nadine.
   B. Bonjour, Nadine.
   C. Eh, Nadine.

4 ▸ En français, s'il vous plaît!

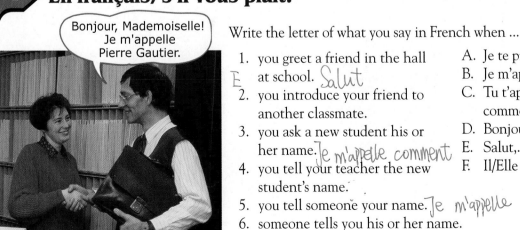

Bonjour, Mademoiselle! Je m'appelle Pierre Gautier.

Write the letter of what you say in French when ...

1. you greet a friend in the hall at school. *Salut* E
2. you introduce your friend to another classmate.
3. you ask a new student his or her name. *Je m'appelle comment*
4. you tell your teacher the new student's name.
5. you tell someone your name. *Je m'appelle*
6. someone tells you his or her name.

A. Je te présente....
B. Je m'appelle....
C. Tu t'appelles comment?
D. Bonjour,....
E. Salut,....
F. Il/Elle s'appelle....

Je m'appelle Anne.

Tu t'appelles comment?

Je m'appelle Malick.

prénoms de filles

Adja
Aïcha
Amina
(Anne)
Anne-Marie
Antonine
Arabéa
Ariane
Assia
Béatrice
Caroline
Catherine
Cécile
Chloé
Christine
Claudette
Clémence
Delphine
Denise
Diane
Élisabeth
Fatima
Florence
Françoise
Gilberte
Isabelle
Jamila
Jeanne
Karima
(Karine)
Laïla
Lamine
Latifa
Magali
Malika

Margarette
Marie
Marie-Alix
Martine
Michèle
Myriam
Nadia
Nadine
Nathalie
Nicole
Nora
Patricia
Renée
Sabrina
Saleh
Sandrine
Sonia
Sophie
Stéphanie
Sylvie
Valérie
Véronique (Véro)
Yasmine
(Zakia)
Zohra

Je m'appelle Zakia.

Je m'appelle Karine.

prénoms de garçons

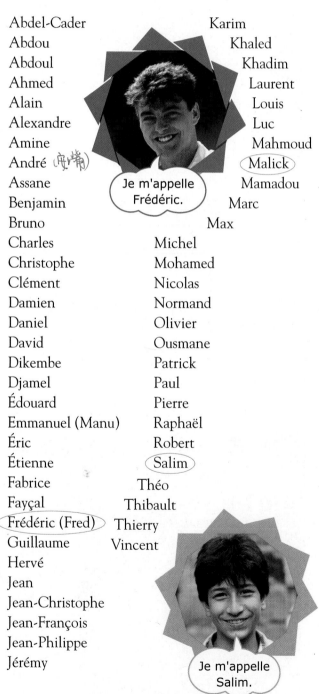

Abdel-Cader
Abdou
Abdoul
Ahmed
Alain
Alexandre
Amine
André (安端)
Assane
Benjamin
Bruno
Charles
Christophe
Clément
Damien
Daniel
David
Dikembe
Djamel
Édouard
Emmanuel (Manu)
Éric
Étienne
Fabrice
Fayçal
(Frédéric (Fred))
Guillaume
Hervé
Jean
Jean-Christophe
Jean-François
Jean-Philippe
Jérémy

Karim
Khaled
Khadim
Laurent
Louis
Luc
Mahmoud
(Malick)
Mamadou
Marc
Max
Michel
Mohamed
Nicolas
Normand
Olivier
Ousmane
Patrick
Paul
Pierre
Raphaël
Robert
(Salim)
Théo
Thibault
Thierry
Vincent

Je m'appelle Frédéric.

Je m'appelle Salim.

What's in a name?

First names can reflect a person's religious or cultural background. For example, children called Paul and Anne may have been named after saints, while the names Charles and Catherine may refer to former French royalty.

M. Dumont

Last names, or surnames, often explain where a family was from originally or the family's occupation. The name Dubois ("from the woods") means that the family lived near a forest; the name Meunier ("miller") indicates that the family milled flour.

Today, names reflect the multicultural makeup of French society. When looking up a last name in the phone book or on the Minitel (a telecommunication system), you will find family names from a variety of French-speaking countries and other areas of the world.

PACHOUTINSKY Alexandre . . 01 49 59 63 71
PAFUNDI Danièle 01 45 31 35 90
PAGANELLI Paul 01 40 44 55 08
PAGET Christèle 01 42 50 87 29
PAI Thérèse 01 43 58 26 61

Elle s'appelle Amina Senghor. (Sénégal)

French-Canadian families pass along first names, such as Serge, Robert, Muguette and Céline, from generation to generation. Paquette, Charbonneau, Levesque and Poitras are examples of surnames from Quebec.

In French-speaking Africa, first names may indicate on what day a child was born, his or her birth order or the name of a nearby lake or town. For example, a boy called Fez or Fes would be named after a city in Morocco. African surnames vary from country to country: Kourouma (the Ivory Coast), Moutawakel (Morocco), Senghor (Senegal).

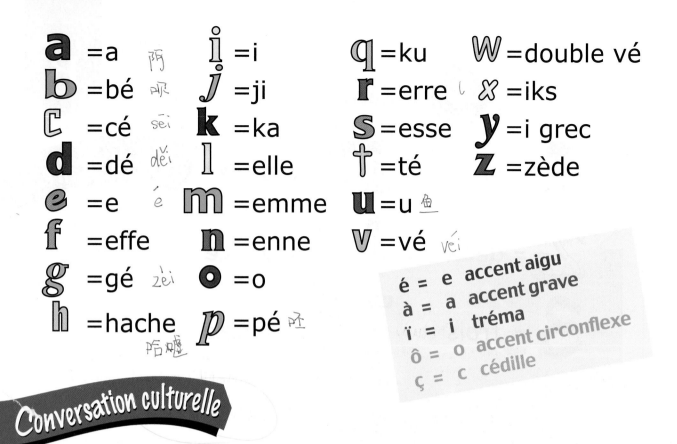

a =a 阿
b =bé 必
c =cé séi
d =dé děi
e =e é
f =effe
g =gé zèi
h =hache 陌嗄

i =i
j =ji
k =ka
l =elle
m =emme
n =enne
o =o
p =pé 丕

q =ku
r =erre
s =esse
t =té
u =u 鱼
v =vé véi

w =double vé
x =iks
y =i grec
z =zède

é = e accent aigu
à = a accent grave
ï = i tréma
ô = o accent circonflexe
ç = c cédille

Conversation culturelle

Jessica Miller, an American high school student, is planning to visit her French pen pal, Stéphanie Dufresne. Jessica calls Stéphanie to tell her when she will be arriving.

Écoute, j'arrive le dix.

Pardon, le six?

Jessica:	**... seize, zéro trois.**
Stéphanie:	**Allô, oui?**
Jessica:	**Stéphanie? Bonjour! C'est Jessica Miller.**
Stéphanie:	**Ah, salut, Jessica! Ça va?**
Jessica:	**Ça va bien, merci. Écoute, j'arrive le dix.**
Stéphanie:	**Pardon, le six?** thank you
Jessica:	**Non, pas le six, le dix, d... i... x.** 不→sorry
Stéphanie:	**Ah, d'accord.**
Jessica:	**À bientôt, Stéphanie.** see you soon
Stéphanie:	**Au revoir.** good bye

às jeudi =see you today
demain =see you tomorrow

Les numéros de téléphone

Note that Stéphanie Dufresne's phone number is 01.42.60.16.03. Phone numbers in France have ten digits and are divided into five groups of two numbers, which are often separated by periods. France is divided into five regions from "01" to "05." The first two digits of a phone number for Paris and the surrounding region (Île-de-France) are "01." When calling Paris from the United States, Jessica begins by dialing "011" (international long distance), "33" (the country code for France) and then "1"(not "01") before the remaining eight digits.

Les adieux

Although **Au revoir** may be used at any time to say good-bye in French, teenagers often say **Salut**. Two other words you may hear are **Ciao**, borrowed from Italian, and even "Bye." **Allô** is used only when answering the phone. **À bientôt** (*See you soon*) may also be said to end a conversation in French.

Au revoir, Céline.

1 Les prénoms

Write the names as you hear them spelled.

2 Répondez!

Choisissez la bonne réponse.

1. What word for hello is used when you answer the phone?
2. What do French speakers say when they want someone to repeat something?
3. How many digits are there in a French phone number?
4. What are the first two digits in a Parisian phone number?
5. What word means both hello and good-bye in French?
6. What is the Italian word for good-bye that French people use?

A. Allô.
B. "01"
C. Pardon?
D. Salut.
E. ten
F. Ciao.

6 ▸ Composez le numéro de téléphone!

You need to call certain people but you don't have their telephone numbers. Fortunately, your partner does. As your partner reads you each person's telephone number in French, use the accompanying telephone to dial these ten-digit numbers, touching each set of numbers in order. Your partner will watch to see that you dial correctly.

1. M. Paquette:
   zéro quatre, dix-neuf, zéro huit, zéro sept, douze
2. Marie-Alix:
   zéro un, vingt, quinze, seize, zéro un
3. Théo:
   zéro trois, treize, dix, quatorze, dix-sept
4. Mme Bérenger:
   zéro deux, zéro six, zéro quatre, onze, dix-huit

Modèle:

A: Stéphanie?
B: Ah… Stéphanie… zéro un, vingt, zéro neuf, quinze, zéro cinq.
A: (Dials 01.20.09.15.05 on the phone.)

Nathalie et Raoul

Vrai — True   Faux — False

✓ Évaluation culturelle

Decide if each statement is true or false.
1. When French teenagers talk to each other, they say **Monsieur**, **Madame** or **Mademoiselle**. *False*
2. In French-speaking Africa, a child's first name may be the name of the weekday on which he or she was born. *True*
3. You say **Allô** when answering the phone in French. *True*
4. The French shake hands the same way Americans do. *False*
5. French last names, such as Meunier and Dubois, indicate what work the family did or where they came from. *True*
6. As soon as you meet someone in France, you should greet that person with two to four kisses on his or her cheeks. *False*
7. French teenagers talk to their friends only in class or on the telephone. *False*
8. French-Canadian first names are passed along from grandparents to parents to children. *True*

How is the French handshake different from the American one?

✓ Évaluation orale

Because you are eager to practice speaking French, you call the new French exchange student in your class.

Answer the phone appropriately.

Greet the French student and introduce yourself.

Greet the American student.

Tell each other your name and spell it so that the other person is sure to understand.

Ask each other how things are going.

Tell each other that things are going well.

Tell each other good-bye and that you will see each other soon.

✓ Évaluation écrite

Write out in dialogue form the entire conversation you had with your partner in the *Évaluation orale*.

✓ Évaluation visuelle

 Complete the two short dialogues below with appropriate expressions from this unit. (You may want to refer to the *Révision de fonctions* on this page and the *Vocabulaire* on page 17.)

Révision de fonctions

Can you do all of the following tasks in French?

- I can say hello, hi, thanks and good-bye, and can greet my friends and adults appropriately.
- I can introduce myself.
- I can introduce my friends to each other and tell their names.
- I can count from 0 to 20.
- I can spell names and other important information.

To greet someone, use:

Salut!	*Hi!*
Bonjour!	*Hello!*
Allô?	*Hello? (on telephone)*
Ça va?	*How are things going?*

To say good-bye to someone, use:

Au revoir.	*Good-bye.*
Ciao.	*Bye.*
Salut.	*Good-bye.*
À bientôt.	*See you soon.*

To introduce yourself, use:

Je m'appelle Valérie.	*My name is Valérie.*
C'est Patrick.	*This is Patrick.*

To introduce someone else, use:

Je te présente Malika.	*Let me introduce you to Malika.*
C'est Luc.	*This is Luc.*

Salut.

To ask someone's name, use:
Tu t'appelles comment? *What's your name?*
To tell someone's name, use:
Il s'appelle Mahmoud. *His name is Mahmoud.*
Elle s'appelle Yasmine. *Her name is Yasmine.*
To thank someone, use:
Merci. *Thanks.*
To give a telephone number, use:
Zéro un, dix-neuf, zéro cinq, *Zero one, nineteen, zero*
dix, douze. *five, ten, twelve.*
To restate information, use:
Raoul, R... a... o... u... l. *Raoul, R . . . a . . . o . . . u . . . l.*

Merci, Benoît.

Vocabulaire

À bientôt. See you soon. *B*
ah oh *B*
allô hello (on telephone) *A*
arriver to arrive *B*
au revoir good-bye *B*

bien well *B*
bonjour hello *A*

c'est this is, it's *B*
ça *B*
   Ça va? How are things going? *B*
   Ça va bien. Things are going well. *B*

ciao bye *B*
cinq five *B*
comment what *A*

d'accord OK *B*
deux two *B*
dix ten *B*
dix-huit eighteen *B*
dix-neuf nineteen *B*
dix-sept seventeen *B*
douze twelve *B*

écoute listen *B*
Eh! Hey! *A*

huit eight *B*

j' I *B*
je I *A*

le (+ *number*) on the (+ ordinal number) *B*

m'appelle: je m'appelle my name is *A*
Madame (Mme) Mrs., Ma'am *A*

Mademoiselle (Mlle) Miss *A*
merci thanks *B*
Monsieur (M.) Mr., Sir *A*

neuf nine *B*
non no *B*

onze eleven *B*
oui yes *A*

pardon excuse me *A*
pas not *B*
présenter to introduce *A*

quatorze fourteen *B*
quatre four *B*
quinze fifteen *B*

s'appelle: elle s'appelle her name is *A*
   il s'appelle his name is *A*
salut hi; good-bye *A*
seize sixteen *B*
sept seven *B*
six six *B*

t'appelles: tu t'appelles your name is *A*
te to you *A*
Tiens! Hey! *A*
treize thirteen *B*
trois three *B*

un one *B*

vingt twenty *B*

zéro zero *B*

Unité

2

Qu'est-ce que tu aimes faire?

In this unit you will be able to:
- express likes and dislikes
- agree and disagree
- give opinions
- ask for information
- invite
- refuse an invitation

www.emcp.com

Vocabulaire

Frédéric aime nager.

Gilberte aime téléphoner.

Philippe aime étudier.

Delphine aime skier.

Damien et Karine aiment bien aller au cinéma.

Françoise et Alain aiment écouter de la musique.

Sophie et Nicole aiment jouer au foot.

Manu aime jouer au basket.

Louis aime regarder la télé.

le foot

le basket

la télé

la musique

le cinéma

Valérie   Karine

It's Wednesday afternoon. Since Valérie and Karine don't have classes, they talk about what they're going to do this afternoon.

Valérie: Dis, qu'est-ce que tu aimes faire?
Karine: J'aime aller au cinéma. Pourquoi?
Valérie: On passe un bon film au Gaumont. On y va?
Karine: Pas possible. J'étudie pour l'interro, demain.
Valérie: D'accord. Alors, à demain.

Les mots apparentés

The word **musique** is a cognate, a word that has a similar spelling and meaning in both French and English. Words like **basketball**, **télévision**, **skier** and **téléphoner** are examples of cognates. Learning to recognize cognates is an easy way to increase your French vocabulary.

What would you expect to find at a *pharmacie*?

Mercredi après-midi

French teenagers usually don't have school on Wednesday afternoon, but they may attend classes on Saturday morning. Students use Wednesday afternoon to see their friends, practice sports, shop and study. Few French teens have part-time jobs. They need to study quite a bit each evening because teachers often assign a lot of homework.

Le cinéma

Going to movies is a popular leisure activity in France. The hundreds of movie theaters in Paris show new releases and classic films from around the world. On certain days of the week movie theaters offer reduced prices for students.

On Wednesday afternoon some students play soccer with their soccer club. (Verneuil-sur-Seine)

---

1 **Qui aime...?**

Write the name of the person who likes to do each activity.

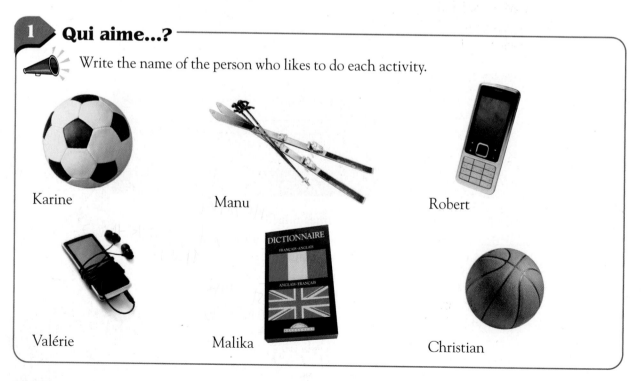

Karine

Manu

Robert

Valérie

Malika

Christian

---

2 ▸ Répondez!

Answer the following questions.

1. How is the daily school schedule of Valérie and Karine different from yours?
2. What can you say in French to refuse an invitation?
3. How does a French speaker say good-bye when he or she will see the person the next day?
4. Why is it difficult for students in France to have part-time jobs?
5. Are only French movies shown in France?

Movies from other countries are dubbed into French or have French subtitles.

3 ▸ Qu'est-ce que vous aimez faire?

Choisissez la bonne réponse.

1. What word does Valérie use to get Karine's attention?
   A. Dis.
   B. D'accord.
   C. Alors.

2. How does Valérie ask Karine what she likes to do?
   A. Pourquoi?
   B. Qu'est-ce que tu aimes faire?
   C. On y va?

3. How does Valérie say that there's a good movie?
   A. On passe un bon film.
   B. J'étudie pour l'interro.
   C. J'aime aller au cinéma.

4. What does Karine say to refuse Valérie's invitation?
   A. D'accord.
   B. Pas possible.
   C. Alors.

5. When does Karine have a test?
   A. À demain.
   B. Le six.
   C. Demain.

6. How does Valérie respond when Karine says she has to study?
   A. D'accord.
   B. Ciao.
   C. Pas possible.

7. How does Valérie tell Karine when they'll see each other again?
   A. Au revoir. *goodbye*
   B. Salut.
   C. À demain. 明天

4 ▸ C'est à toi!

Questions personnelles.

1. Qu'est-ce que tu aimes faire?
2. Tu aimes aller au cinéma?
3. Tu aimes jouer au foot?
4. Tu aimes jouer au basket?
5. Tu aimes écouter de la musique?
6. Tu aimes regarder la télé?

> J'aime bien jouer au basket.

Subject pronouns

To talk to or about people, use subject pronouns to replace their names. Subject pronouns are either singular (referring to one person) or plural (referring to more than one person). Here are the subject pronouns in French.

Singular		Plural	
je	I	nous	we
tu vous }	you	vous	you
il elle on	he she one/they/we	ils elles }	they

Tu aimes aller au cinéma?　　*Do you like to go to the movies?*

Oui, **j'**aime aller au cinéma.　　*Yes, I like to go to the movies.*

Note that **je** becomes **j'** when the next word begins with a vowel sound.

The pronoun **on** is singular even though it often refers to more than one person.

On passe un bon film au Rex.　　*They're showing a good movie at the Rex.*

Sophie? Elle aime écouter de la musique.

Il replaces a masculine name; **elle** replaces a feminine name.

Valérie? **Elle** va au cinéma.　　*Valérie? She is going to the movies.*

Elles refers to two or more women. **Ils** refers to two or more men or to a combination of men and women.

Nicolas et Renée?　　*Nicolas and Renée?*

Ils aiment skier.　　*They like to ski.*

Pratique

5　Trouvez le sujet!

Find the subject pronoun in each headline or advertisement.

1. *Il jouait du piano assis...*
2. *Vous avez gagné 20€*
3. JE DESIRE M'ABONNER A **MATCH**
4. **TU AS JOUÉ?**
5. Nouvelle Peugeot 405 MI 16. Elle met tout son talent à vos pieds.
6. On aime... on déteste / fleurs CD tomates
7. *Ils ont dit « oui », comme au cinéma !*
8. *Nous allons à la plage!*

Choisissez le sujet!

Select the appropriate subject pronoun to describe each person or group of people from the following list:

il	elle	ils	elles

1. elle
2. ils
3. il
4. ils
5. elles
6. ils

tu VS. *vous*

In French **tu** and **vous** both mean "you," but they are used in different ways. When you talk to one person,

use **tu** with:	use **vous** with:
1. a friend	1. an adult you don't know
2. a close relative	2. a distant relative
3. a person your own age	3. a person older than you
4. a child	4. an acquaintance
5. a pet	5. a person of authority, such as a teacher

Tu...?
Vous...?

Dis, Toutounne, qu'est-ce que tu aimes faire?

Bonjour, Mlle Dufresne! Vous skiez?

When you talk to more than one person, always use **vous**.

Qu'est-ce que **tu** aimes faire, Nadine?	*What do you like to do, Nadine?*
Vous skiez, Mlle Dufresne?	*Do you ski, Miss Dufresne?*
Karine et Luc, **vous** étudiez?	*Karine and Luc, are you studying?*

Pratique

Tu ou vous?

Indicate whether you should use **tu** or **vous** with each person or group of people.

1. Karine's mother   *vous*
2. a lost five-year-old   *tu*
3. your math teacher   *vous*
4. your friend Bruno   *tu*
5. Bruno's dog, Milou   *tu*
6. two secretaries from the office at school   *vous*
7. your 15-year-old cousin Thierry   *tu*
8. your grandfather's brother   *vous*
9. your classmates Sophie and Béatrice   *vous*
10. a police officer   *vous*

Vous aimez aller au cinéma, Monsieur?

Infinitives

A verb expresses action or a state of being. The basic form of a verb is the infinitive, the verb form found in the end vocabulary of this textbook and in French dictionaries. Many French infinitives end in **-er**, such as **présenter, arriver, étudier, nager, jouer, skier, regarder, écouter, téléphoner, aimer** and **passer**.

Pratique

Le dictionnaire

List the infinitives ending in **-er** that are found on the following page taken from a beginning French dictionary.

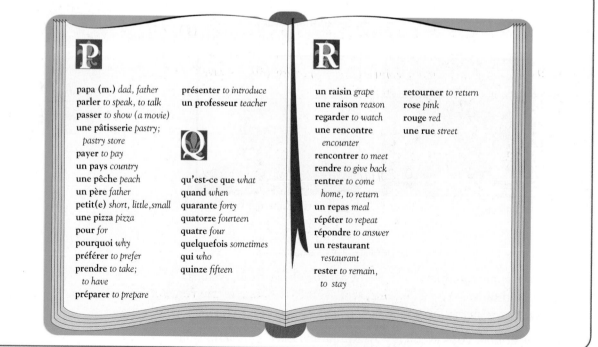

P

papa (m.) *dad, father*
parler *to speak, to talk*
passer *to show (a movie)*
une pâtisserie *pastry; pastry store*
payer *to pay*
un pays *country*
une pêche *peach*
un père *father*
petit(e) *short, little, small*
une pizza *pizza*
pour *for*
pourquoi *why*
préférer *to prefer*
prendre *to take; to have*
préparer *to prepare*

présenter *to introduce*
un professeur *teacher*

Q

qu'est-ce que *what*
quand *when*
quarante *forty*
quatorze *fourteen*
quatre *four*
quelquefois *sometimes*
qui *who*
quinze *fifteen*

R

un raisin *grape*
une raison *reason*
regarder *to watch*
une rencontre *encounter*
rencontrer *to meet*
rendre *to give back*
rentrer *to come home, to return*
un repas *meal*
répéter *to repeat*
répondre *to answer*
un restaurant *restaurant*
rester *to remain, to stay*

retourner *to return*
rose *pink*
rouge *red*
une rue *street*

Qu'est-ce qu'on aime faire?

Tell what some of your friends like to do, according to the illustrations.

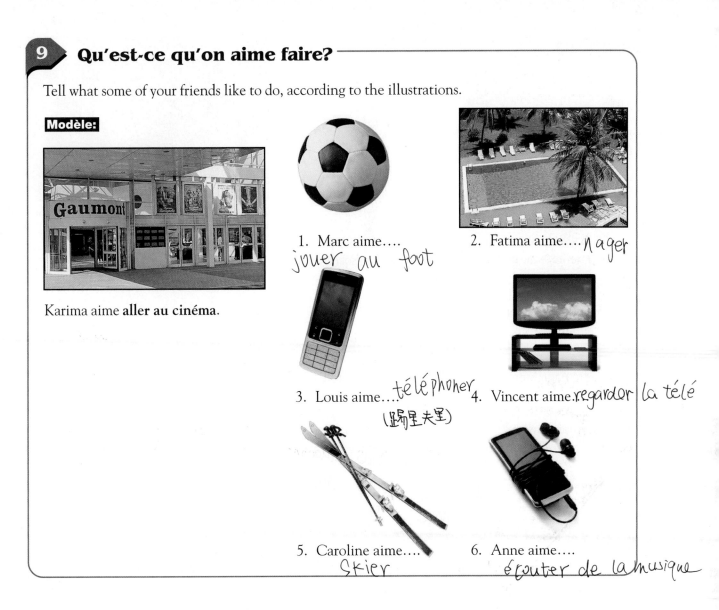

Modèle:

Karima aime **aller au cinéma**.

1. Marc aime.... *jouer au foot*

2. Fatima aime.... *nager*

3. Louis aime.... *téléphoner* (踢屋夫里)

4. Vincent aime. *regarder la télé*

5. Caroline aime.... *skier*

6. Anne aime.... *écouter de la musique*

Present tense of regular verbs ending in *-er*

Many verbs whose infinitives end in **-er** are called regular verbs because their forms follow a predictable pattern. Regular **-er** verbs, such as **jouer**, have six forms in the present tense. To form the present tense of a regular **-er** verb, first find the stem of the verb by removing the **-er** ending from its infinitive.

jou er

Now add the endings (**-e, -es, -e, -ons, -ez, -ent**) to the stem of the verb depending on the corresponding subject pronouns.

jouer		
Subject Pronoun + Stem + Ending		
je	jou	e
tu	jou	es
il/elle/on	jou	e
nous	jou	ons
vous	jou	ez
ils/elles	jou	ent

Florence et Marie-Alix étudient.

Vous **jouez** demain?　　　*Are you playing tomorrow?*

Oui, je **joue** au foot.　　　*Yes, I'm playing soccer.*

Remember that **je** becomes **j'** when the next word begins with a vowel sound: **J'étudie pour l'interro.**

Each present tense verb form in French consists of only one word but has more than one meaning.

André **nage** bien.　　　$\Big\{$ *André swims well.*
　　　　　　　　　　　　　André is swimming well.

André **nage** bien?　　　*Does André swim well?*

If an infinitive ends in **-ger**, its **nous** form ends in **-eons**.

Nous **nageons**.　　　*We are swimming.*

Pratique

eg. je nage　　nous nageons
tu nages　　vous nagez
Elle nage　　Ils nagent

10 ▸ Le foot ou le basket?

Tell whether the following people play soccer or basketball.

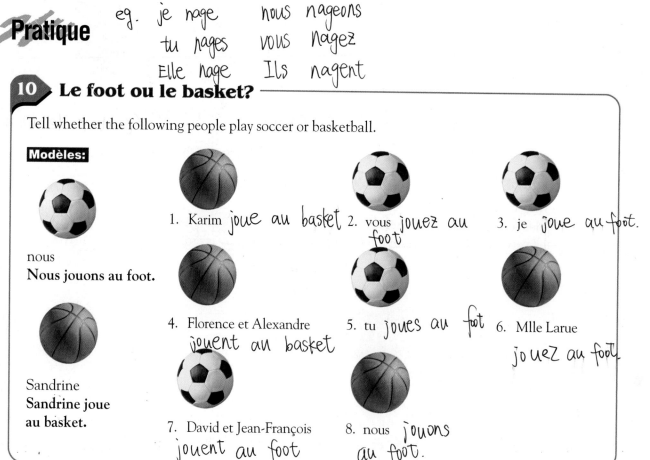

Modèles:

nous
Nous jouons au foot.

Sandrine
Sandrine joue au basket.

1. Karim *joue au basket*

2. vous *jouez au foot*

3. je *joue au foot.*

4. Florence et Alexandre *jouent au basket*

5. tu *joues au foot*

6. Mlle Larue *jouez au foot*

7. David et Jean-François *jouent au foot*

8. nous *jouons au foot.*

11 ▸ Complétez!

Write the correct form of the appropriate verb from the following list. Use each verb at least once.

regarder étudier aimer passer écouter jouer arriver

1. Qu'est-ce que vous… faire? **aimez**
   Nous… nager. *aimez* **aimons** ~~regarde~~
2. Tu… la télé? **regardes**
   Non, j'… de la musique. *écouter* **J'écoute**
3. Tu… au basket? *jouer* **joues**
   Non, je… au foot. **joue**
   jouer

4. Vous… le sept? **arrivez**
   Non, nous… le neuf. **arrivons**
5. On… un bon film au Gaumont. On y va? **passe**
   Pas possible. J'… pour l'interro. **J'étudie**

12 ▸ Chez les Bouchard au Canada

The Bouchards have invited the Robidoux family to spend the day at their cabin. Describe what everyone is doing.

Modèle:

1. Édouard joue au basket.

2. Claudette et Marie jouent au foot.
3. M. Robidoux et Minou
4. Normand et Robert nagent
5. Mme Robidoux écoutez de la musique.
6. Mme Bouchard téléphonez

13 ▸ Qu'est-ce qu'on fait?

With a partner, talk about what various people are doing. Student A asks questions and Student B answers them. Follow the model.

Modèle:

Éric (nager/skier)
A: **Éric nage?**
B: **Non, il skie.**

1. Mme Gagner (regarder la télé/téléphoner) **regarde. téléphone**
2. Karine et Manu (étudier/jouer au basket) **étudient. jouent**
3. tu (jouer au foot/écouter de la musique) **joues écoute**
4. Diane et Nadia (arriver le dix/arriver le neuf) **arrivent. arrivent**
5. tu (aimer aller au cinéma/aimer regarder la télé) **aimes. aime**

Communication

14 ▸ Une enquête

To find out what some of your classmates' favorite activities are, draw a grid like the one that follows. In the grid write the question you will ask and add any three activities you can express in French. Then poll ten of your classmates to determine which of these three activities is the most popular.

Qu'est-ce que tu aimes faire?

	1	2	3	4	5	6	7	8	9	10
nager	✔									
jouer au basket										
regarder la télé										

Modèle:

Cécile: **Qu'est-ce que tu aimes faire? Nager? Jouer au basket? Regarder la télé?**

Daniel: **J'aime nager.**

1. Ask each classmate what he or she likes to do, giving him or her your three choices.
2. Make a check by each activity that your classmate likes to do.
3. Count how many people like each activity.

15 ▸ En partenaires

Working in pairs, take turns asking each other what you like to do. Make a grid like the one that follows and put a check in the appropriate column.

Modèle:

Frédéric: **Tu aimes aller au cinéma?**
Laurent: **Oui.**

Tu aimes téléphoner? (Paris)

Tu aimes...	oui	non
aller au cinéma?	✔	
étudier?		
nager?		
jouer au foot?		
jouer au basket?		
skier?		
regarder la télé?		
écouter de la musique?		
téléphoner?		

16 ▸ Mes activités préférées

Which activities in this lesson are your favorites? Classify them by making a list beginning with the one you like the most and ending with the one you like the least. When you have finished, read your list to a partner and compare your preferences.

17 ▸ À vous de jouer!

You and a friend pass notes back and forth to make plans for after school.

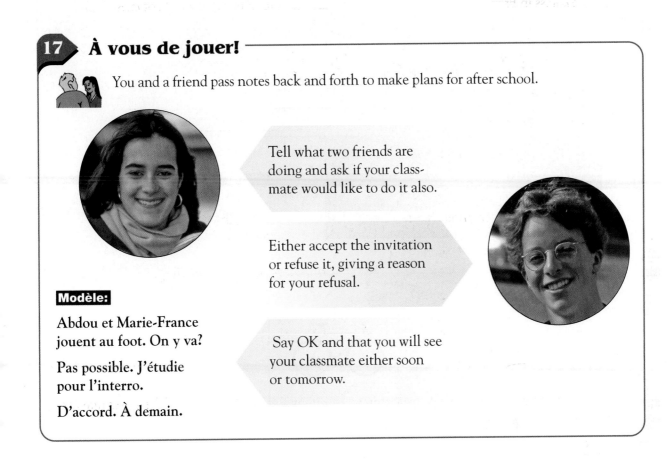

Tell what two friends are doing and ask if your classmate would like to do it also.

Either accept the invitation or refuse it, giving a reason for your refusal.

Say OK and that you will see your classmate either soon or tomorrow.

Modèle:

Abdou et Marie-France jouent au foot. On y va?

Pas possible. J'étudie pour l'interro.

D'accord. À demain.

Prononciation

Unpronounced consonants

A consonant in French generally is not pronounced when it is the last letter of a word. Say each of these words:

salut   alors   comment   pas   pardon   d'accord

The consonant **h** is never pronounced in French. Say each of these words:

Catherine   Hervé   Nathalie   Thierry

Ils aiment faire du sport.

Vocabulaire

Julien et Nicole aiment faire du roller.

Marc et Renée aiment faire du footing.

Chloé et Karine aiment faire du vélo.

le footing

le vélo

le roller

M. Vinay aime un peu
le camping.

Yasmine et Anne-Marie
aiment bien les sports.

Patrick aime beaucoup les films.

Martine   Jérémy

Jérémy wants to ask Sophie out. To find out what Sophie likes to do, he asks her friend Martine some questions.

Jérémy: **J'aime bien Sophie. Elle aime faire du sport?**

Martine: **Oui. Elle aime bien faire du roller, du footing, du vélo.**

Jérémy: **Elle écoute de la musique?**

Martine: **Oui. Elle aime beaucoup le rock et le reggae. Elle aime un peu le jazz.**

Jérémy: **Super! Moi aussi, j'aime beaucoup le rock. Bon, je téléphone à Sophie.**

As long as they order something to eat or drink, teens may sit for hours at a café talking to their friends.

Le temps libre

[handwritten: Soir: evening   Bonsoir: Good night]
[handwritten: jour: day   Bonjour: Good day]

After school many French teenagers play sports, listen to music or watch TV. When they have free time in the evening, they often get together with their friends at sidewalk cafés or at home. Many high school students like to dance at weekend parties, called **soirées**. Younger teens usually call their parties **boums**. Older teens and adults often go out to dance and listen to music at **les boîtes** and **les clubs** (*dance clubs*).   [handwritten: bars]

[handwritten: Bonne journée: have a good day]
[handwritten: Bonne soinée: have a good night]

La musique

Many French speakers listen to music from other countries, including England and the United States. Teens may like **le rock, le hip-hop, le break-dance, le reggae, la musique pop, la techno, le jazz, le funk, la musique du monde** or **la musique classique**, for example.

[handwritten: la musique country: country music]

Le transport

In France teenagers can't get a driver's license until they are 18 years old. They often walk, bike, ride scooters, use inexpensive public transportation or even hitchhike to get to school or to recreational activities.

Le Tour de France

Le Tour de France, the most prestigious sporting event in France, is an annual endurance test of bicycling skill that was first organized in 1903. For 23 days in July, racers cover over 2,000 miles. The distance covered each day depends on the difficulty of the terrain. The most challenging laps wind through the mountain passes of the Alps and the Pyrenees. The **Tour de France féminin** also takes place in July.

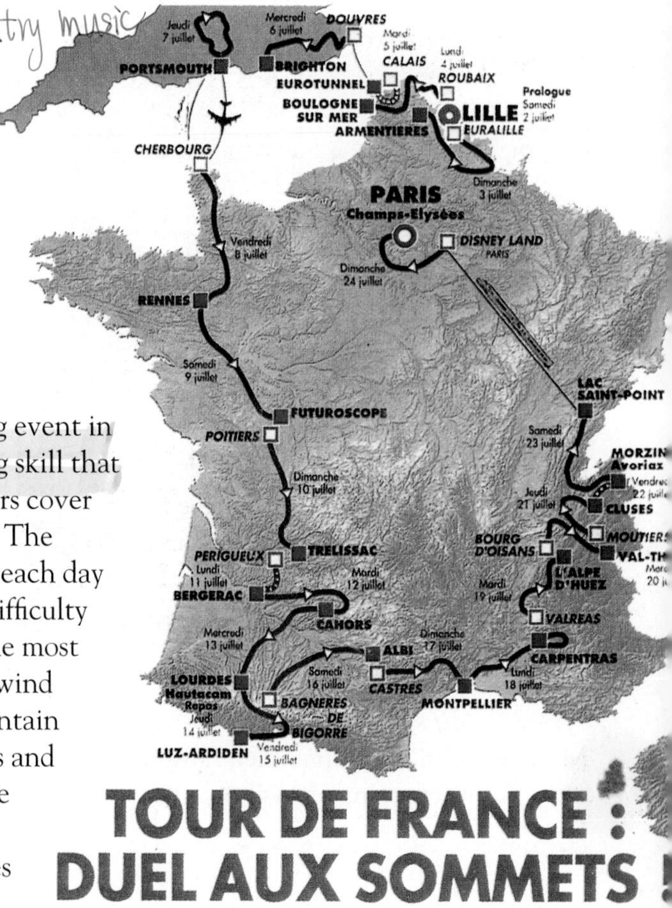

Cyclists who excel in scaling mountains, such as *les Pyrénées*, are called *grimpeurs*.

TOUR DE FRANCE : DUEL AUX SOMMETS !

1 Un peu, bien ou beaucoup?

Draw three hearts if the speaker likes the activity a lot; two hearts if the speaker likes it; one heart if the speaker likes it a little.

♥♥♥ = **beaucoup** *like a lot*

♥♥ = **bien** *like.*

♥ = **un peu** *like a little*

2 Répondez!

Choisissez la bonne réponse.

1. What is the French word for "running"? H
2. Where do French teenagers often get together after school or in the evening? E
3. What is the word 11- to 13-year-old students use for a "party"? F
4. What do older students call a "party"? G
5. Where would you go to dance in a French-speaking country? A
6. Name a kind of music that is popular in France. C
7. At what age can the French get a driver's license? B
8. What is the name of the most famous sporting event in France? D

A. boîte
B. 18
C. techno
D. Le Tour de France
E. café
F. boum
G. soirée
H. footing

3 Jérémy et Sophie

Répondez en français. (Answer in French.)

1. Jérémy aime bien Sophie?
2. Qu'est-ce que Sophie aime faire?
3. Sophie écoute de la musique?
4. Sophie aime un peu le rock?
5. Jérémy aime aussi la musique?
6. Jérémy téléphone à Martine?

Sophie aime faire du sport. Elle aime bien faire du footing.

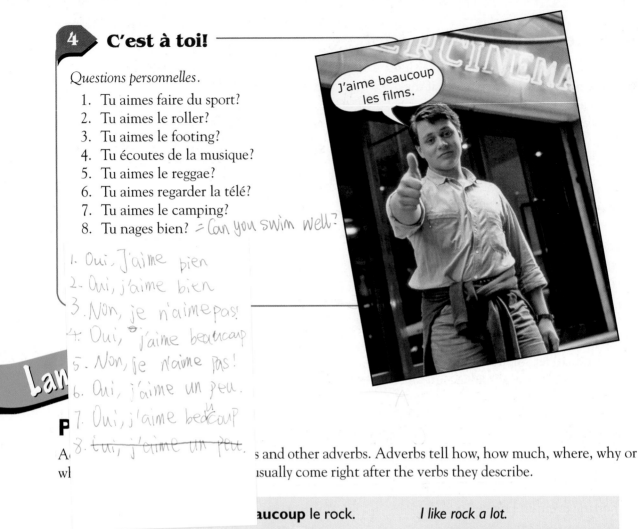

4 C'est à toi!

Questions personnelles.

1. Tu aimes faire du sport?
2. Tu aimes le roller?
3. Tu aimes le footing?
4. Tu écoutes de la musique?
5. Tu aimes le reggae?
6. Tu aimes regarder la télé?
7. Tu aimes le camping?
8. Tu nages bien? = Can you swim well?

1. Oui, J'aime bien
2. Oui, j'aime bien
3. Non, je n'aime pas!
4. Oui, j'aime beaucoup
5. Non, je n'aime pas!
6. Oui, j'aime un peu.
7. Oui, j'aime beaucoup
8. Oui, j'aime un peu.

J'aime beaucoup les films.

La

P

A....................s and other adverbs. Adverbs tell how, how much, where, why or
wh.................usually come right after the verbs they describe.

	...aucoup le rock.	I like rock a lot.
bien	J'aime **bien** la musique.	I (really) like music.
un peu	J'aime **un peu** le jazz. J'aime **un peu** écouter le reggae.	I like jazz a little. I like to listen to reggae a little.

Ils aiment beaucoup faire du vélo.

Pratique

5 ▸ Vous aimez...?

Tell how much you like what is indicated by using **beaucoup**, **bien** or **un peu**.

Modèle:

le rock
J'aime beaucoup le rock.

1. faire du roller
2. regarder la télé
3. le jazz
4. faire du vélo
5. le camping
6. faire du footing
7. le reggae
8. téléphoner

On aime bien le camping.

6 ▸ Beaucoup, bien ou un peu?

Look at the survey on how much your friends like certain sports. Tell how much they like each individual sport and how much they like sports in general.

	le footing	le roller	le foot	le basket
Max	beaucoup	un peu	un peu	un peu
Sylvie	un peu	un peu	un peu	un peu
Nadia	beaucoup	un peu	beaucoup	beaucoup
Salim	beaucoup	beaucoup	beaucoup	beaucoup
Pierre	un peu	un peu	beaucoup	un peu
Chloé	un peu	beaucoup	un peu	un peu

Modèle:

Max aime beaucoup le footing. Il aime un peu le roller, le foot et le basket. Il aime un peu les sports.

7 ► On joue bien.

Tell what you and your friends like to do. Then say that you do it well.

Modèle:

Martine/jouer au basket
Martine aime jouer au basket. Elle joue bien.

1. Bruno/jouer au foot
2. je/skier
3. Marc et Benjamin/jouer au basket
4. Latifa/nager
5. Anne-Marie et Alain/skier
6. nous/étudier

Alice et Marc aiment skier. Ils skient bien.

Communication

8 ► Devinez!

To guess how much your partner likes certain activities, number from 1 to 8. Predict whether your partner likes each activity a lot or a little. Beside the number, write **beaucoup** or **un peu**. Then check the accuracy of your guesses with your partner. Ask each other questions based on your predictions. Circle the correct predictions.

Modèle:

Emmanuel: **Tu aimes beaucoup le camping?**
Diane: **Oui, j'aime beaucoup le camping.**
Emmanuel: (Circles **beaucoup** on his sheet of paper.)

1. faire du vélo
2. le rock
3. le camping
4. faire du roller
5. le reggae
6. faire du footing
7. le jazz
8. les films

1. beaucoup
2. un peu
3. un peu

Write captions for the photos in your album. Give the name of the person and tell what he or she likes to do. Add **beaucoup**, **bien** or **un peu** to tell how much the person likes doing the activity.

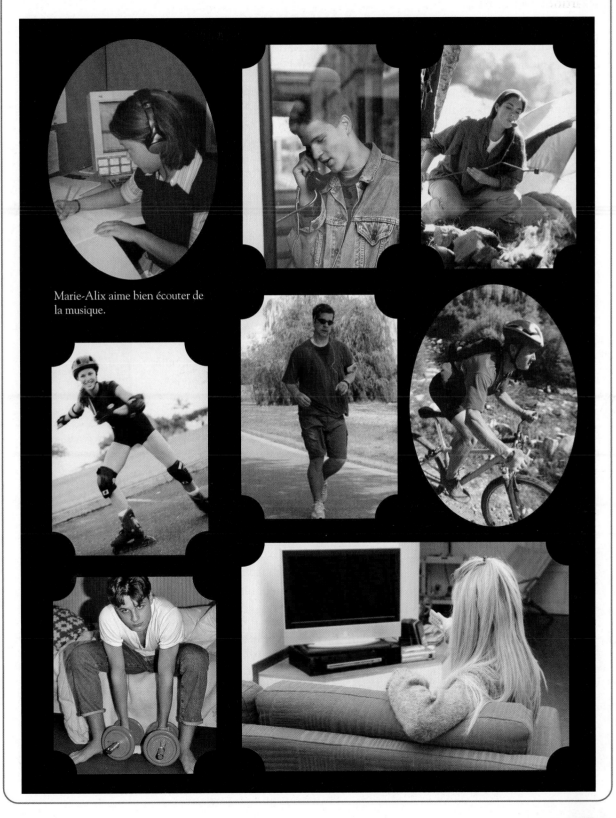

Marie-Alix aime bien écouter de la musique.

La musique

Music is an international language. **Le rock**, **le jazz** and **le reggae** sound familiar to teenagers all over the globe because of an increasing trend toward world music.

What kinds of music do you listen to? Chances are that French speakers listen to the same sounds that you do. Music is an important part of a teenager's life in French-speaking countries, just as it is for English-speaking teens. Of course, tastes in music vary from person to person.

Shopping for CDs is a favorite activity of many adolescents in France. In fact, one popular large music store in Paris occupies four stories!

Performers from all over the world appear at the Zénith and at Bercy, two popular concert halls in Paris. When students' favorite artists perform at these halls, concerts sell out in no time.

Traditional French songs are usually poetic and melodious. The lyrics often have a message or a feeling to convey to the listener. The messages change, but the songs typically deal with love, peace, family, daily life and politics.

The words of contemporary songs are more daring than those of the past. Topics include women's issues, antiracism, the environment and the difficulty of city life. The music and the lyrics are fairly aggressive, especially those of **le rock**, whose strong rhythm encourages dancing. French teens also like **le RNB**, a sort of melodious rap. **Le hip-hop**, still popular in France, was influenced by the same movement in the United States. In fact, many French-speaking teenagers listen to songs in English and know the words, even though they may not know what these words mean.

Music legends, such as ex-Beatle Paul McCartney, perform at Bercy. (Paris)

At dance clubs and on the radio, teenagers listen to a variety of music formats, such as **le funk** and **le rock**. Young people who have a taste for hard rock listen to **le métal**. **Le raï** could be called the North African version of rhythm and blues. **La techno**, another popular type of music, is based on an industrial, synthetic sound. Even though **le jazz** originated in the United States, many teens in France listen to it as well. Clubs, such as Le Petit Journal Montparnasse, New Morning and the Jazz Club Lionel Hampton, have helped establish Paris as one of the jazz capitals of the world.

Khaled, called the "king of raï," popularized this North African music in France.

Teenagers all over the world listen to a wide variety of sounds. A wave of multiculturalism has swept across the music scene, influencing and expanding tastes. For example, Céline Dion, a singer from Québec, has become an international star. Other examples of the trend toward international music are **la musique créole**, exported from Martinique, and **le world beat** from French West Africa. But no matter where a song originates, its music and lyrics reflect the lifestyles of its writers and performers.

10 ▸ La musique

Répondez aux questions.

1. What is the major music trend in France? *Familiar to teenagers all over the globe*
2. What are the names of two concert halls in Paris? *Zénith & Bercy*
3. What are two words that describe traditional French songs? *Poetic & melodious*
4. What are three topics that may be included in contemporary songs? *Women's issues, antiracism, the environment and the difficulty of city life.*
5. What is a style of music that is based on a synthetic sound? → *La techno*
6. What kind of music is played at Le Petit Journal Montparnasse? *Le jazz*
7. What is a type of music that has been exported from Martinique? *La musique créole*

11 ▸ Au Café Arlequin

Choose the best answer to each question based on the advertisement you see.

1. What is being advertised here?
   A. A restaurant.
   B B. A café.
   C. A dinner theater.

2. What is the name of this place?
   A. Arlequin.
   A B. Trio Dany Revel.
   C. Déjeuners Musicaux.

3. What is the name of the group that is playing here from April 24 to June 26?
   A. Carte Menu.
   C B. Café Arlequin.
   C. Trio Dany Revel.

4. What time is this group performing? (Times are often given using the 24-hour clock.)
   B A. 12:30 — 5:00.
   B. 12:30 — 3:00.
   C. 12:30 — 2:00.

5. How much does the suggested meal cost for each person?
   A. 25 euros.
   A B. 150 francs.
   C. 15 euros.

6. What telephone number do you call to make a reservation?
   A A. 01.40.68.30.85.
   B. 25.
   C. 12.30.15.

DÉJEUNERS MUSICAUX

Tous les dimanches
du 24 avril au 26 juin
découvrez les déjeuners musicaux
au

Café
ARLEQUIN

ambiance musicale avec le
TRIO DANY REVEL
de 12h30 à 15h

–

Notre suggestion
CARTE MENU
25 €
(par personne)
comprenant (1 entrée, 1 plat, 1 dessert et Café)

Vocabulaire

Fifi aime dormir.

Amélie aime faire les devoirs.

Annie et Éric aiment jouer aux jeux video.

Thierry et Christine aiment sortir.

Mme Lafont et Dominique aiment lire.

Mme Delon aime faire du shopping.

le volley

le tennis

la pizza

les devoirs (m.)

le shopping

les jeux vidéo (m.)

Paul

Éric

Chantal

Paul, Éric and Chantal are making plans to get together over the weekend.

Paul: Qui aime danser?

Éric: Émilie et moi, nous aimons aller en boîte. Mais Laurent et Claire, ils n'aiment pas danser.

Paul: Alors, qui aime jouer au tennis?

slang for well then

Chantal: Je joue au tennis. Mais je préfère jouer au volley.

Paul: Bon ben, j'invite tout le monde chez moi. Tout le monde aime manger de la pizza!

Les sports

Since sports are not usually associated with schools in France, students often go to **le club** to exercise. Many also take private lessons there. Local communities offer opportunities for students to participate in sports and arrange competitions as well. In Canada many teenagers ski or play hockey or ringette. On the Caribbean island of Martinique they play soccer or participate in many kinds of water sports, for example, **la planche à voile** (*windsurfing*).

The French love windsurfing...

... but the Canadians are wild about hockey.

1 Oui ou non?

Make a plus sign if the speaker does the activity; make a minus sign if not.

2 Le weekend

Répondez en français.

1. Émilie et Éric aiment danser?
2. Qui aime aller en boîte? Oui.
3. Qui n'aime pas danser? Émilie et Éric
4. Qui joue au tennis? Chantel
5. Qu'est-ce que Chantal préfère? Jouer au volley.
6. Qui invite tout le monde à manger de la pizza? Paul.
7. Tout le monde aime manger de la pizza? Oui.

3 Qu'est-ce qu'elles aiment faire?

Complétez le dialogue suivant.
(Complete the following dialogue.)

Aimée: Bonjour. Ça va?
Danielle: Ça va…. Tu aimes faire…?
Aimée: …. Je préfère….
Danielle: Qui aime…?
Aimée: Moi, je n'aime pas….
Danielle: …, à bientôt.
Aimée: ….

Beginning to Read in French:
Context, Organization, Guessing and Cognates

How do you develop reading habits that will help you be a successful reader in French? Try to identify and apply the skills that you have learned when reading in English to what you read in French.

1. Figure out the **context** (setting or purpose) of the reading by looking at it as a whole. What is the title of the reading below? What activities might be included in a description of a teen's week?
2. Look at the **organization** of the sentences. How might "A Typical Week" in the life of a teenager be organized? What do you think *lundi, mardi, mercredi, jeudi* and *vendredi* mean?
3. Read each sentence and **guess** about the words you don't know based on the title, context and what you <u>do</u> understand. For example, in which season would this person most likely ski?
4. A new skill you will need to develop is recognizing **cognates**, or words that look and mean the same as English words you already know. For example, *les cours* means "courses."

Ma Vie Hebdomadaire (A Typical Week in My Life)

Le lundi. Je salue mon amie Christine. Nous décidons d'écouter de la musique après les cours. Je préfère le RNB, mais pas Christine. Alors, nous écoutons du métal.

Le mardi. J'invite tout le monde chez moi. Qu'est-ce que nous aimons faire? Alors, nous jouons au volley parce qu'il fait beau.

Le mercredi. Trois heures de classe. À l'école, je dis "Bonjour" à Jean-Marc. Il demande "Tu joues au foot aujourd'hui?" Mais je refuse parce que j'ai une interro vendredi. "Non. Désolé. J'étudie pour l'interro de maths."

Le jeudi. J'adore regarder la télé lundi, mardi, mercredi, jeudi... mais c'est pas possible. J'aime aussi nager en été, skier en hiver et jouer aux jeux vidéo. Qui aime étudier? Pas moi. Mais j'ai une interro.

Le vendredi. L'interro? Pas trop difficile! Après les cours, je téléphone à Serge. Je lui demande "Qu'est-ce que tu aimes faire?" Serge aime faire du roller. Alors, nous invitons Thibaud, Karim et Nathalie aussi et nous allons faire du roller. Et comme d'habitude, j'invite tout le monde chez moi. Tout le monde arrive chez moi. "On y va?" dis-je. "D'accord. Faisons du roller!" Super!

Ça, c'est ma vie hebdomadaire.

12 ▸ Ma Vie Hebdomadaire

Answer some general questions about this reading.

1. On which days of the week is this student focusing? ~~Le lundi. Le vendredi.~~ *Monday to Friday*
2. Is this person popular? How can you tell? *Yes. Many friends with him every day*
3. What types of activities does this person enjoy? What is his or her least favorite activity? *Sports. Study*
4. Is this person a good student? How do you know?

Yes. Because "Désolé. J'étudie pour l'interro de math." She studied for math test for two days.

Nathalie et Raoul

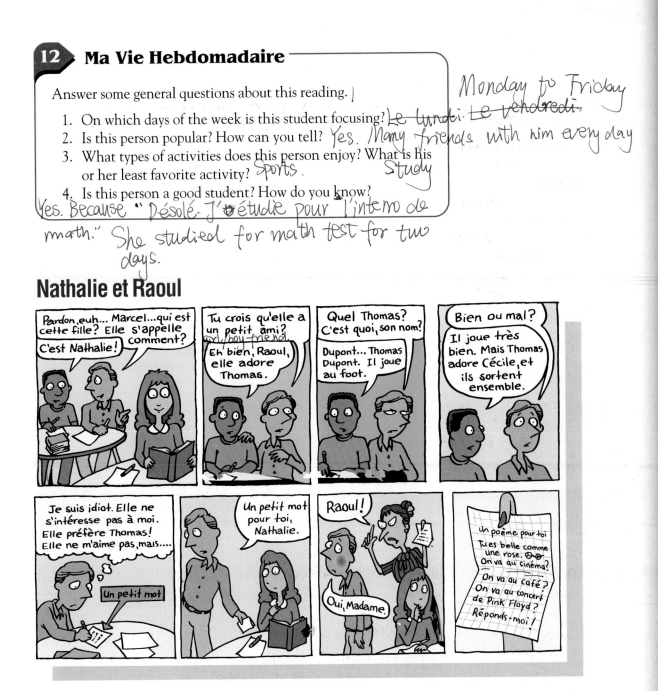

✓ Évaluation culturelle

Decide if each statement is true (**vrai**) or false (**faux**).

1. Most French teenagers don't go to school on Wednesday afternoons and spend this time at their part-time jobs. ~~True~~ False *(They don't have part-time jobs)*
2. Movies are a popular leisure activity for French teens. ~~False~~ True
3. High school students often dance at parties called **soirées**. False
4. French teenagers limit their interest in music to **le rock** and **le funk**. ~~True~~ False
5. In France you have to be 18 years old to get a driver's license. False ~~True~~ False
6. **Le Tour de France** is a 2,000-mile French bike race that takes place every summer. True
7. Music in France has a multicultural influence that makes it very international. True
8. Many French teens know the words to songs in English even if they don't know what the words mean. True
9. Just as they do in the United States, organized sports play an important role in a French teenager's life at school. False

✓ Évaluation orale

You are applying to be a junior counselor at a camp in France where French teenagers practice speaking English. With a partner, play the roles of the American student and the French camp official.

Greet each other in French, introduce yourselves and ask each other how things are going.

Ask the student what he or she likes to do.

Tell the camp official at least three activities that you like to do (which are appropriate for camp) and how much you like to do each one.

Ask the student what he or she does not like to do.

Tell the camp official at least one activity that you do not like to do.

Ask the student if he or she likes to listen to music.

Say that you like to listen to music and specify what kinds.

Thank each other and tell each other good-bye.

✓ Évaluation écrite

Imagine that you interviewed with the camp official for the job of junior counselor. Write a letter to the camp director, Mr. Desrosiers, restating what you said in your interview. Begin your letter with **Monsieur**, and at the end thank him and sign your letter.

✓ Évaluation visuelle

Tell what Delphine likes to do.

In terms of sports, tell what Christophe and Jean-Pierre do and don't do.

 Complete the short dialogue below in which Luc asks Karine out. Use appropriate expressions that you have learned so far. (You may want to refer to the *Révision de fonctions* on page 54 and the *Vocabulaire* on page 55.)

Révision de fonctions

Can you do all of the following tasks in French?

- I can tell what I like and what I dislike.
- I can give my opinion by saying what I prefer.
- I can agree or disagree with someone.
- I can ask for information about "who," "what" and "why."
- I can invite someone to do something.
- I can refuse an invitation.

To say what you like, use:

J'aime le rock.   *I like rock (music).*
J'aime danser.   *I like to dance.*
J'aime aller au cinéma.   *I like to go to the movies.*
J'aime faire du sport.   *I like to play sports.*

To say what you dislike, use:

Je n'aime pas le camping.   *I don't like camping.*
Je n'aime pas étudier.   *I don't like to study.*
Je n'aime pas aller en boîte.   *I don't like to go to the dance club.*
Je n'aime pas faire du footing.   *I don't like to go running.*

Jean-Luc n'aime pas faire les devoirs.

To agree or disagree with someone, use:

D'accord.   *OK.*
Oui.   *Yes.*
Moi aussi.   *Me, too.*
Non.   *No.*

To give your opinion, use:

Je préfère le jazz.   *I prefer jazz.*
Je préfère jouer au volley.   *I prefer to play volleyball.*

To ask for information, use:

Qu'est-ce que tu aimes faire?   *What do you like to do?*
Qui aime skier?   *Who likes to ski?*
Pourquoi?   *Why?*

To invite someone to do something, use:

On y va?   *Shall we go (there)?*
J'invite tout le monde chez moi.   *I'm inviting everybody to my house.*

To refuse an invitation, use:

Pas possible.   *Not possible.*

On y va? — D'accord.

Qui aime faire du sport? Tout le monde!

Vocabulaire

à to *A*
    À demain. See you tomorrow. *A*
aimer to like, to love *A*
aller to go *A*
alors (well) then *A*
△ **au** to (the), at (the) *A*
aussi also, too *B*
le **basket (basketball)** basketball *A*
beaucoup a lot, (very) much *B*
ben: bon ben well then *C*
△ **bien** really *A*
une **boîte** dance club *C*
bon, bonne good *A*
    bon ben well then *C*
le **camping** camping *B*
chez to the house/home of *C*
    chez moi to my house *C*
le **cinéma** movies *A*
danser to dance *C*
demain tomorrow *A*
les **devoirs (m.)** homework *C*
△ **dis** say *A*
dormir to sleep *C*
écouter to listen (to) *A*
    écouter de la musique to listen to music *A*
elle she, it *A*
elles they (f.) *A*
en to (the) *C*
et and *A*
étudier to study *A*
faire to do, to make *A*
    faire du footing to go running *B*
    faire du roller to go in-line skating *B*
    faire du shopping to go shopping *C*
    faire du sport to play sports *B*
    faire du vélo to go biking *B*
    faire les devoirs to do homework *C*
un **film** movie *A*
le **foot (football)** soccer *A*
le **footing** running *B*
il he, it *A*
ils they (m.) *A*
une **interro (interrogation)** quiz, test *A*
inviter to invite *C*
le **jazz** jazz *B*
des **jeux vidéo (m.)** video games *C*
jouer to play *A*
    jouer au basket to play basketball *A*
    jouer au foot to play soccer *A*

l'
la
le t
les t
lire t
mais
mange
mar
moi me
la **musique**
nager to s
ne (n')... ... not *C*
nous we *A*
on they, we, one *A*
    On y va? Shall we go (there)? *A*
passer to show (a movie) *A*
(un) **peu** (a) little *B*
une **pizza** pizza *C*
possible possible *A*
pour for *A*
pourquoi why *A*
préférer to prefer *C*
qu'est-ce que what *A*
qui who, whom *C*
regarder to watch *A*
le **reggae** reggae *B*
le **rock** rock (music) *B*
le **roller** in-line skating *B*
le **shopping** shopping *C*
skier to ski *A*
sortir to go out *C*
un **sport** sport *B*
super super, terrific, great *B*
téléphoner to phone (someone), to make a call *A*
la **télé (télévision)** TV, television *A*
le **tennis** tennis *C*
tout le monde everybody *C*
tu you *A*
un a, an *A*
un **vélo** bicycle, bike *B*
le **volley (volleyball)** volleyball *C*
vous you *A*

3

Au café

In this unit you will be able to:
- invite
- accept and refuse
  an invitation
- order food and beverages
- ask for a price
- state prices
- ask what time it is
- tell time on the hour
- ask how someone is
- tell how you are

www.emcp.com

Vocabulaire

How's it going?

Comment vas-tu?

Très bien! very good.

Comment vas-tu?

Pas mal. Not bad.

Comment vas-tu?

So so.

Comme ci, comme ça.

J'ai faim. hungry

J'ai soif. thirsty

Quelle heure est-il? What time is it?

Il est une heure.

Il est midi. mid-day.

Il est quatre heures.

Il est minuit. mid night

Il est neuf heures.

Caroline

Marie

Caroline runs into her classmate Marie downtown.

Caroline: **Bonjour, Marie. Comment vas-tu?**
Marie: **Très bien, merci. Et toi?**
Caroline: **Pas mal, mais j'ai faim.**
Marie: **Moi aussi.**

Marie: **Quelle heure est-il?**
Caroline: **Il est déjà une heure. On va au café ou au fast-food?**
Marie: **Moi, je préfère aller au fast-food.**
Caroline: **D'accord, allons-y!**

Les fast-foods

French fast-food restaurants like Quick, Free Time, and Pizza del Arte serve food and beverages that many teenagers like: hamburgers, French fries, pizza, hot dogs and soft drinks. American fast-food restaurants can also be found in the French-speaking world; teenagers often eat at McDonald's and Domino's.

McDonald's, often called McDo, was the first American fast-food chain to cross the Atlantic. Approximately 1000 McDonald's restaurants have opened in France since 1974, and they serve over one million customers daily.

Quick, *un hamburger restaurant*, sometimes offers outdoor seating.

The French often end their meals with fruit and cheese.

Le régime français

Traditionally, the French emphasize healthy eating and good-tasting food. Fresh bread and vegetables are frequently purchased each day. Dessert often consists of fruit, cheese or yogurt. More and more products are appearing with the expression **light** in the name. You can find **Coca-Cola light**, **ketchup light** and even **chocolat light** at supermarkets in France.

1 Quelle heure est-il?

Write each time you hear in numerals.

2 Comment allez-vous?

Respond to each situation using **Très bien, Pas très bien** or **Comme ci, comme ça.**

1. You get an "A" on a math test. *Très bien*
2. It rains on the day of your trip to the amusement park. *Pas...*
3. You win your tennis match. *Très bien*
4. You have to clean your room. *Comme ci, comme ça*
5. It's the first day of school. *Pas très bien*
6. You win concert tickets from a local radio station.
7. Your date cancels at the last minute.
8. You receive an unexpected gift.

Comment vas-tu?

Pas très bien.

3 C'est qui?

Based on the dialogue, match the expression with whom it describes.

1. Pas mal.
2. Très bien.
3. J'ai faim.
4. Elle préfère aller au fast-food.
5. On va au fast-food.

A. Marie
B. Caroline
C. Marie et Caroline

4 En français, s'il vous plaît!

Write the letter of how you ask your friend in French... to go

1. what time it is? C
2. how he or she is feeling? F
3. if he or she wants to go to the café? B
4. what he or she likes to do? D
5. if he or she likes to go to the fast-food restaurant? A
6. who likes to eat pizza? E

A. Tu aimes aller au fast-food?
B. On va au café?
C. Quelle heure est-il?
D. Qu'est-ce que tu aimes faire?
E. Qui aime manger de la pizza?
F. Comment vas-tu?/Ça va?

to go?

Quelle heure est-il? (Lyon)

5 C'est à toi!

Questions personnelles.

1. Comment vas-tu?
2. Tu aimes aller au fast-food?
3. Qu'est-ce que tu préfères, Le McDo ou Domino's?
4. Tu préfères aller au fast-food ou au café?
5. Tu aimes le Coca-Cola light?

On va au fast-food?

Present tense of the irregular verb *aller*

The verb **aller** (*to go*) is called an irregular verb because its forms follow an unpredictable pattern. It's the only **-er** verb that is irregular.

aller			
je	**vais**	nous	**allons**
tu	**vas**	vous	**allez**
il/elle/on	**va**	ils/elles	**vont**

Comment **vas**-tu?   *How are you?*

Nous **allons** au café.   *We're going to the café.*

As you can see, the verb **aller** has more than one meaning. It can be used:

1) to talk about going somewhere.

On **va** au café.   *We're going to the café.*

2) to talk about how things are going in general.

Ça **va**?   *How are things going?*

3) to talk about someone's health.

Comment **allez**-vous?   *How are you?*

Je **vais** bien, merci.   *I'm fine, thanks.*

Ils vont au cinéma.

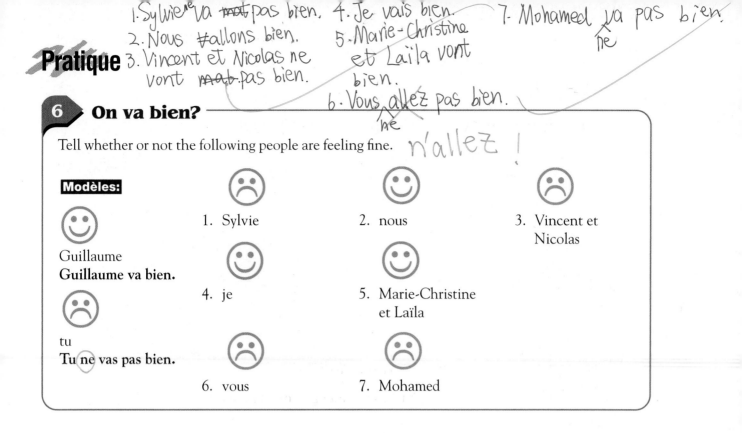

Pratique

Handwritten answers at top:
1. Sylvie va ~~va~~ ne pas bien. 4. Je vais bien. 7. Mohamed va pas bien. ne
2. Nous ~~#~~ allons bien. 5. Marie-Christine et Laïla vont bien.
3. Vincent et Nicolas ne vont ~~pas~~ pas bien. 6. Vous allez pas bien. ne n'allez !

6 ▸ On va bien?

Tell whether or not the following people are feeling fine.

Modèles:

Guillaume
Guillaume va bien.

tu
Tu ne vas pas bien.

1. Sylvie
2. nous
3. Vincent et Nicolas

4. je
5. Marie-Christine et Laïla

6. vous
7. Mohamed

7 ▸ Samedi soir

Tell where the following people are going, according to the illustrations.

1. Tu vas au fast-food?
2. Tout le monde va au café.
3. Théo et Martine vont ~~dansent~~ boîte. en

4. Vous allez au cinéma.
5. Je vais chez moi.

With a partner, play the roles of each of the following pairs of people.
Ask how your partner is feeling and where he or she is going.
Follow the model.

Modèle:

A: **Comment vas-tu?**
B: **Très bien. Et toi?**
A: **Pas mal. Tu vas au fast-food?**
B: **Non, je vais en boîte.**

Telling time on the hour

To ask what time it is in French, say **Quelle heure est-il?** To tell what time it is, say **Il est... heure(s).** You must always use the word **heure(s)**, even though the expression "o'clock" may be omitted in English. To say that it's noon or midnight, use **Il est midi** or **Il est minuit.**

Quelle heure est-il?	*What time is it?*
Il est une heure.	*It's one (o'clock).*
Il est neuf heures.	*It's nine (o'clock).*

The abbreviation for **heure(s)** is **h:** 1h00 = 1:00.

Quelle heure est-il? Il est midi.

Pratique

9 **Quelle heure est-il?**

Répondez à la question.

Modèle:

Il est cinq heures.

1. Il est trois heures.

2. Il est midi.

3. Il est cinq heures.

4. Il est dix heures.

5. Il est sept heures.

6. Il est un heures.

7. Il est minuit.

8. Il est six heures

12 La journée de Cédric

Cédric lives on the island of Martinique. Help him tell how he spends a typical vacation day by writing a caption for each picture.

Modèle:

8:00
Il est huit heures.
J'écoute de la musique.

1. 9:00
Il est neuf heures. Je ~~faire~~ joue au tennis

2. 11:00
Il est onze heures. ~~Je~~ J'nage.

3. 1:00
Il est un heures. Je ~~mange fast-food~~ vais

4. 2:00
Il est deux heures. Je ~~fa~~ joue au foot.

5. 4:00 quatre
Il est ~~cinq~~ heures. Je vais ~~Il faut~~ au cinéma

6. 6:00
Il est six heures. Je vais ~~Je faller~~ au café.

7. 10.00
Il est dix heures. Je regarde ~~da~~ la télé

Prononciation

The sound [a]

The sound of the French vowel a is similar to the sound of the letter "a" in the English words "calm" and "father." However, the French sound [a] is shorter than the English "a" sound. In fact, all French vowels are shorter than English vowels. Say each of these words:

mal   Malika   déjà   d'accord   allons-y   basket

The sound [i]

The sound of the French vowel i is similar to the sound of the letters "ee" in the English word "see." Say each of these words:

midi   merci   Christine   idée   cinéma   musique

Vocabulaire

des desserts (m.):

une glace à la vanille

une glace au chocolat

des boissons (f.):

un coca

une eau minérale

une limonade

une crêpe

un jus de raisin

un café

un jus de pomme

une quiche

un steak-frites

une omelette

un jus d'orange

un sandwich au fromage
chese sandwich

un hamburger

un sandwich au jambon
ham sandwich

une salade

un hot-dog

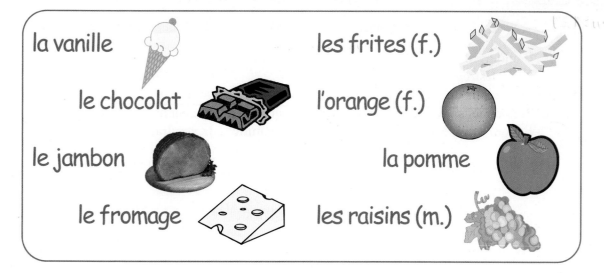

la vanille

le chocolat

le jambon

le fromage

les frites (f.)

l'orange (f.)

la pomme

les raisins (m.)

Serveur

Madame Paganini

Monsieur Paganini

Monsieur and Madame Paganini are having lunch at a small café on **le boulevard Saint-Michel** in Paris. The server arrives to take their order.

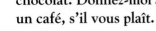

Serveur:	**Bonjour, Messieurs-Dames. Vous désirez?**
Mme Paganini:	**Je voudrais une salade et un jus de pomme, s'il vous plaît.**
Serveur:	**Et pour vous, Monsieur?**

M. Paganini:	**Je voudrais un steak-frites et une eau minérale, s'il vous plaît.**
Serveur:	**Et comme dessert?**
M. Paganini:	**Je voudrais une glace au chocolat. Donnez-moi aussi un café, s'il vous plaît.**

Le Quartier latin

Le boulevard Saint-Michel runs through the heart of the Latin Quarter in Paris. Located near France's most famous university, la Sorbonne, this street is one of the centers of student life.

Les frites

Steak-frites refers to a steak that is served with French fries. **Frites** are also popular in Belgium, where they originated. French fry snack bars in Belgium are called **friteries**.

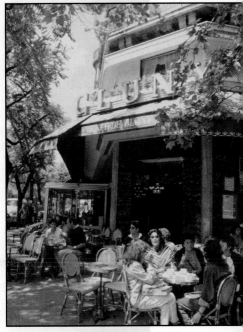

Students at the Sorbonne take a break from their studies at a café on *le boulevard Saint-Michel.*

Les boissons

Some popular brands of mineral water are Vittel, Perrier, Vichy, Contrex, Évian and Badoit. Fruit juices are not just for breakfast but are served throughout the day. Usually, only young children drink milk. **Un diabolo menthe** is a sweet drink made by mixing lemon-lime soda with mint-flavored syrup. Other drinks can be made with different flavored syrups. French speakers also buy popular American soft drinks.

Un diabolo menthe is one of many beverages that can be made by mixing a flavored syrup with lemon-lime soda.

Le café

The French, even teenagers, have coffee at the end of a meal, rather than during it. They may order **un express** (*espresso coffee*) or **un café crème** (*coffee with cream*) during the day when at a café with their friends. Coffee is made and served one cup at a time rather than by the pot.

Les crêpes

Students often stop with their friends at **crêperies** (*crêpe shops*), where they snack on a dessert crêpe. Resembling thin pancakes, crêpes can be filled with jam or with butter and sugar or even with chocolate. They originated in the province of Brittany in northwestern France but are now a popular dessert throughout the country. As a meal, these pancakes can be made with buckwheat flour. Then called **galettes**, they may be filled with ham, eggs or cheese.

It's easy to find an outdoor *crêperie* where you can buy hot *crêpes.*

1 Vous désirez?

Write the letter of the food item that you hear.

CEDAB

A.   B.   C.   D.   E.

2 Vous avez faim ou soif?

Répondez en français.

Modèle:

J'ai soif.

1.   2.   3.   4.   5.   6.   7.   8.

3 ▸ Qu'est-ce que c'est?

Identifiez.

Modèle:

C'est une....
C'est une **omelette**.

1. C'est une....
2. C'est un....
3. C'est un....
4. C'est un....
5. C'est une....
6. C'est une....
7. C'est un....
8. C'est un....

C'est une quiche spéciale… une quiche lorraine.

4 **Qu'est-ce que vous désirez?**

Répondez en français.

困死了！ *(handwritten)*

give me *(handwritten)*

Modèle:

Vous désirez un café ou un jus d'orange? — or *(handwritten)*
Donnez-moi un jus d'orange, s'il vous plaît.

What do U want? *(handwritten)* please *(handwritten)*

Vous désirez?

Donnez-moi un sandwich au jambon et un diabolo menthe.

1. Vous désirez une glace à la vanille ou une glace au chocolat? Donnez-moi à la vanille, s'il vous plaît. *(handwritten)*
2. Vous désirez un sandwich au fromage ou un steak-frites? Donnez-moi un steak-frites, s'il vous plaît *(handwritten)*
3. Vous désirez un jus de pomme ou un jus de raisin? Donnez-moi un jus de raisin, s'il vous plaît *(handwritten)*
4. Vous désirez un coca ou une limonade? Donnez-moi un coca, s'il vous plaît. *(handwritten)*
5. Vous désirez une quiche ou une salade? Donnez-moi une salade, s'il vous plaît. *(handwritten)*
6. Vous désirez un hamburger ou un hot-dog? Donnez-moi un hot-dog, s'il vous plaît *(handwritten)*
7. Vous désirez une pomme ou une orange? Donnez-moi une orange, s'il vous plaît *(handwritten)*

Langue active

Gender of nouns and indefinite articles

A noun is the name of a person, place or thing. Unlike nouns in English, every French noun has a gender, either masculine or feminine. You will need to remember the gender of each French noun that you learn. You can usually tell if a noun is masculine or feminine by what precedes it. For example, a noun preceded by **un** is masculine, and a noun preceded by **une** is feminine. **Un** and **une**, meaning "a" or "an," are called indefinite articles. If you don't know whether a noun is masculine or feminine, you can find out by looking it up in the end vocabulary of this textbook.

C'est une omelette.

我也要吃！ *(handwritten)*

Pratique

5 ▶ Au café

Count the number of masculine items and the number of feminine items on each café receipt.

Café de l'Univers

un jus de pomme	2,29
un thé	2,74
une eau minérale	3,20
une salade verte	4,12
un steak-frites	10,67
une crêpe	3,51
Total	**26,53**

Café Olé

un coca	
une limonade	3,05
un sandwich au jambon	2,90
un croque-monsieur	4,27
	4,57
Total	
	14,79

Café Brocéliande

un diabolo menthe	3,35
un jus de raisin	2,29
une glace à la vanille	4,88
une glace au chocolat	4,88
Total	**15,40**

Café de la place de l'Horloge

	2,29
un express	2,74
un café-crème	3,05
un chocolat	4,12
une tarte aux fraises	1,37
un croissant	13,57
Total	

6 ▶ En euros, s'il vous plaît!

Using the café receipts from Activity 5, name one item you could order for each price.

Modèle:

2,74
un café-crème

1. 2,90
2. 3,20
3. 10,67
4. 3,51
5. 4,88
6. 3,05

Vous désirez une salade verte?

En partenaires

 With a partner, play the roles of various customers at a sidewalk café and a server. The customer orders certain things to eat and drink; the server repeats each order. Follow the model.

Modèle:

A: **Je voudrais un sandwich au fromage et une eau minérale, s'il vous plaît.**
B: **Alors, un sandwich au fromage et une eau minérale?**
A: **Oui, Monsieur/Madame/Mademoiselle.**

Communication

and you? = et vous?

8 ## En groupes de trois

With two of your classmates, play the roles of two customers who order a snack and something to drink at a sidewalk café and the server who waits on them.

1. The server and the two customers greet each other.
2. The server asks what the customers would like.
3. Each customer politely orders a <u>snack</u> and something to drink.
4. As the server repeats the two orders, he or she gets them mixed up, switching the beverages.
5. Each customer again says his or her order.
6. The server repeats both orders correctly.

Je voudrais un jus d'orange, s'il vous plaît.

Je voudrais un hamburger et un jus d'orange, sil vous plait.
(vú-tèi) *(jui dề hống jiǔ)*

9 ## En famille

You are going to order for your entire family at a French fast-food restaurant. Before you place your order, make a list in French of what everyone wants. Organize your list by categories so that you can order efficiently.

Your mother wants a salad and mineral water.

Your father wants something hot to eat and a hot drink.

Your sister wants ice cream and a cold drink.

Your brother wants a sandwich and fruit juice.

You want...

On désire manger au fast-food.

10 ## On bouffe ensemble.

不要放大行吗

Pick up something to eat and drink at a fast-food restaurant for you and four friends. Write down your order in advance.

Qu'est-ce que tu aimes manger au fast-food?

La cuisine française

French food

Even on Paris's most famous street, *les Champs-Élysées*, you can get a quick bite to eat.

French restaurants have earned the reputation of serving some of the best cuisine in the world. You can grab a sandwich from a sidewalk stand, spend some time at a café or eat a meal consisting of many courses at an elegant restaurant.

While walking downtown, people often grab a simple snack, such as a sandwich, hot dog, crêpe or slice of pizza, from a sidewalk stand. People with more time usually stop at a café where they can talk with friends, read the newspaper or watch people strolling by as they eat their food. Since menus are displayed outside cafés, you know in advance what is available and how much it will cost. In nice weather people usually sit on **la terrasse** (*terrace*) outside in front of a café. Tourists in Paris visit some of the world-famous cafés, such as the Deux Magots, the Café de Flore and Fouquet's.

In Brittany, as in other regions of France, people enjoy sitting on the *terrasse* of their favorite café when it's bright and sunny.

Can you recognize what's in a *salade niçoise*? It gets its name from the city of Nice.

Since each region of France and each French-speaking country has its own specialty, there is something available for every taste and budget. You can order **choucroute garnie** (*sauerkraut with meat*) from the Alsace region near Germany, a **crêpe** from Brittany or a **salade niçoise** (*salad made with lettuce, cold vegetables,* *hard-cooked eggs, olives, anchovies, tuna and a vinaigrette dressing*) from the city of Nice on the Riviera. Of course, each region produces its own cheese, wine and even candy to share with the rest of the country. North African restaurants serve couscous, a dish of steamed semolina usually accompanied by a meat stew and a variety of sauces. Creole cuisine, from Martinique and Guadeloupe, is fairly spicy and uses many different fruits and seafoods. **La tourtière**, a meat potpie, originated in Quebec. Spicy Cajun cuisine from New Orleans is popular throughout the world.

Couscous, a spicy meat stew on a bed of semolina, is a popular main course.

The chef at *La Tour d'Argent*, a world-renowned restaurant in Paris, displays some of his specialties in front of a breathtaking view of *Notre-Dame*.

In eating formally at a restaurant, people can choose either certain courses from the menu or a full-course meal at a fixed price. They may eat various courses, starting with an **hors-d'œuvre**, such as **crudités** (*raw vegetables, often shredded*), then a meat and vegetable course, a salad, cheese and finally dessert. Some fixed-price meals may have only three courses. Diners eat fresh bread throughout the entire meal. A small cup of espresso is served at the end. You can expect to wait a while between courses at a French restaurant. French people do not like to eat quickly and often spend hours at the table. They take great pleasure in eating well. It is often said that a good meal is composed of three parts: good food, plenty of time and good conversation.

11 ▶ La cuisine française

Répondez aux questions.

1. What are three types of French eating establishments? *[handwritten: café, restaurant, sidewalk stand]*
2. What can you order to eat at a sidewalk stand? *[handwritten: sandwich, hot dog, crêpe or slice of pizza]*
3. Besides eating, what do people do at cafés? *[handwritten: talk with friends, read newspaper, watch people strolling by]*
4. How can you decide where you want to eat before sitting down? *[handwritten: U can see the menu outside cafés]*
5. What are two regional specialties in France? *[handwritten: choucroute garnie, salade niçoise]*
6. What is a specialty from North Africa? *[handwritten: cheese and couscous]*
7. What are five courses a typical French restaurant serves? *[handwritten: a meat, vegetable courses, a salad, cheese and finally dessert]*
8. Why may the service seem slow to an American who dines at a French restaurant? *[handwritten: French people dont like eat quickly]*
9. For a French person, what three ingredients compose a good meal? *[handwritten: good food, plenty of time and good conversation.]*

When the French dine out, they often spend hours enjoying a good meal.

12 ▶ Au restaurant

Imagine that you are a server at Le Rétro. Your table ordered a salad, a steak with fries, an omelette, a quiche, a cup of coffee, a bottle of Badoit mineral water and a Coke. Prepare the check for your table of three customers, using the receipt from the Chez Paul restaurant as a model. Your check should show the name, address and phone number of the restaurant, the number of the table you have been serving, the number of people at the table (**couverts**) and a list of the food and prices as well as the total amount to be paid.

[handwritten: bill → la facture (invoice) restaurant → L'addition (付諸帳單)]

Restaurant

CHEZ PAUL
"Le Bistrot Traditions"

13, rue de Charonne
75011 PARIS
Tél. 01.47.00.34.57

Ouvert tous les jours, midi et soir (commande jusqu'a 0h30)

```
*×*×*×*×*CHEZ    PAUL*
        COMME CHEZ SOI
    13 RUE DE CHARONNE 75011
        TEL 01 47 00 34 57


TABLE       7

COUVERTS:   3

    1 POULET A L ESTRAGON
    1 LEGUMES SAISON
    1 ESCALOPE SAUMON
    1 SOUPE DE MELON
    1 DOUBLE CAFE
    1 BADOIT BT
    1 PICHET 50 SAUVIGNON

        S/TOTAL

*  TOTAL  *          40

MAISON RECOMMANDEE PAR LES GUIDES R

DIM 08  JUL 07      Garçon *
```

Restaurant LE RÉTRO

Babeth et Roger

1, rue Paul Fort
75014 PARIS
Tél. 01 45 40 97 56

20 VINGT
21 vingt et un
22 vingt-deux
23 vingt-trois

30 TRENTE （以下结尾也发音）
31 trente et un
32 trente-deux
33 trente-trois

40 QUARANTE
41 quarante et un
42 quarante-deux
43 quarante-trois

50 CINQUANTE
51 cinquante et un
52 cinquante-deux
53 cinquante-trois

60 SOIXANTE
61 soixante et un
62 soixante-deux
63 soixante-trois

70 SOIXANTE-DIX
71 soixante et onze
72 soixante-douze
73 soixante-treize
74 soixante-quatorze
75 soixante-quinze
76 soixante-seize
77 soixante-dix-sept
78 soixante-dix-huit
79 soixante-dix-neuf

80 QUATRE-VINGTS
81 quatre-vingt-un 没有et
82 quatre-vingt-deux
83 quatre-vingt-trois

90 QUATRE-VINGT-DIX
91 quatre-vingt-onze 没有et
92 quatre-vingt-douze
93 quatre-vingt-treize
94 quatre-vingt-quatorze
95 quatre-vingt-quinze
96 quatre-vingt-seize
97 quatre-vingt-dix-sept
98 quatre-vingt-dix-huit
99 quatre-vingt-dix-neuf

100 CENT （末）

Vocabulaire

法国人什么奇葩思维!!

20: vingt 加单位数
30: trente 加单位数
40: quarante 加单位数
50: cinquante 加单位数
60: soixante 加单位数
☆ 70: soixante 加双位数
☆ 80: quatre-vingt (4×20) – 单位数
☆ 90: quatre-vingt- (4×20) – 双位数
100: cent

quatre-vingt-un
Leçon C

Jean-François   Serveuse   Myriam

Jean-François and Myriam have just finished eating and are ready to pay the bill.

Jean-François: **Ça fait combien, Madame?**
Serveuse: *waitress*

Serveur waiter

Voyons, le sandwich au jambon coûte quatre euros vingt-sept, la quiche… cinq euros trente-quatre, et les deux boissons… cinq euros dix-huit. Ça fait quatorze euros soixante-dix-neuf.

Myriam: **Voilà quinze euros. Merci, Madame.**
Serveuse: **Je vous en prie.** *You're welcome*

L'addition

On a menu the words **service compris** mean that the tip (a 15% service charge) is included in the bill, but most people leave some small change as an extra tip for good service.

L'euro

The **euro (l'euro)** is the basic unit of money in France and in 11 other European countries. In each of these countries **l'euro** has the same value. Previously, **le franc** was the national currency of France.

Each **euro** is divided into 100 **cents** (or **centimes**). Bills are issued in denominations of 5, 10, 20, 50, 100, 200 and 500 **euros**. The greater the value, the larger the bill. There are also eight **euro** coins in denominations of one and two **euros** and 1, 2, 5, 10, 20 and 50 **cents**. Prices in **euros** are written with an € and sometimes a comma (**36,50 €** or **36 € 50 = trente-six euros cinquante**). The value of the **euro** depends on the daily exchange rate. Some other currencies used in French-speaking countries are **le dinar** (Algeria and Tunisia), **le dirham** (Morocco) and **le dollar canadien** (Quebec).

1 Ça fait combien?

Write the numbers that you hear in words.

2 Comment dit-on?

Répondez en français.

1. How do you ask in French how much something costs? *Ça fait combien?*

   Go head. welcome

2. How do you say "You're welcome" in French? *Je vous en p[...]*

3. What words appear on a menu to let you know that the tip is included in the bill? *service compris*

4. What is the basic unit of money in France? *euro*

5. How many other countries use money with this name? ~~*euro*~~ *eleven*

6. How do you write **dix-huit euros cinquante?**

   18,50€ or 18€50

Magali counts her *euros.*

3 Ça fait combien?

Répondez en français.

1. Douze et vingt-trois? *35*
2. Quatorze et quarante-deux? *82*
3. Trente-sept et vingt-huit? ~~*75*~~ *65*
4. Quarante et trente-trois? *73*
5. Cinquante et trente? *80*
6. Soixante et vingt et un? *81*
7. Soixante-dix et vingt? *90*
8. Treize et trente-quatre? *~~47~~*

4 ▸ En euros, s'il vous plaît!

Say how much the following food and beverage combinations cost.

sandwich au fromage	3,51 €
steak-frites	11,43 €
crêpe	3,20 €
quiche	3,66 €
omelette	4,27 €
salade	3,20 €
glace à la vanille	4,57 €
eau minérale	2,59 €
café	2,44 €
jus d'orange	2,74 €
jus de pomme	2,74 €
limonade	2,90 €
coca	3,05 €

1. une crêpe et un jus d'orange 3,2 + 2,74 = 5,94
2. un sandwich au fromage et un jus de pomme 3,51 + 2,74 = 6,25
3. une quiche et une limonade 11,43 + 2,9 = 14,33
4. un steak-frites et un coca 11,43 + 3,05 = 14,48
5. une glace à la vanille et un café 4,57 + 2,44 = 7,01
6. une salade et une eau minérale 3,2 + 2,59 = 5,79

5 ▸ C'est à toi!

Questions personnelles.

1. Tu aimes aller au café? Oui
2. Qu'est-ce que tu manges au café? café. frites
3. Tu aimes beaucoup aller au fast-food? Oui
4. Qu'est-ce que tu manges au fast-food? hamburger coca
5. Qu'est-ce que tu aimes comme dessert? glace
6. Qu'est-ce que tu aimes comme boisson? coca

Jun aime bien aller au café.

Langue active

Definite articles

To refer to a specific person, place or thing, you use a definite article. In French the singular definite articles are **le**, **la** and **l'**, all meaning "the." **Le** precedes a masculine word beginning with a consonant sound.

Le sandwich au jambon coûte cinq euros.	*The ham sandwich costs five euros.*

La precedes a feminine word beginning with a consonant sound.

La quiche est délicieuse.	*The quiche is delicious.*

J'aime bien la quiche.

L' is used instead of **le** or **la** before a masculine or feminine word beginning with a vowel sound.

Je préfère **l'**eau minérale.	*I prefer mineral water.*
L'omelette est pour Marie-Hélène.	*The omelette is for Marie-Hélène.*

A definite article may also designate a noun in a general sense.

J'aime **la** glace.	*I like ice cream (in general).*

The subject pronoun **il** (*it*) may replace a masculine singular noun.

Le dessert est superbe.	*The dessert is superb.*
Il est superbe.	*It is superb.*

The subject pronoun **elle** (*it*) may replace a feminine singular noun.

La salade est fraîche.	*The salad is fresh.*
Elle est fraîche.	*It is fresh.*

J'aime le chocolat. Il est délicieux.

Pratique

6 **Vous aimez ou pas?**

Tell whether or not you like the following foods and beverages.

Modèles:

J'aime la glace à la vanille.

1. J'aime le pizza.

2. J'aime l'eau minérale

Je n'aime pas le jus d'orange.

3. Je n'aime pas le jambon.

4. Je n'aime pas le coca.

5. Je n'aime pas le café.

6. Je n'aime pas le fromage.

7. Je n'aime pas le chocolat 好想吃 😊

8. Je n'aime pas la quiche

9. Je n'aime pas le steak.

10. Je n'aime pas la lemonade.

Cognates

If you recognize a word in French because there is a similar word in English, it may be a cognate. Being able to distinguish which words are cognates will help you to make sense of the reading as a whole and increase your vocabulary in French. For example, in the context of school, can you figure out what **histoire** and **cours** mean, knowing that they are cognates? **Histoire** means "history" and **cours** means "course."

Here are two hints to help you find other cognates.
1. For French words that contain a letter with a circumflex (^), replace that letter or the following one with an "s." When you do this, **coûter** resembles "cost."
2. For French words that begin with an é, replace the é with an "s." For example, **école** looks like "school."

But you must watch out for false cognates, words that look like English words but that have completely different meanings, such as **but** ("goal") and **chose** ("thing"). You can identify false cognates by reading in context and determining the part of speech of the word in question. Read the conversation that follows, remembering to pay attention to the title, the context, the order of sentences and possible cognates.

Au café

Isabelle rencontre son copain Michel à l'école.
— Salut, Michel. Ça va?
— Bien.
— Tu vas au café maintenant?
— Non, j'ai un cours.

Michel n'accepte pas l'invitation. Il va à son cours d'histoire. Isabelle a faim et elle va au café Printemps pour déjeuner. À la terrasse du café Printemps, le serveur arrive à sa table.

— Qu'est-ce que vous désirez, Mademoiselle?

— Je ne sais pas. Qu'est-ce qu'il y a aujourd'hui?

—Des steaks-frites, des crêpes au jambon et au fromage, une belle salade niçoise, de la soupe du jour, des sandwichs....

— Combien coûtent les sandwichs?

— Trois euros quatre-vingt-un.

— Je voudrais un sandwich au thon, aux œufs et au maïs, avec de la mayonnaise, s'il vous plaît. Et puis, comme j'ai soif aussi, je prendrais....

— Du thé? Du café? Du coca? Une eau minérale? Un jus d'orange?

— Je voudrais un coca, s'il vous plaît, et une glace au chocolat. Merci!

Après le déjeuner, le serveur lui apporte l'addition.

— Ça fait combien?

— Ça fait six euros quatre-vingt-six.

— Voilà sept euros. Merci, Monsieur.

— À votre service, Mademoiselle.

Après son cours, Michel rencontre son amie Isabelle devant le café. Quelle bonne surprise!

[handwritten notes:]
cours : course
frites : fries
salade : salad
sandwichs : sandwiches
coca : coke
minérale : mineral
six : six
service : service
su

15 ▸ **Les mots apparentés**

Make a list of all the cognates in the reading. If the French word is not spelled the same as its English counterpart, write the English word next to it.

Nathalie et Raoul

Évaluation

✓ Évaluation culturelle

Decide if each statement is **vrai** or **faux**.

1. Because France has strict rules about eating balanced meals, fast-food restaurants are not allowed in the country.
2. French families usually buy fresh bread and vegetables daily.
3. French fries originated in France.
4. Vichy, Perrier and Évian are popular brands of mineral water.
5. Crêpes resemble thin pancakes and can be filled with jam or with butter and sugar.
6. French cafés post their menus outside.
7. The French usually eat a salad before they begin their meat and vegetable course.
8. **Service compris** means that a service charge or tip is included in the price of the food and beverages.
9. **L'euro** is the basic unit of French money.

✓ Évaluation orale

Your French class is setting up and running a French café for International Day. With a partner, practice a typical café conversation by playing the roles of a server and a customer.

Greet each other in French. Ask each other how you are and answer.

Ask the customer what he or she would like.

Order something to eat and drink as well as a dessert. After finishing your meal, ask the server how much it costs.

Give the price of each item and the total.

Say how much you are leaving to cover the bill and tip.

Thank the customer.

Tell each other good-bye.

✓ Évaluation écrite

Each café set up for International Day reflects a different region of France and its typical foods. As a group, choose a region of France and do research on its specific dishes. Next, give your café a name. Then create your café's menu with prices in euros.

✓ Évaluation visuelle

 With three classmates, write and then role-play a scene in which you choose, order and pay for something to eat and drink at a French café. Use the menu in the illustration. (You may want to refer to the *Révision de fonctions* on page 96 and the *Vocabulaire* on page 97.)

Menu

sandwich au jambon	4,30 €
sandwich au fromage	4,20 €
hot-dog	3,00 €
quiche	4,50 €
glace	3,80 €
crêpe	3,50 €
coca	3,10 €
jus d'orange	2,95 €
eau minérale	3,25 €

Révision de fonctions

Can you do all of the following tasks in French?
* I can invite someone to do something.
* I can accept or refuse an invitation.
* I can order something to eat and drink.
* I can ask for and state the price of something.
* I can ask what time it is and tell time on the hour.
* I can ask people how they are and tell them how I am.
* I can say whether I'm hungry or thirsty.

To invite someone to do something, use:

On va au café? *Shall we go to the café?*
Allons-y! *Let's go (there)!*

To accept an invitation, use:

D'accord. *OK.*

To refuse an invitation, use:

Moi, je préfère aller au fast-food. *I prefer going to the fast-food restaurant.*

To order food and beverages, use:

Je voudrais une salade, **s'il vous plaît.** *I would like a salad, please.*
Donnez-moi un café, **s'il vous plaît.** *Give me (a cup of) coffee, please.*

To ask for a price, use:

Ça fait combien? *How much is it/that?*

To state a price, use:

Ça fait trois **euros.** *That's/It's 3 euros.*
Ça coûte neuf **euros** quinze. *That costs 9,15 euros.*

To ask what time it is, use:

Quelle heure est-il? *What time is it?*

To tell time on the hour, use:

Il est trois **heures.** *It's three o'clock.*
Il est midi. *It's noon.*
Il est minuit. *It's midnight.*

To ask how someone is, use:

Comment vas-tu? *How are you?*
Comment allez-vous? *How are you?*

To tell how you are, use:

Très bien. *Very well.*
Bien. *Well.*
Pas mal. *Not bad.*
Mal. *Bad.*
Comme ci, comme ça. *So-so.*
J'ai faim. *I'm hungry.*
J'ai soif. *I'm thirsty.*

quatre-vingt-seize

Unité 3

96

Vocabulaire

allons-y let's go (there) A

une **boisson** drink, beverage B

ça that, it C

Ça fait.... That's/It's C

Ça fait combien? How much is it/that? C

un **café** café A; coffee B

cent (one) hundred C

le **chocolat** chocolate B

cinquante fifty C

un **coca** Coke B

combien how much C

comme like, for A

comme ci, comme ça so-so A

comment how A

Comment vas-tu? How are you? A

coûter to cost C

une **crêpe** crêpe B

déjà already A

des some B

désirer to want B

Vous désirez? What would you like? B

un **dessert** dessert B

donner to give B

Donnez-moi.... Give me .... B

l' **eau (f.)** water B

l'eau minérale (f.) mineral water B

est is A

un **euro** euro C

la **faim: J'ai faim.** I'm hungry. A

fait C

Ça fait.... That's/It's C

un **fast-food** fast-food restaurant A

des **frites (f.)** French fries B

le **fromage** cheese B

une **glace** ice cream B

une glace à la vanille vanilla ice cream B

une glace au chocolat chocolate ice cream B

un **hamburger** hamburger B

l' **heure (f.)** hour, time, o'clock A

Quelle heure est-il? What time is it? A

un **hot-dog** hot dog B

le **jambon** ham B

le **jus d'orange** orange juice B

le **jus de pomme** apple juice B

le **jus de raisin** grape juice B

une **limonade** lemon-lime soda B

mal bad, badly A

Messieurs-Dames ladies and gentlemen B

midi noon A

minuit midnight A

une **omelette** omelette B

une **orange** orange B

ou or A

une **pomme** apple B

prie: Je vous en prie. You're welcome. C

quarante forty C

quatre-vingt-dix ninety C

quatre-vingts eighty C

quel, quelle what, which A

une **quiche** quiche B

un **raisin** grape B

s'il vous plaît please B

une **salade** salad B

un **sandwich** sandwich B

un sandwich au fromage cheese sandwich B

un sandwich au jambon ham sandwich B

un **serveur, une serveuse** server B

la **soif: J'ai soif.** I'm thirsty. A

soixante sixty C

soixante-dix seventy C

un **steak** steak B

un steak-frites steak with French fries B

toi you A

trente thirty C

très very A

une **a, an, one** A

voilà here is/are, there is/are C

voudrais would like B

voyons let's see C

Unité

4

À l'école

In this unit you will be able to:

- express need
- ask what something is
- identify objects
- tell location
- ask for information
- give information
- agree and disagree
- express emotions
- describe daily routines
- invite
- state exact time

www.emcp.com

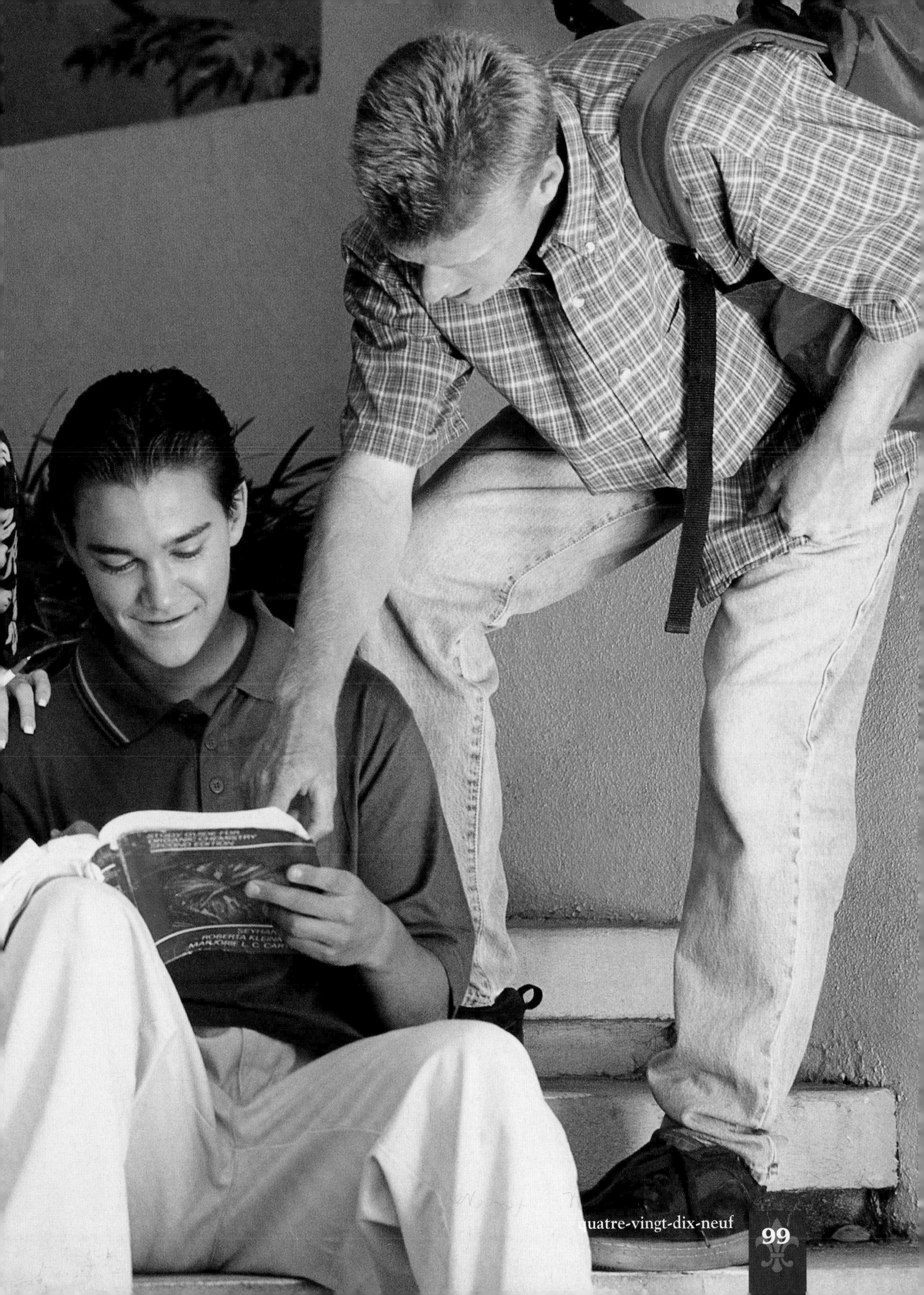

Vocabulaire

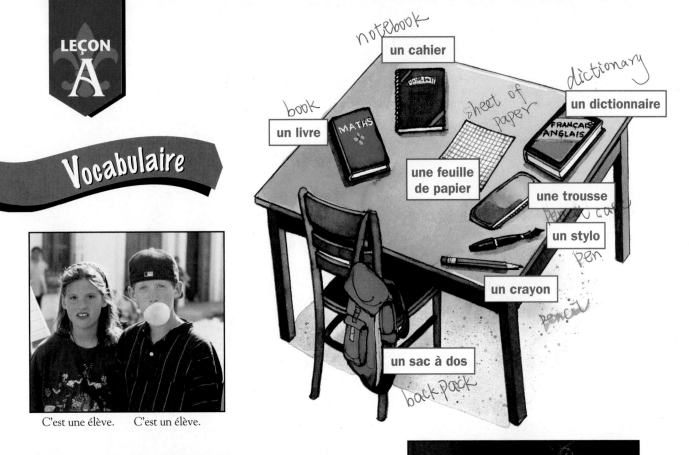

un cahier — *notebook*

un livre — *book*

un dictionnaire — *dictionary*

une feuille de papier — *sheet of paper*

une trousse

un stylo — *pen*

un crayon — *pencil*

un sac à dos — *backpack*

C'est une élève.   C'est un élève.

C'est une école. — *school*

C'est une étudiante.   C'est un étudiant. — *student*

C'est un professeur. C'est une prof. — *teacher teacher*

C'est un professeur. C'est un prof.

une salle de classe

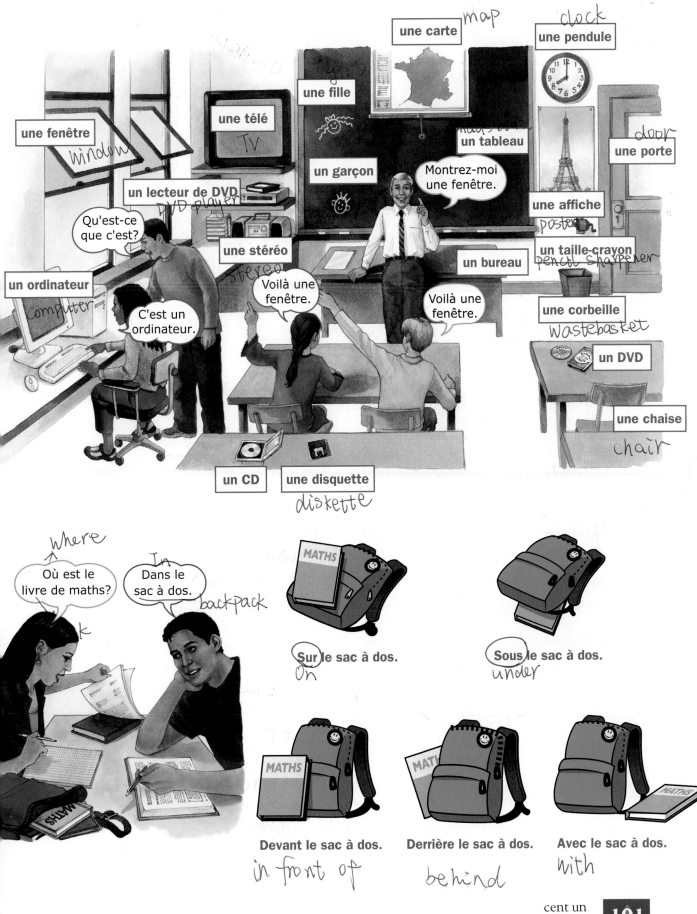

Alexandre

Louis

Où est le cahier de maths?

Alexandre and Louis are doing homework together.

Alexandre: **Zut! J'ai besoin d'étudier pour l'interro de maths, mais je n'ai pas le cahier. Où est le cahier de maths?**

Louis: **Dans le sac à dos?**

Alexandre: **Non, j'ai juste le livre de maths et la trousse dans le sac à dos.**

Louis: **Tiens! Qu'est-ce que c'est?**

Alexandre: **Quoi?**

Louis: **Là, devant toi, sur le bureau.**

Alexandre: **Oh, c'est le cahier de maths. Tant mieux. Bon ben, étudions!**

Où : where (wù)
ou : or

là : there/here
la : the

Trousse ou sac à dos?

French students often use **une trousse** to carry pens, pencils, rulers and other small school supplies. Students carry larger items in **un sac à dos**. In most French schools students do not have lockers; only teachers have a place to store their belongings.

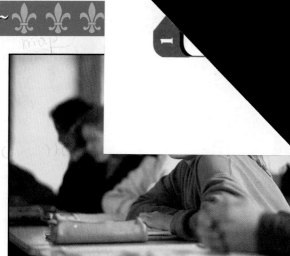

French *trousses* come in different shapes, colors and sizes.

Tiens!

Les interjections

Just as you do, French speakers use short words to express strong emotion. For example, **zut!** shows disgust. You have already seen **eh!** and **tiens!** used to mean "hey!" when someone is surprised. Short French words are also used to fill pauses in conversations. For instance, **ben**, the shortened form of **bien**, means "well."

Élève ou étudiant(e)?

Un élève refers to a male student; **une élève** refers to a female student. The words **un étudiant** and **une étudiante** traditionally refer to university students, but high school students like to use these terms to refer to themselves.

Would these students refer to themselves as *élèves* or *étudiantes*?

Dans la salle de classe

 Write the letter of the person or object that you find in a classroom.

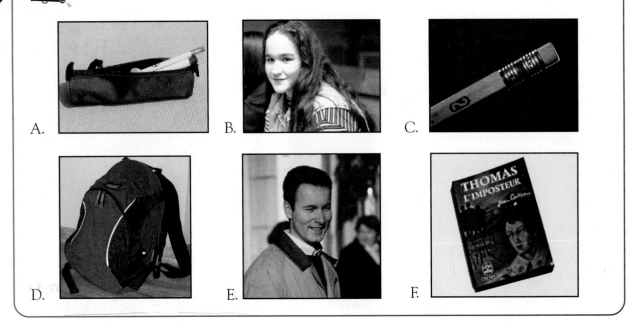

A.

B.

C.

D.

E.

F.

2 ▸ Les devoirs

Répondez en français.

1. Qui étudie avec Alexandre?
2. Alexandre étudie pour l'interro de maths?
3. Le cahier de maths est dans le sac à dos?
4. Le livre de maths est dans le sac à dos?
5. Où est la trousse?
6. Où est le cahier de maths?

3 ▸ En classe

Identifiez la personne ou l'objet.

Modèle:

C'est une pendule.

A. *Où est Luc?* Say where Luc is in relation to the teacher's desk.

Modèle:

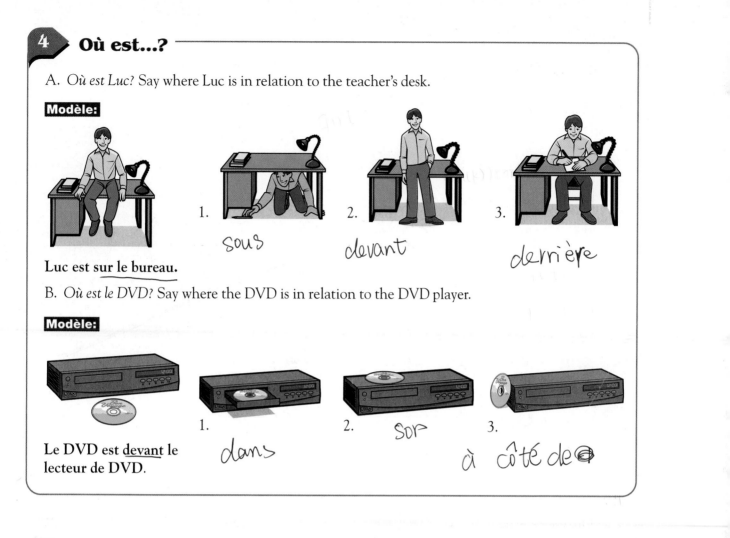

Luc est <u>sur</u> le bureau.

1. *sous*

2. *devant*

3. *derrière*

B. *Où est le DVD?* Say where the DVD is in relation to the DVD player.

Modèle:

Le DVD est <u>devant</u> le lecteur de DVD.

1. *dans*

2. *sor*

3. *à côté de*

Questions personnelles.

1. Tu étudies avec qui?
2. Tu aimes faire les devoirs?
3. Dans la salle de classe, qui est devant toi?
4. Dans la salle de classe, qui est derrière toi?
5. Qu'est-ce que tu préfères, un crayon ou un stylo?

Christelle étudie avec Simone et Anne.

Present tense of the irregular verb *avoir*

The verb **avoir** (*to have*) is irregular.

avoir			
j'	**ai**	nous	**avons**
tu	**as**	vous	**avez**
il/elle/on	**a**	ils/elles	**ont**

Vous **avez** une feuille de papier? *Do you have a sheet of paper?*
J'**ai** le cahier. *I have the notebook.*

Les Diop ont un ordinateur. (Les Courtillières)

Pratique

6 Dans la trousse

Dites si (Tell if) les élèves ont des crayons ou des stylos.

Modèles:

Jérémy

Jérémy a des crayons.

Diane et Anne-Marie

Diane et Anne-Marie ont des stylos.

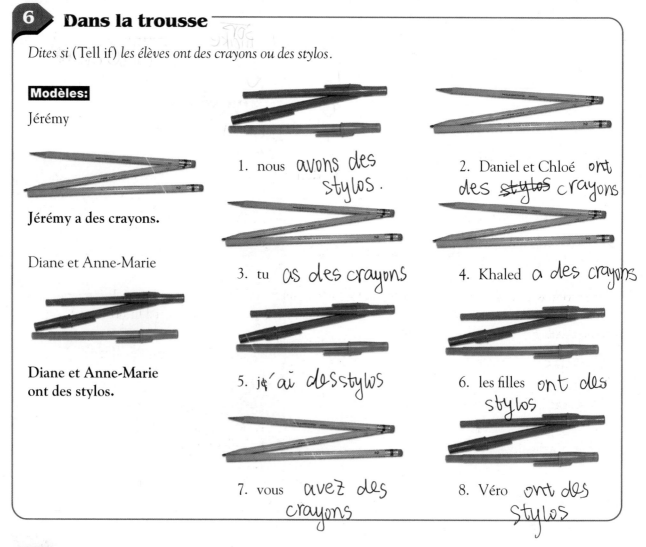

1. nous avons des stylos.
2. Daniel et Chloé ont des stylos crayons
3. tu as des crayons
4. Khaled a des crayons
5. j'ai desstylos
6. les filles ont des stylos
7. vous avez des crayons
8. Véro ont des stylos

Qu'est-ce qu'on a?

Dites quels objets chacun (everyone) a.

Modèle:

Abdoul

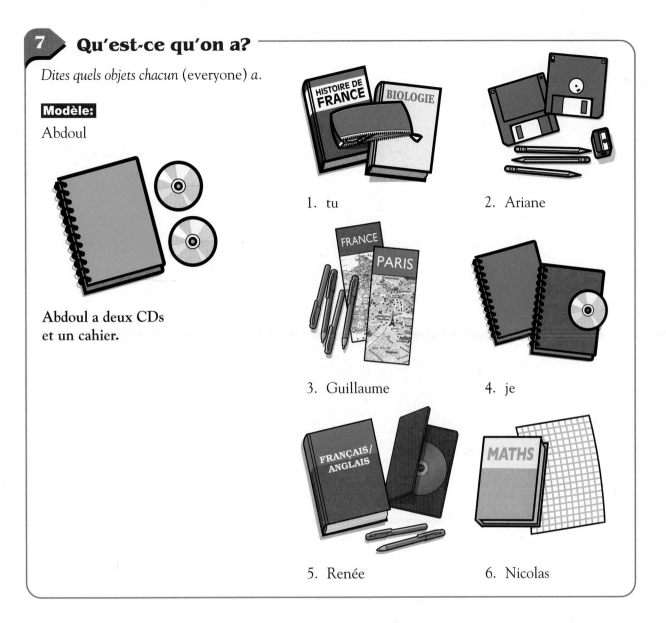

**Abdoul a deux CDs
et un cahier.**

1. tu

2. Ariane

3. Guillaume

4. je

5. Renée

6. Nicolas

Le pique-nique

Everyone who was supposed to bring food for the French class picnic remembered. But everyone who was assigned beverages forgot. Tell who has what they were supposed to bring and who doesn't.

Modèles:

Delphine et Saleh/les sandwichs
Delphine et Saleh ont les sandwichs.

Théo/le jus de pomme
Théo n'a pas le jus de pomme.

1. Nicole et Olivier/la salade
2. vous/la limonade
3. nous/les hot-dogs
4. tu/le fromage
5. les garçons/le coca
6. je/les pommes
7. Michèle/la glace
8. le prof/l'eau minérale

Expressions with *avoir*

You have already seen that forms of **avoir** are used in some French expressions where the verb "to be" is used in English. Two of these expressions are **avoir faim** (*to be hungry*) and **avoir soif** (*to be thirsty*).

J'**ai faim**.	*I'm hungry.*
Vous **avez soif**?	*Are you thirsty?*

To say that you need to do something or that you need something, use the expression **avoir besoin de** (*to need*). Remember that **de** becomes **d'** before a word beginning with a vowel sound.

Tu **as besoin de** téléphoner?	*Do you need to call?*
Oui, et j'**ai besoin d'**un euro.	*Yes, and I need a euro.*

Véro a besoin d'étudier.

9 ▸ **À la cantine**

Dites si les personnes à la cantine ont faim ou soif.

1. Théo et Nadia....
2. Nous....
3. Monsieur Bobot....
4. Yasmine....
5. Vous....
6. J'....
7. Les professeurs de maths....
8. Tu....

10 ▶ Interro ou excursion?

Les élèves de Mme Vaillancourt ont une interro demain. Les élèves de M. Messier vont à Disneyland Paris. Qui a besoin d'étudier?

Modèles:

Alexandre
A: **Alexandre a besoin d'étudier?**
B: **Oui, il a besoin d'étudier.**

Sophie et Karine
A: **Sophie et Karine ont besoin d'étudier?**
B: **Non, elles n'ont pas besoin d'étudier.**

Les élèves de Mme Vaillancourt	Les élèves de M. Messier
Arabéa	Jean-Philippe
Charles	Fatima
Nora	Sophie
Alain	Christine
Éric	Salim
Paul	Sonia
Alexandre	Karine
Cécile	Anne

1. Salim
2. Paul et Charles
3. Nora
4. Christine et Sonia
5. Fatima
6. Éric
7. Jean-Philippe et Anne
8. Arabéa et Cécile

Communication

11 ▶ La rentrée

You're going shopping to buy the back-to-school supplies that you need this year. Make a shopping list.

Tu as besoin de quoi?

3 ▸ Le calendrier

Quel jour est après (after)?

Modèle:

mardi
C'est mercredi.

1. dimanche   4. lundi
2. vendredi   5. jeudi
3. mercredi   6. samedi

4 ▸ L'emploi du temps de Marie-Ève

Look at Marie-Ève's **emploi du temps** (*schedule*). Write the appropriate day that matches each description.

Modèle:

Elle a musique.
le vendredi

EMPLOI DU TEMPS

heures	LUNDI	MARDI	MERCREDI	JEUDI	VENDREDI	SAMEDI
8h - 9h	Allemand	Géographie		Français	Sciences Naturelles	Latin (option)
9h - 10h	Fxs / E.E.	Mathématiques		Français	Étude	Mathématiques
10h - 11h	Mathématiques	Technologie		Latin (option)	Mathématiques	Sciences Physiques
11h - 12h	Français	Étude		Étude	Anglais	Anglais
12h - 13h30	Repas	Repas		Repas	Repas	
13h30 - 14h30	Étude	Allemand		Sciences Physiques	Allemand	
14h30 - 15h30	Sport	Anglais		Latin (option)	Musique	
15h30 - 16h30	Histoire	Français		Histoire	Sport	
16h30 - 17h30	Dessin					

1. Elle a juste quatre cours. *le samedi*
2. Elle a sport. *le lundi*
3. Elle n'a pas cours. *le mercredi*
4. Elle a allemand. *le mardi*
5. Elle a histoire. *le lundi et le jeudi*
6. Elle n'a pas maths. *le jeudi*
7. Elle a géographie. *le mardi*
8. Elle a anglais. *le vendredi*
9. Elle a deux heures de français et deux heures de latin. *le jeudi*

5 ▸ C'est à toi!

Questions personnelles.

1. Tu préfères quel jour de la semaine?
2. Tu as combien d'heures de sciences par semaine?
3. Tu aimes un peu ou beaucoup les sciences?
4. Tu as combien de minutes de français par jour?
5. Tu as combien de cours le mercredi?

Nous préférons mercredi et le foot.

Present tense of regular verbs ending in *-ir*

The infinitives of many French verbs end in **-ir**. Most of these verbs, such as **finir** (*to finish*), are regular because their forms follow a predictable pattern. To form the present tense of a regular **-ir** verb, first find the stem of the verb by removing the **-ir** ending from its infinitive.

Now add the endings (**-is, -is, -it, -issons, -issez, -issent**) to the stem of the verb depending on the corresponding subject pronouns.

finir — to finish			
je	**finis**	nous	**finissons**
tu	**finis**	vous	**finissez**
il/elle/on	**finit**	ils/elles	**finissent**

Vous **finissez** à quelle heure? *At what time do you finish?*
Le cours **finit** à midi. *The class ends at noon.*

Jérémy et Bruno finissent les devoirs.

Pratique

6 ▸ Les restes

Student A likes only fruits and desserts. Student B likes everything but fruits and desserts. Who will finish the leftovers?

Modèle:

le steak/la salade
A: **Tu finis le steak?**
B: **Oui, je finis le steak.**
    Tu finis la salade?
A: **Non, je ne finis pas**
    la salade.

1. la glace/les frites
2. la quiche/les raisins
3. le chocolat/les pommes
4. le jambon/le fromage

Tu finis le dessert?

cent quinze
Leçon B

115

7 Qui va au café?

David asks you who is going to the café after school. Only those who finish their last class before 3h30 can go. Answer his questions.

Modèles:

Assane va au café? (2h00)
Oui, il finit à deux heures.

Et Élisabeth et Louis vont au café? (4h00)
Non, ils finissent à quatre heures.

1. Et Catherine va au café? (5h00)
2. Et Laïla et toi, vous allez au café? (3h00)
3. Et Florence et Sabrina vont au café? (4h00)
4. Et Daniel va au café? (2h00)
5. Et André et Nicole vont au café? (3h00)
6. Et Max et moi, nous allons au café? (6h00)

Non, elle ̶i̶l̶s̶ finit à cinq heures.
Non, vous finissez à trois heures.
Non, elles finissent à quatre heures.
Oui, il finit à deux heures.
Non, ils finissent à trois heures
Non, nous finissons à six heures.

Communication

Les élèves vont au café. Ils finissent à 3h00.

你们是有多热？裤子要穿的那么不明显么？

8 Une enquête

To find out how much your classmates like various school subjects, draw a grid like the one that follows. In the grid write the names in French of five subjects and the expressions **beaucoup**, **un peu** and **ne... pas**. Then poll ten of your classmates.

1. Ask each classmate if he or she likes each subject and make a check by the response you hear.
2. After you have finished asking questions, tell how many students like each subject a lot, a little or not at all.

Modèle:

Henri: **Tu aimes l'histoire?**
Marie-Claire: **J'aime beaucoup l'histoire.**

....

Henri: **Six élèves aiment beaucoup l'histoire, trois élèves aiment un peu l'histoire et un élève n'aime pas l'histoire.**

	beaucoup	un peu	ne...pas
Tu aimes l'histoire?	✓✓✓✓✓✓	✓✓✓	✓
Tu aimes...?			
Tu aimes...?			
Tu aimes...?			
Tu aimes...?			

L'emploi du temps de Pierre-Jean

Voilà une lettre de Pierre-Jean. Créez son (Create his) emploi du temps sur une feuille de papier.

J'ai une heure de maths à 9h00.

J'ai dix cours différents par semaine. J'ai une heure de chimie le lundi à 10h00, de 10h00 à 12h00 le mardi et le jeudi, et de 9h00 à 10h00 le vendredi. Le lundi, le mardi, le mercredi, le jeudi et le samedi, j'ai une heure de maths à 9h00. Le français est de 14h00 à 15h00 le lundi et de 15h00 à 17h00 le jeudi. Le lundi, le mardi et le vendredi, j'ai une heure de géographie à 15h00. J'ai sport le mercredi de 14h00 à 17h00. J'aime beaucoup le sport! J'ai anglais de 10h00 à 11h00 le mercredi, le vendredi et le samedi, et j'ai une heure d'allemand le lundi et le mercredi à 11h00 et de 14h00 à 15h00 le vendredi. Le samedi à 11h00 j'ai une heure de musique. J'ai une heure de philosophie à 14h00 le mardi et le jeudi, et j'ai une heure d'histoire à 13h00 le lundi et à 11h00 le vendredi. Je finis à 12h00 le samedi.

10 ▸ Combien de minutes?

Based on the schedule you created in Activity 9, figure out how many minutes Pierre-Jean spends in each class per week. Write this number in French. Finally, total the number of minutes he spends in class each week.

Modèle:

la chimie - trois cents minutes par semaine

L'enseignement secondaire en France

Métro, take the trains   **boulot,** work   **dodo!** sleep

"Métro, boulot, dodo!" This expression sums up how people who live in Paris describe their daily routine of taking the subway, going to work and then going to bed. This rhyme also describes the busy schedule of students, since education is a full-time job for French teenagers.

Secondary education begins when 11-year-olds enter **le collège**, or **C.E.S. (Collège d'Enseignement Secondaire)**. They stay here for four years: **sixième (6ème)**, **cinquième (5ème)**, **quatrième (4ème)** and **troisième (3ème)**. These years correspond to junior high school or middle school in the United States. (Note that the way of labeling school years is the opposite of the American system.)

Since the public educational system is the same all over the country, all French students use similar textbooks, follow similar course schedules and take the same major tests. Students spend up to ten hours a day at school, since classes begin as early as 8:00 A.M. and sometimes continue as late as 6:00 P.M. However, all classes do not meet every day. For example, one day a student may have six classes, and another day just two; he or she may have history twice a week, French three times a week, and drawing once a week. Students have Wednesday afternoons off to study, play sports or meet friends. Some classes are held on Saturday mornings. Students must take a second language. They begin learning their first foreign language, usually English or German, in **sixième** and then add a second language a few years later. Teenagers usually have hours of homework to do every night.

Martine is a student in cinquième at le Collège Montaigne.

At the end of **troisième**, students take their first big exam, **le brevet des collèges**. The results of this test do not affect entrance into high school (**le lycée**), but a high grade is naturally a morale boost. After four years at **le collège**, some students choose to go to a vocational school, while others who are academically inclined attend **le lycée**.

Students go to **le lycée** in **seconde** (2ème), **première** (1ère) and **terminale**. Here they choose a major area of study in preparation for **le baccalauréat** (**bac**), the national exam which usually determines whether or not students may continue their studies at a university. In **première**, students take the first part of **le bac**, which concentrates on the French language. The second half of **le bac**, given in **terminale**, focuses on each student's area of concentration.

A typical French **lycée** classroom is sparsely decorated. Students sit at tables instead of desks. Classroom instruction focuses on the teacher and textbook, with few of the visual aids seen on the walls of many American classrooms. Likewise, the relationship between teacher and students, which is often personal in the United States, is more formal in France.

Two students share a table in a typical French *lycée*.

As for grades, the French use a point system, with 20 points being the top score. Instead of an "A," a student might receive 18 out of 20. Teachers grade strictly and students are often happy when they get a score of 12 out of 20. Students need to have an overall average of 10 out of 20 to pass to the next grade, otherwise they must repeat it. Repeating a grade is fairly common in France: over half of the students in **le lycée** repeat at least one year of school. They may take **le bac** over if they don't pass it the first time, but if they fail a second time, they must repeat the whole school year.

During the school day, students meet in the school courtyard or at lunch to talk with friends. A long lunch period in **la cantine** or **la caféteria** usually breaks up the school day. However, many students choose to leave the school grounds to have lunch in a café or at home. After school, teenagers may stop for **un goûter** (*afternoon snack*) at a sidewalk stand or for a beverage at a local café. Cocurricular activities generally take place away from school in France, and organized sports are less important in French **lycées** than they are in American high schools.

For their *goûter*, French students might also stop at a pastry shop for *un pain au chocolat*.

11 ▸ L'enseignement secondaire en France

Répondez aux questions.

1. What is junior high school called in France? *le collège & C.E.S*
2. What is one similarity between French and American secondary schools? *Schools begin at 8am* / *have cafeteria*
3. What is one difference between French and American secondary schools? *French students have Wednesday after off*
4. What is the name of the test that students take at the end of **le collège**? *le brevet des collège* / *leaver → points*
5. What is senior high school called in France? *le lycée*
6. What may French students do instead of attending a **lycée**? *Go to vocational schools*
7. Why is **le baccalauréat** so important? *It determines whether or not students may continue their studies in Univers...*
8. What is one difference between classrooms in France and the United States? *A typical classroom lycée is sparsely decorated*
9. What overall score do students need to pass to the next grade? *10/20*
10. Where might students go to eat lunch during the school day? *la cantine or cafeteria* *(or home)*

Solange gets a well-balanced lunch in her school's *cantine*.

12 ▸ Le bulletin de notes de Michel

Looking at Michel's **bulletin de notes** (*report card*) for a three-week period, answer the following questions.

1. How many different courses did Michel take? *14*
2. In what class did Michel receive the highest grade? *Langue vivante I*
3. What were Michel's three scores in French composition? *14, 16, 15*
4. What four languages did he take? *Anglais Espagnal. Latin French*
5. How many periods of science did Michel have? *French*
6. What grade did Michel receive for his **leçons** (*lessons*) in art?
7. How many teachers signed the report card? *one*
8. Was Michel an honor student? *Oui*
9. The **appréciations** (*comments*), such as **très bien, bien, assez bien** (*fairly well*) and **vous pouvez mieux faire** (*you can do better*), show the teachers' opinions of Michel's efforts. What would your French teacher write about your efforts in class? *I've no idea.*
10. In what class did Michel do **assez bien**? *Musique*

PÉRIODE DU _____			AU _____	
	Leçons	Devoirs de contrôle	Autres devoirs	APPRÉCIATIONS
Composition française	14	16	15	
Orthographe Grammaire	17	17,5	18	C'est bien. Continuez.
Récitations	18	16	17	
Mathématiques	17,5	15,5	16	Bien, vous pouvez mieux faire.
Langue vivante I Anglais Allemand	17	19	18,5	Très bien.
Langue vivante II Anglais Allemand Espagnol	15,5	16	17,5	Bien, vous avez fourni des efforts.
Latin ou Grec ou langue renforcée	15	14,5	16	Bien, Continuez
Histoire Géographie	16	16	17	C'est bien. Apprenez plus la Géographie.
Biologie Géologie	17,5	15,5	16	C'est bien. Travaillez encore la Géologie
Sciences Physiques	18	15	17,5	Très bien.
Technologie	18	18	18	Très bien.
Dessin	17,5	17	17	
Musique	17	15,5	16	Assez bien
Education Physique	17	15	16	Continuez
Le Professeur Principal			TABLEAU D'HONNEUR	ENCOURAGEMENT
Ph. De la Pastelle				Les Parents

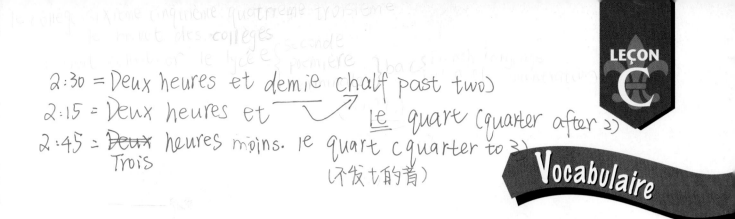
2:30 = Deux heures et demie (half past two)
2:15 = Deux heures et → le quart (quarter after)
2:45 = ~~Deux~~ heures moins. le quart (quarter to)
   Trois
(不发t的音)

Il est une heure et quart.

Il est deux heures et demie.

Il est quatre heures moins le quart.

On finit à 12h40.

Nora

Patricia

Nora and Patricia meet in the hall before school.

Nora: On mange ensemble? *We eat together?*

Patricia: Voyons, c'est vendredi. J'ai trois *Friday*
cours - musique, dessin et philosophie.
Je finis à 12h30. On va à la cantine
à 12h45?

Nora: D'accord. Tu as un bon emploi
du temps. *That's your schedule*

Patricia: Mais c'est vendredi. Le lundi je
commence à 8h00 et je finis
à 17h30.

L'heure

Many French-speaking countries use the 24-hour clock to give the times for TV programs, films, plays, sporting events, class schedules, plane and train schedules, etc. This 24-hour system eliminates the need for specifying A.M. or P.M. To convert the P.M. system to the 24-hour system, add 12 hours. For example, 3:00 P.M. is the same as 15h00. Conversely, to convert the 24-hour system to the P.M. system, subtract 12 hours.

L'heure précise

To clarify the difference between A.M. and P.M., the French say **du matin** (*in the morning*), **de l'après-midi** (*in the afternoon*) and **du soir** (*in the evening*).

Il est dix heures du matin.

Il est dix heures du soir.

1 Quelle heure est-il?

Write the time that you hear in numbers.

2 À l'école

Répondez en français.

1. C'est quel jour?
2. Patricia a combien de cours?
3. Patricia finit à quelle heure?
4. Nora et Patricia vont manger où?
5. Patricia commence à quelle heure le lundi?
6. Patricia finit à quelle heure le lundi?

3 Votre emploi du temps

Écrivez votre (Write your) *emploi du temps en français.*

C'est à toi!

Questions personnelles.

1. Qu'est-ce que tu étudies à 9h00? ~~religious~~
2. Tu manges avec qui à midi? *Qui*
3. Tu manges à l'école? *Oui*
4. Tu as combien de cours le vendredi? *Non*
5. Tu finis à 12h30 le vendredi? *Non*
6. Qu'est-ce que tu aimes faire à 17h00?
   What   *J'aime étudier*

Je finis à trois heures moins vingt le vendredi.

Langue active

Telling exact time

You have already learned how to ask what time it is and to tell time on the hour in French.

Quelle heure est-il?   *What time is it?*
Il est dix heures.   *It's 10:00.*

To tell that it's quarter after the hour, add **et quart** or **quinze**.

Il est huit heures **et quart**. ⎫
Il est huit heures **quinze**.   ⎭   *It's 8:15.*

> **Il est trois heures et quart.**

To tell that it's half past the hour, add **et demi(e)** or **trente**.

Il est midi **et demi**.   *It's 12:30.*
Il est trois heures **et demie**. ⎫
Il est trois heures **trente**.   ⎭   *It's 3:30.*
⟶ minus 减去

> **Il est six heures et demie.**

To tell that it's quarter to the hour, add **moins le quart** before the next hour or **quarante-cinq** after the hour.

Il est **six heures moins le quart**. ⎫
Il est **cinq heures quarante-cinq**. ⎭   *It's 5:45.*

> **Il est neuf heures moins le quart.**

To tell that it's minutes after the hour but before the half hour, say the number of minutes after the hour.

Il est quinze heures **vingt**.   *It's 3:20 P.M.*

To tell that it's minutes before the hour, say either **moins** and the number of minutes subtracted from the next hour or say the number of minutes after the hour.

Il est **quatre heures moins cinq**.   ⎫
Il est **trois heures cinquante-cinq**.   ⎭   *It's 3:55.*

To ask at what time something happens, use **à quelle heure**.

On mange **à quelle heure**?   *At what time are we eating?*

Pratique

5 Quelle heure est-il?

好像错啊！我和我的小伙伴们都傻眼了！

Répondez à la question.

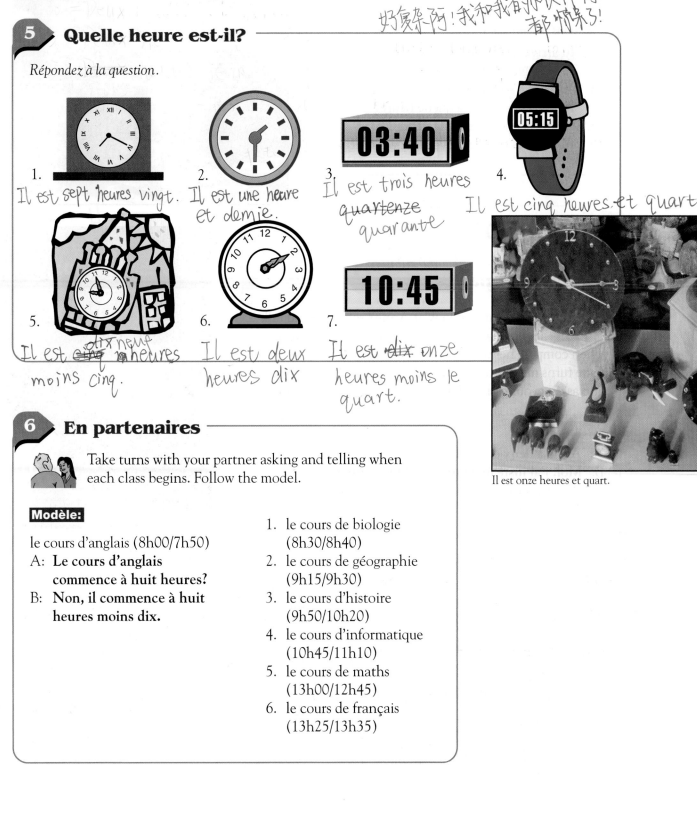

1. Il est sept heures vingt.

2. Il est une heure et demie.

3. Il est trois heures ~~quartenze~~ quarante

4. Il est cinq heures et quart

5. Il est ~~cinq~~ dix neuf ~~ma~~ heures moins cinq.

6. Il est deux heures dix

7. Il est ~~dix~~ onze heures moins le quart.

Il est onze heures et quart.

6 En partenaires

Take turns with your partner asking and telling when each class begins. Follow the model.

Modèle:

le cours d'anglais (8h00/7h50)

A: **Le cours d'anglais commence à huit heures?**

B: **Non, il commence à huit heures moins dix.**

1. le cours de biologie (8h30/8h40)
2. le cours de géographie (9h15/9h30)
3. le cours d'histoire (9h50/10h20)
4. le cours d'informatique (10h45/11h10)
5. le cours de maths (13h00/12h45)
6. le cours de français (13h25/13h35)

cent vingt-cinq
Leçon C
125

Lecture

Context and Text Organization

To understand what a reading in French is all about, first determine its setting or purpose (context). Reading for context is easy because you are reading for the big picture, not for all the details. For example, after glancing at the reading that follows, it is easy to determine that it shows the results of a questionnaire. Once you have established the context or subject, read the information more thoroughly. Understanding the context will help you understand the details of what you are reading.

In the questionnaire be sure to read the heading and section titles, which will give you important clues about how the reading is organized. What will you be reading first? Second? Look at the section **Les réponses** to find out how to interpret the numbers in the survey.

Voici un questionnaire distribué à quelques élèves âgés de 15 ans dans un collège à Tours en France.

Les réponses: 1 = Oui, tout à fait d'accord.
2 = Plutôt d'accord.
3 = Plutôt pas d'accord.
4 = Non, pas du tout d'accord.

Mon opinion sur l'école et les études:	La moyenne des résultats:
J'ai besoin d'étudier pour l'école.	1,7
J'utilise un agenda.	1,2
J'ai beaucoup de devoirs.	1,0
J'en ai marre de l'école.	1,6
Je préfère:	
les maths.	3,2
les langues.	2,0
la littérature.	3,0
la biologie.	2,7
le dessin.	1,6
Mon opinion sur les sports et les loisirs:	
J'aime manger au resto.	2,5
J'aime aller au café.	1,2
J'aime sortir avec mes ami(e)s.	1,1
J'aime:	
le tennis.	2,0
le foot.	1,6
le basket.	2,0
le volley.	1,4
Je vais souvent au cinéma.	2,0
J'écoute de la musique.	1,2
Je skie souvent.	3,3
Je téléphone souvent.	2,4

---

12 ▸ Le questionnaire

The statements that follow are generally correct or incorrect, according to the opinions expressed by the teenagers surveyed in Tours. Write **vrai** or **faux** for each sentence.

1. Les ados aiment sortir avec leurs ami(e)s.
2. Les ados aiment les sports.
3. Les ados vont souvent au ciné.
4. Les ados écoutent de la musique.
5. Les ados téléphonent souvent.
6. Les ados n'ont pas besoin d'un calendrier.
7. Les ados ont beaucoup de devoirs.
8. Les ados en ont marre de l'école.
9. Les ados préfèrent les maths et la biologie.
10. Les ados préfèrent les langues et le dessin.

Les ados aiment beaucoup le volley.

Nathalie et Raoul

Évaluation

✓ Évaluation culturelle

Decide if each statement is **vrai** or **faux**.

(handwritten: Faux P1037) 1. Students in French schools store their belongings in lockers, just as American students do.
(handwritten: Faux P1032) 2. French students often use slang expressions, such as **J'en ai marre!**, when they greet their teachers as they enter class each day.
(handwritten: Faux vari P1P) 3. French students study **la philosophie** and **la géographie**, subjects which are not always offered in high schools in the United States.
(handwritten: Faux "seldom") 4. An 11-year-old French student enters **le collège** to begin a six-year university program.
(handwritten: Faux "4yrs") 5. French students usually don't have classes on Wednesday and Saturday afternoons.
(handwritten: Vrai) 6. The exam which decides whether French students may go on to a university is called the **terminale**. *(handwritten: le bac)*
(handwritten: Faux) 7. The walls of classrooms in French high schools are filled with examples of students' work, pictures, posters, etc., and look similar to those of American classrooms.
(handwritten: P19 Faux) 8. French students are often happy with a score of 12 out of 20.
(handwritten: vrai) 9. Time in France is always expressed according to the 24-hour clock.
(handwritten: vrai) 10. If you use the 24-hour clock, you don't need to specify A.M. or P.M.

(handwritten: Faux vrai)

✓ Évaluation orale

With a partner, play the roles of a student in your school and a visiting French exchange student.

Greet each other in French and introduce yourselves.

Ask each other how things are going and respond.

Ask and tell each other which courses you are taking now.

Ask and tell each other the teacher's name for each of these courses.

Ask and tell each other when each of these classes begins.

Ask and tell each other which courses you like.

Ask and tell each other what supplies you need.

Tell each other good-bye and say that you'll see each other soon.

130 cent trente
Unité 4

✓ Évaluation écrite

As a follow-up to your conversation, write a paragraph telling what you have discovered about your partner's daily schedule, courses and needed school supplies. Organize your thoughts by filling in a graphic organizer like the one below. Use this information to write your paragraph.

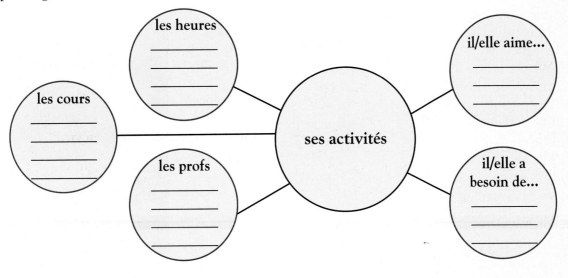

✓ Évaluation visuelle

Write a paragraph that describes the people and objects in this classroom. Remember to use prepositions to tell where these people and objects are. (You may want to refer to the *Révision de fonctions* on page 132 and the *Vocabulaire* on page 133.)

Révision de fonctions

Can you do all of the following tasks in French?

- I can say what I need.
- I can ask what something is.
- I can identify school objects.
- I can tell where people or things are.
- I can ask for information about "where" and "what."
- I can describe my school schedule.
- I can disagree with someone.
- I can express emotions.
- I can invite someone to do something.
- I can tell exact time.

To express need, use:

J'ai besoin de dormir.　　　　　*I need to sleep.*
J'ai besoin d'étudier.　　　　　*I need to study.*

To ask what something is, use:

Qu'est-ce que c'est?　　　　　*What is it/this?*

To identify something, use:

C'est le cahier de maths.　　　　*This is the math notebook.*

To tell location, use:

Il/Elle est devant le café.　　　　*It's in front of the café.*
Il/Elle est derrière la chaise.　　　*It's behind the chair.*
Il/Elle est sur le bureau.　　　　*It's on the desk.*
Il/Elle est sous le sac à dos.　　　*It's under the backpack.*
Il/Elle est dans la trousse.　　　　*It's in the pencil case.*
Il/Elle est avec le stylo.　　　　*It's with the pen.*
Il/Elle est là.　　　　　　　*It's there/here.*

To ask for information, use:

Où est la trousse?　　　　　*Where is the pencil case?*
Quoi?　　　　　　　　　*What?*
Tu as juste un cours le mercredi?　*Do you have just one class on Wednesday?*

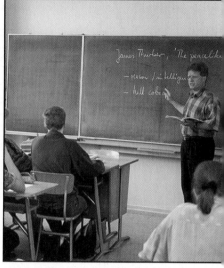

M. Bouteille est devant le tableau.

To give information, use:

Je finis à 10h00.　　　　　*I finish at 10:00.*

To disagree with someone, use:

Si, j'aime la biologie.　　　　*Yes (on the contrary), I like biology.*

To express emotions, use:

Tant mieux.　　　　　　　*That's great.*
J'en ai marre!　　　　　　*I'm sick of it! I've had it!*
Zut!　　　　　　　　　*Darn!*

To describe daily routines, use:

J'ai une heure de chimie.　　　*I have one hour of chemistry.*
J'ai trois **cours.**　　　　　*I have three classes.*
Je commence à 8h00.　　　　*I begin at 8:00.*
Je finis à 17h30.　　　　　*I finish at 5:30.*

To invite someone to do something, use:

On mange **ensemble?**　　　　*Shall we eat together?*

On étudie ensemble?

To state exact time, use:

Il est deux heures **et quart.**　　*It's 2:15.*
Il est deux heures **quinze.**　　*It's 2:15.*
Il est quatre heures **et demie.**　*It's 4:30.*
Il est quatre heures **trente.**　　*It's 4:30.*
Il est six heures **moins le quart.**　*It's 5:45.*
Il est cinq heures **quarante-cinq.**　*It's 5:45.*
Il est sept heures **dix.**　　　*It's 7:10.*
Il est neuf heures **moins vingt.**　*It's 8:40.*
Il est huit heures **quarante.**　　*It's 8:40.*

Vocabulaire

à at A
une affiche poster A
l' allemand (m.) German (language) B
l' anglais (m.) English (language) B
avec with A
avoir to have A
    avoir besoin de to need A
    avoir faim to be hungry A
    avoir soif to be thirsty A

le besoin: avoir besoin de to need A
la biologie biology B
un bureau desk A

un cahier notebook A
un calendrier calendar B
une cantine cafeteria C
une carte map A
un CD CD A
une chaise chair A
la chimie chemistry B
commencer to begin C
une corbeille wastebasket A
un cours course, class B
un crayon pencil A

dans in A
de (d') of A; from B
demi(e) half C
    et demi(e) thirty (minutes), half past C
derrière behind A
le dessin drawing B
devant in front of A
un dictionnaire dictionary A
dimanche (m.) Sunday B
une disquette diskette A
un DVD DVD A

une école school A
un(e) élève student A
un emploi du temps schedule C
ensemble together C
l' espagnol (m.) Spanish (language) B
un(e) étudiant(e) student A
Étudions.... Let's study . . . . A

une fenêtre window A
une feuille de papier sheet of paper A
une fille girl A
finir to finish B
le français French (language) B

un garçon boy A
la géographie geography B

l' histoire (f.) history B

l' informatique (f.) computer science B

jeudi (m.) Thursday B
un jour day B
juste just, only A

là there, here A
le latin Latin (language) B
le (+ *day of the week*) on (+ day of the week) B
un lecteur de DVD DVD player A
un livre book A
lundi (m.) Monday B

mardi (m.) Tuesday B
marre: J'en ai marre! I'm sick of it! I've had it! B
les maths (f.) math A
mercredi (m.) Wednesday B
mille (one) thousand B
une minute minute B
moins minus C
    moins le quart quarter to C
montrer to show A
    Montrez-moi.... Show me . . . . A

oh oh A
un ordinateur computer A
où where A

par per B
une pendule clock A
la philosophie philosophy B
la physique physics B
une porte door A
un(e) prof teacher A
un professeur teacher A

Qu'est-ce que c'est? What is it/this? A
un quart quarter C
    et quart fifteen (minutes after), quarter after C
    moins le quart quarter to C
quoi what A

un sac à dos backpack A
une salle de classe classroom A
samedi (m.) Saturday B
les sciences (f.) science B
une semaine week B
si yes (on the contrary) B
sous under A
une stéréo stereo A
un stylo pen A
sur on A

un tableau (ch
un taille-cray
Tant mieu
une trousse

vendre

Zut! D

Unité

5

En famille

In this unit you will be able to:
- ask for information
- give information
- explain something
- point out family members
- describe physical traits
- describe character
- express emotions
- ask and tell how old someone is
- ask and tell what the date is
- tell when someone's birthday is
- tell location

www.emcp.com

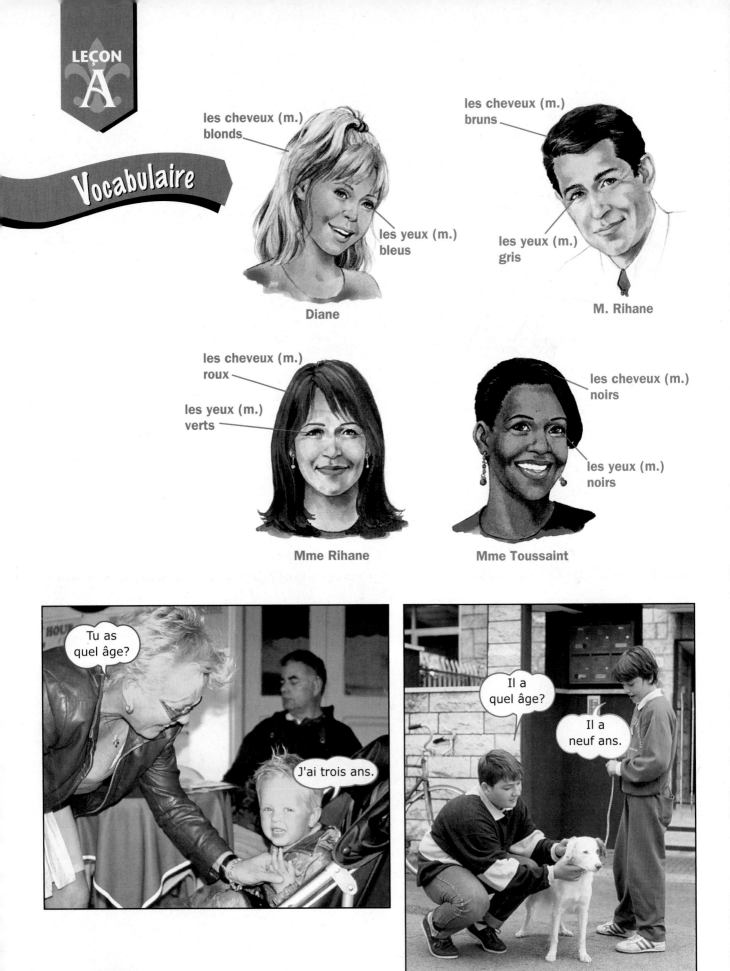

le grand-père   la grand-mère

Ce sont les
parents de Diane.

le beau-père   la mère

le père   la belle-mère   la tante   l'oncle (m.)

la belle-sœur   le beau-frère

le frère   la sœur   la cousine   le cousin

Diane

la demi-sœur   le demi-frère

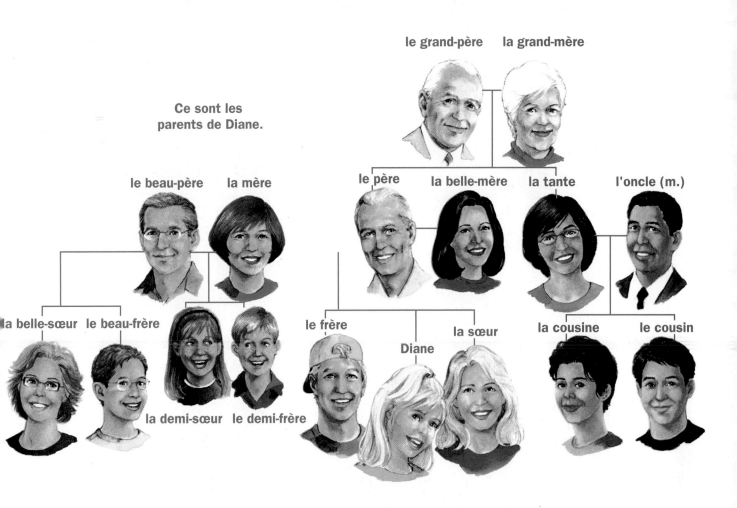

Ce sont les parents de M. Rihane.

M. Rihane   la femme

le fils

la fille

les enfants (m., f.)

Ce sont les parents de Mme Toussaint.

les parents (m.)   le mari

Mme
Toussaint

Max

Thierry

Max is looking at a photo of a young boy in Thierry's room.

une photo

Max: C'est toi?
Thierry: Non, c'est Justin, mon demi-frère. Il a deux ans. C'est le fils de mon
         père et de ma belle-mère.
Max: Il a tes yeux bleus et tes cheveux bruns.
Thierry: Il est beau comme moi, n'est-ce pas? Nous ressemblons tous les
         deux à notre père.

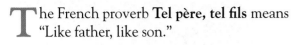
Proverbe

The French proverb **Tel père, tel fils** means "Like father, like son."

le beau-père   la belle-mère

C'est la belle-famille de Delphine.

Delphine   Francis   le beau-frère   la belle-sœur

Tel père, tel fils.

Beau- ou belle-

The French use the same prefix, **beau-** or **belle-**, for members of stepfamilies and in-laws. For example, the word **beau-frère** means both "stepbrother" and "brother-in-law."

1 La famille de Diane

According to the top illustration on page 137, write **vrai** if the sentence is true; write **faux** if it is false.

2 La photo de Thierry

Répondez en français.

1. Qui est avec Thierry?
2. C'est une photo de Thierry?
3. Qui est Justin?
4. Justin a quel âge?
5. Qui a les yeux bleus et les cheveux bruns?
6. Le père de Thierry a aussi les yeux bleus?

---

3 Complétez!

Trouvez dans la liste suivante le mot qui complète correctement chaque phrase. (In the following list find the word that correctly completes each sentence.)

| grand-père | verts | sœur | âge | ressemble | belle-sœur | blonds | oncle |

1. Pierre a les yeux.... ~~blonds~~ *verts*
2. Le frère de ma mère est mon.. *grand-père*
3. J'ai les yeux gris et les cheveux blonds. Mon père a aussi les yeux gris et les cheveux blonds. Je... à mon père. *ressemble*
4. Tu as quel...? *âge*
5. Nicole a les cheveux.... *blonds* ~~belle~~
6. Le père de ma mère est mon... *ressemble* *oncle*
7. La fille de mon père est ma.... *ressemble* *sœur*
8. La femme de mon frère est ma.... ~~sœur~~ *belle-sœur*

4 ▸ C'est à toi!

Questions personnelles.

1. Tu as quel âge?
2. Tu ressembles à qui?
3. Tu as les cheveux blonds, bruns, noirs ou roux?
4. Tu as les yeux noirs, gris, verts ou bleus?
5. Tu as combien de cousins?

> Je ressemble à Véronique.

Langue active

Possessive adjectives

Possessive adjectives show ownership or relationship, for example, "my" computer or "his" sister. In French, possessive adjectives have different forms depending on the nouns they describe. Note how possessive adjectives agree in gender (masculine or feminine) and in number (singular or plural) with the nouns that follow them.

	Singular		Plural
	Masculine	**Feminine before a Consonant Sound**	
my	**mon**	**ma**	**mes**
your	**ton**	**ta**	**tes**
his, her, one's, its	**son**	**sa**	**ses**
our	**notre**	**notre**	**nos**
your	**votre**	**votre**	**vos**
their	**leur**	**leur**	**leurs**

(masculine: frère · feminine: sœur · plural: parents)

The possessive adjective agrees with the noun that follows it, not with the owner.

C'est une photo de **mes** cousins et de **ma** tante.	*This is a picture of my cousins and my aunt.*
Leur père est très beau.	*Their father is very handsome.*

Son, **sa** and **ses** may mean "his," "her," "its" or "one's," depending on the gender of the owner.

Luc aime bien **sa** belle-mère.	*Luc really likes his stepmother.*
Claire et **son** frère étudient ensemble.	*Claire and her brother are studying together.*

Before a feminine singular word beginning with a vowel sound, **ma**, **ta** and **sa** become **mon**, **ton** and **son**, respectively.

Ton interro est demain?	*Is your test tomorrow?*
Ma sœur, Renée, a **mon** affiche.	*My sister, Renée, has my poster.*

140 cent quarante
Unité 5

Pratique

5 · L'arbre généologique de Sabrina

Répondez aux questions.

Modèles:

Nadine est la tante de Sabrina?
Oui, Nadine est sa tante.

Pierre est le père
de Sabrina?
**Non, Pierre est
son grand-père.**

1. Max est le frère de Sabrina?
2. Éric est le beau-père de Sabrina?
3. Cécile est la grand-mère de Sabrina?
4. Isabelle est la cousine de Sabrina?
5. Vincent est l'oncle de Sabrina?
6. David est le cousin de Sabrina?
7. Diane est la mère de Sabrina?
8. Alain est le père de Sabrina?
9. Sylvie est la sœur de Sabrina?

Handwritten answers:
Non, Max est son cousine.
2. Oui, Éric est son grand-mère
4. Non, Sabrina est son sœur.
5. Non, Sabrina est sa fille
6. Non, Sabrina est son sœur.
7. Oui, Diane est sa mère.
8. Non, Alain est son oncle.
9. Non, Sylvie est sa cousine

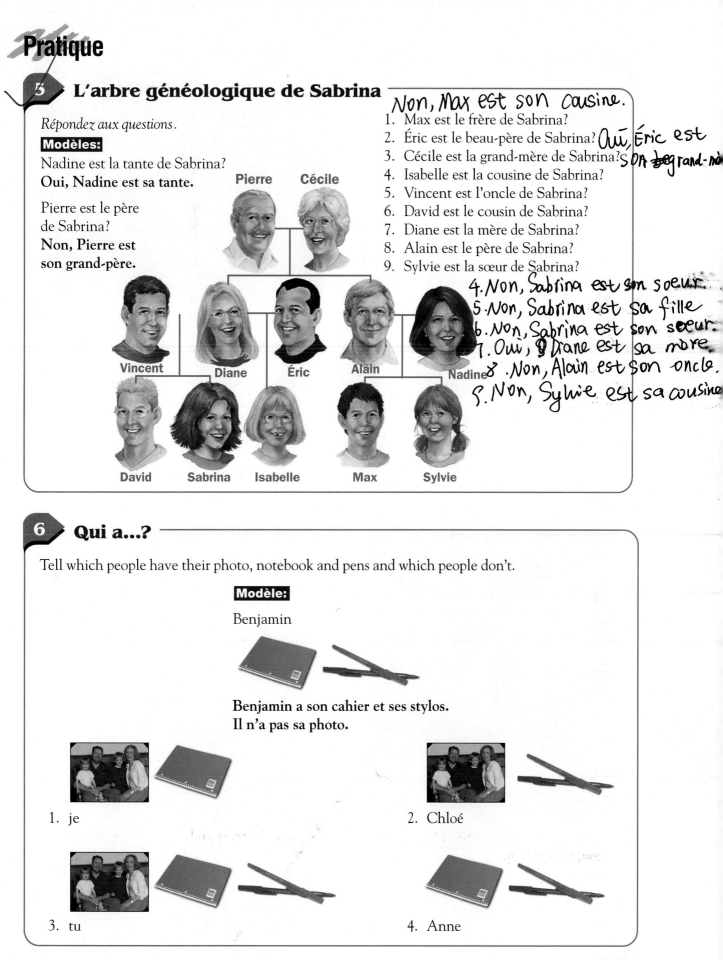

Pierre **Cécile**

Vincent **Diane** **Éric** **Alain** **Nadine**

David **Sabrina** **Isabelle** **Max** **Sylvie**

6 · Qui a...?

Tell which people have their photo, notebook and pens and which people don't.

Modèle:

Benjamin

**Benjamin a son cahier et ses stylos.
Il n'a pas sa photo.**

1. je

2. Chloé

3. tu

4. Anne

7 ▸ Tout le monde va au café.

Qui va au café et avec qui?

Modèle:

Luc (mère/frère)
Luc va au café avec sa mère et son frère.

1. je (parents/grand-père)
2. Monsieur Eberhardt (femme/enfants)
3. vous (père/belles-sœurs)
4. Sophie et Ariane (beau-père/frères)
5. Manu et Christophe (belle-mère/sœurs)
6. Madame Magouet (mari/fille)
7. nous (mère/cousins)

Raphaël va au café avec ses cousines.

8 ▸ On se ressemble.

Complétez chaque phrase avec l'adjectif possessif convenable (appropriate).

Modèle:

Justin et Thierry ressemblent
à **leur** père.

Guy ressemble beaucoup à son grand-père. (Avignon)

1. Je ressemble beaucoup à... cousins.
   Je ressemble un peu à... mère.
   Je ne ressemble pas à... oncle.
2. Michel et Karine ressemblent beaucoup à...
   demi-sœur. Ils ressemblent un peu à... père.
   Ils ne ressemblent pas à... cousins.
3. Vous ressemblez beaucoup à... grand-père.
   Vous ressemblez un peu à... parents.
   Vous ne ressemblez pas à... sœur.
4. Ahmed ressemble beaucoup à... mère.
   Il ressemble un peu à... sœurs.
   Il ne ressemble pas à... demi-frère.
5. Tu ressembles beaucoup à... frère.
   Tu ressembles un peu à... cousins.
   Tu ne ressembles pas à... tante.
6. Nous ressemblons beaucoup à... père.
   Nous ressemblons un peu à... grand-mère.
   Nous ne ressemblons pas à... cousins.

Expressions with *avoir*

You have already learned several expressions where the verb "to be" is used in English but forms of **avoir** are used in French. Two more of these _____ someone's age and **avoir... an(s)** to

How old are you?
I'm fourteen (years old).

J'ai quinze ans.

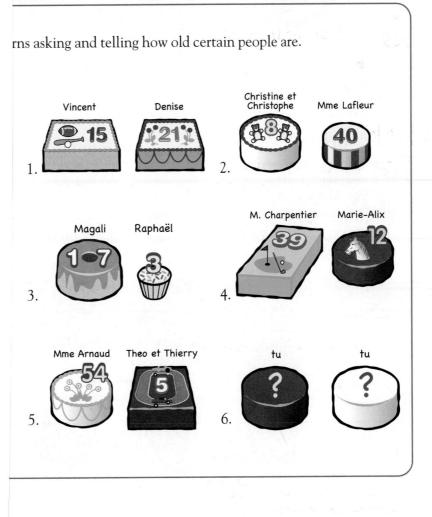

...ns asking and telling how old certain people are.

1. Vincent — 15   Denise — 21   2. Christine et Christophe — 8   Mme Lafleur — 40

3. Magali — 1·7   Raphaël — 3   4. M. Charpentier — 39   Marie-Alix — 12

5. Mme Arnaud — 54   Theo et Thierry — 5   6. tu — ?   tu — ?

Communication

10 ▶ Mon album de photos

Match each photo of your family with the appropriate label.

Modèle:

C'est ma sœur Claire.
Elle a 6 ans.
G

A.

B.

C.

D.

E.

F.

G.

1. C'est mon grand-père.
2. C'est mon beau-père.
3. C'est mon frère, Alexandre.

4. C'est ma mère.
5. C'est ma grand-mère.
6. C'est ma sœur Anne. Elle a 19 ans.

rough outline

11 ▶ En partenaires

 Write a description of each member of your real or imaginary family including name, relationship to you and age. Then, with a partner, take turns reading your description aloud. As your partner speaks, draw his or her family tree and label each person by name, family relationship and age.

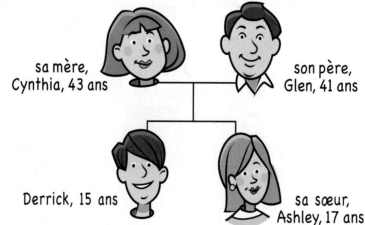

sa mère,
Cynthia, 43 ans

son père,
Glen, 41 ans

Derrick, 15 ans

sa sœur,
Ashley, 17 ans

Modèle:

Moi, je m'appelle Derrick. J'ai 15 ans.
Ma mère s'appelle Cynthia. Elle a 43 ans.
Mon père s'appelle Glen. Il a 41 ans.
Ma sœur s'appelle Ashley. Elle a 17 ans.

12 ▸ Ma famille imaginaire

Choose any <u>two pictures</u> of your imaginary family and write <u>three sentences</u> for each one. The first sentence should tell how this <u>person is related to you;</u> the second one should tell <u>this person's age;</u> the third one should tell <u>what color eyes and hair this person has.</u> Then leave your descriptions on your desk, choose a partner and switch seats. Read your partner's descriptions and then write the letter of the appropriate picture next to each one. Return to your seat and see if your partner correctly identified the people you described.

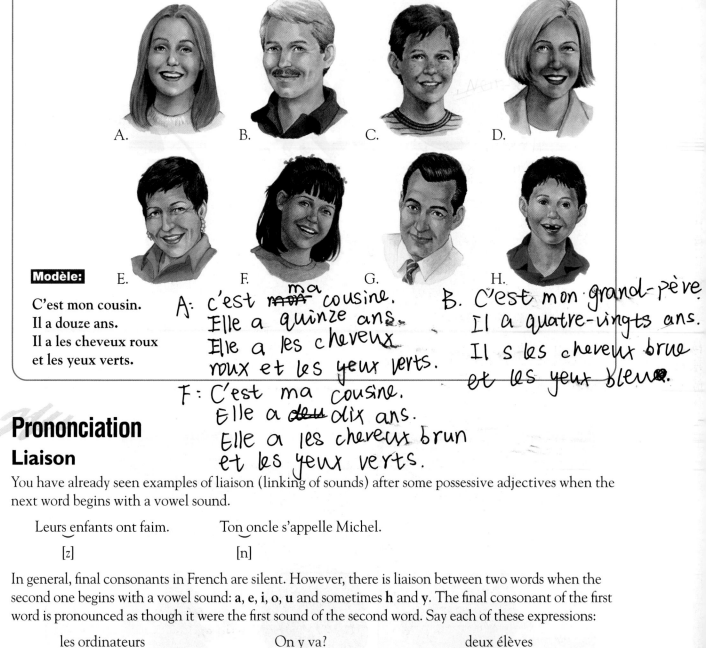

A.　B.　C.　D.

E.　F.　G.　H.

Modèle:

C'est mon cousin.
Il a douze ans.
Il a les cheveux roux
et les yeux verts.

(handwritten)
A: C'est ~~moi~~ *ma* cousine.
Elle a quinze ans.
Elle a les cheveux
roux et les yeux verts.

B. C'est mon grand-père.
Il a quatre-vingts ans.
Il s les cheveux brue
et les yeux bleue.

F: C'est ma cousine.
Elle a ~~deux~~ dix ans.
Elle a les cheveux brun
et les yeux verts.

Prononciation

Liaison

You have already seen examples of liaison (linking of sounds) after some possessive adjectives when the next word begins with a vowel sound.

Leurs‿enfants ont faim.　Ton‿oncle s'appelle Michel.

[z]　[n]

In general, final consonants in French are silent. However, there is liaison between two words when the second one begins with a vowel sound: **a, e, i, o, u** and sometimes **h** and **y**. The final consonant of the first word is pronounced as though it were the first sound of the second word. Say each of these expressions:

les‿ordinateurs　On‿y va?　deux‿élèves

[z]　[n]　[z]

neuf‿ans　cinq‿heures　Il est‿au café.

[v]　[k]　[t]

Les vacances

Most French workers get six weeks of paid vacation each year. Many families spend the entire month of July or August on vacation.

Les chiens

There are 54 million pets in France, or an average of one pet per family. France has more dogs per person than any other country in western Europe. Paris has 40 animal clinics open day and night, animal ambulances, a therapy center for dogs and dog-sitter agencies. By law, the French must clean up after their pets. **Caninettes**, bright green motorbikes with rotating brushes and suction hoses, keep the city's sidewalks spotless. French dogs are welcome in hotels, stores and even the fanciest restaurants. They are often treated as part of the family and given affectionate nicknames. Some common names for dogs include Médor, Rex, Reine, Fidèle and Fifi. Pedigreed dogs born in a particular year must all have a name starting with a certain letter of the alphabet. In one recent year, the names of all pedigreed dogs began with the letter "A"; names such as Attila and Angèle were very popular.

The seaside is one of the most popular destinations for summer vacationers. (La Baule)

Some people bring their dogs to cafés and restaurants. (Paris)

1 ▸ **Les mois**

Write the month that comes after the one you hear.

2 ▸ **Les vacances des Lévesque**

Répondez en français.

1. C'est le 20 avril?
2. Les vacances de M. et Mme Lévesque, elles commencent le 25 avril?
3. Les Lévesque vont où en vacances?
4. Où sont la Martinique et la Guadeloupe?
5. Qui est Milou?
6. Qui va en vacances avec M. et Mme Lévesque? Pourquoi?

3 Les animaux domestiques

Répondez en français.

Modèle:

Le chat de la famille Durocher
s'appelle comment?
Leur chat s'appelle Minou.

la famille Durocher — Minou

Coco — Laurent et Olivier

Khaled — Joséphine et Napoléon

Ariane et Bruno — Prince

Tornade — Denise

1. Qui a un cheval? *Tornade Denise.*
2. Combien de poissons rouges a Khaled? *Non. deux.*
3. La famille Durocher a un chien? *Non.*
4. L'oiseau de Laurent et Olivier s'appelle comment? *Coco*
5. Ariane et Bruno ont un chat? *Non, ils ont un chien.*
6. Combien de chats a la famille Durocher? *Un.*
7. Le cheval de Denise s'appelle Napoléon? *Non.*
8. Qui a un chien? *Ariane et Bruno.*

4 C'est à toi!

Questions personnelles.

1. Tu préfères quel mois?
2. Tu vas où en vacances?
3. Tu vas en vacances avec qui?
4. Qu'est-ce que tu aimes faire en vacances?
5. Tu préfères les chats ou les chiens?
6. Qui sont les membres de ta famille?

Je préfère les chats.

Present tense of the irregular verb être

The verb **être** (*to be*) is irregular.

être			
je	**suis**	nous	**sommes**
tu	**es**	vous	**êtes**
il/elle/on	**est**	ils/elles	**sont**

Vous **êtes** ensemble?　　*Are you together?*
Il **est** beau.　　*He's handsome.*

Grégoire est à (*in*) la cantine.

 Pratique

5 **En vacances ou pas?**

Dites si l'on est en vacances ou pas.

Modèles:

Karine
Karine est en vacances.

Luc et Ousmane
Luc et Ousmane ne sont pas en vacances.

1. M. Simon

2. Delphine et sa sœur

3. la prof de français

4. tu

5. vous

6. M. et Mme Dupont

6 ▸ Complétez!

Écrivez la forme convenable du verbe **être**.

1. C'...est... quelle date?
   C'...est... le 20 décembre. Nous...sommes... mercredi.
2. Tes chiens...sont... en vacances avec toi?
   Oui, Rex et Reine... des membres de la famille. sont
3. Tu...es... avec Étienne?
   Oui, nous...sommes... ensemble.
4. C'...est... ton frère?
   Oui, il... beau comme moi. est

5. Tu...es... à l'école?
   Non, je...suis... au café.
6. Vous...êtes... les sœurs de Catherine?
   Non, nous...sommes... ses cousines.
7. Vous...êtes... de Nantes?
   Non, je... de Paris. suis

Non, je suis chez moi.

Tu es au fast-food?

7 ▸ Où sont-ils?

Complétez chaque phrase avec la forme convenable du verbe **être** *et choisissez une expression de la liste.*

| à l'école   au café   au cinéma   au fast-food |

1. Les Maurel mangent des hamburgers et des frites.
   Ils...sont... au fast-food
2. J'écoute le professeur de biologie.
   Je...suis... à l'école
3. Christine mange une quiche et une crêpe.
   Elle...est... au café
4. Nous étudions.
   Nous...sommes... à l'école
5. Tu es serveur.
   Tu...es... au café
6. Jeanne et toi, vous avez une interro.
   Vous...êtes... à l'école
7. Alain regarde un film.
   Il...est... au cinéma

Jacqueline et ses frères sont aux Gaumont.

実在風TT

12 ▸ En kilomètres, s'il vous plaît!

Help a French salesperson complete a mileage report for the month by telling the number of kilometers traveled between Aix-en-Provence and each of the cities listed. (Note that the chart gives only one-way distances from Aix-en-Provence to each city.) Finally, give the total number of kilometers traveled. Follow the model.

Distances kilométriques d'Aix-en-Provence à:

Antibes 165	Marseille 30
Arles 75	Montpellier 145
Avignon 75	Nice 190
Bordeaux 645	Orange 100
Cannes 155	Paris 765
Genève 430	Saint-Tropez 150
Grenoble 290	Toulon 80
Lyon 300

Paris est à 765 kilomètres d'Aix-en-Provence.

Modèle:

Lyon
six cents kilomètres

Orange	Arles	Montpellier	Paris
Genève	Marseille	Nice	Cannes

(handwritten annotations:) deux cents, cent et cinquante, deux cents, quatre-vingt-dix, huit cents, soixante, soixante, trois cents et quatre-vingts, trois cents et dix, 只有200 cents

13 ▸ Perdu-Trouvé

Read the pet lost and found section in the classified ads. Then answer the questions.

> Perdu le 1/4, chien noir et brun, yeux noirs. S'appelle Rex. Porte un large collier noir. Contacter le 01.43.98.45.23.

> Perdu le 3/4, chien noir et brun, yeux gris. S'appelle Hugo. Contacter le 01.44.56.70.91. Forte récompense.

> Perdu le 31/3, grand chat gris, yeux verts. S'appelle César. Tél: 01.42.09.23.18.

1. What two kinds of pets are lost? *cat & dog*
2. Which pet has been lost the longest? *cat*
3. What are the names of the other two animals? *Rex & Hugo*
4. In what way are the two dogs similar? *They both are black*
5. What is one difference in the appearance of the two dogs? *eyes' colors*
6. For which animal is there a reward?
7. Which animal is wearing a black collar?

Les familles françaises

When Americans talk about their families, they usually mean their immediate families: parents, children, brothers and sisters. In France, the term **la famille** is used to refer to the extended family, including grandparents, uncles, aunts, nephews, nieces and cousins. With today's ever-changing family structure, it has become more and more difficult to define the word **famille**.

The changing family structure is reflected by the decrease in the birth rate in France. In order to maintain the population at its current level, the French government gives money to families upon the birth of each child after the first two.

Family members enjoy getting together to celebrate special occasions, especially weddings. In France, couples often have two wedding ceremonies. First, there is a required official ceremony at **la mairie** (*town hall*). Instead of choosing a maid or matron of honor and a best man, the bride and groom select two or more witnesses to listen to their vows. Other family members and friends also attend this civil ceremony. A second, optional ceremony takes place at the couple's place of worship. The entire wedding celebration may last for several days and include dancing, singing and lots of good food. Couples with more modest tastes simply invite their friends and family to a restaurant for a special dinner afterward.

Today the average French family has 1.89 children; families with two or more children are increasingly rare. (Paris)

A bride and groom wait for their wedding ceremony to begin at *la mairie*.

Madame Joseph Richer
Monsieur et Madame Jean-Pierre Jourdan
sont heureux de vous faire part du
mariage de leur
petite-fille et fille Frédérique, avec Monsieur
Sébastien Martel.

En vous priant d'assister ou de vous unir
d'intention à la Cérémonie Religieuse qui sera
célébrée le
Samedi 22 Décembre 2014, à 15 h. 30, en
l'Église de
Saint-Suliac (Ille-et-Vilaine).

Un Cocktail sera servi à l'issue de la
Cérémonie.

9, rue du Moulin aux Pauvres
35300 Fougères

In France, young women must be 15 years old (with parental permission) to marry; young men must be 18 years old. After her marriage, a woman may choose to keep her maiden name or to take the surname of her husband. She may also hyphenate her name, *i.e.*, Martin-Dubois. But the legal name of a woman remains the name that she was given at birth.

French families don't need special occasions in order to get together. Some families have **une maison de campagne** (*country home*) to go to when they want to get away from the stress of city life. They often personalize this home with a name, such as **Mon Repos** (*My Place to Relax*).

Families usually spend a month-long summer vacation together. During July or August they head for their country home, go camping, travel, rent a home by the sea or visit relatives.

Many French families go to their country homes in July or August. (Espelette)

14 ▸ Les familles françaises

Répondez aux questions.

1. When Americans talk about their family, whom do they include?
2. When the French talk about their family, whom do they include?
3. Why does the French government give money to families upon the birth of each child after the first two?
4. How are wedding ceremonies in France and in the United States similar?
5. How are they different?
6. How old must French people be in order to marry?
7. Where do French families go when they want to escape the stress of city life?

Francis and Isabelle Cazette were married in Beauregard.

15 ▶ Un faire-part de mariage

On a wedding invitation, the bride's family is listed on the left side; the groom's family is listed on the right side. The names of the grandparents come before the names of the parents. The parents' addresses are given at the bottom of the invitation. Answer the questions about Anne and Frédéric's wedding.

Anne et Frédéric

Monsieur et Madame Marcel Fossal
Monsieur et Madame André Biancheri
Madame Colette Fossal
Monsieur Michel Biancheri

Madame Richard Pretzner
Monsieur et Madame Florent Meyer

ont la joie de vous faire part du mariage de leurs petits-enfants et enfants

Anne et Frédéric

La Bénédiction Nuptiale leur sera donnée
en l'Eglise Notre-Dame du Monastère de Cimiez
le Samedi 16 Juin 2014 à 16 heures

2, Av. du Monastère de Cimiez
06000 Nice

3, Rue Pugel
06100 Nice

1. What is Frédéric's last name?
2. What is Anne's last name?
3. Who are Colette and Michel?
4. How many of Frédéric's grandparents will be at the wedding?
5. What is the name of the church where Anne and Frédéric will be married?
6. What is the date of the wedding?
7. At what time does the wedding begin?
8. Who lives on the street where the church is located?
9. In what city do Anne and Frédéric's parents live?
10. Where is the zip code placed in relation to the name of the city in a French address?

Cultural Viewpoint

As an American, you probably filter what you read in French through an American cultural lens, seeing things the American way. For example, if you are reading about **une maison** in France, you might picture a house in the suburbs with a two-car garage. But to many French people who live in the city, **une maison** is a high-rise apartment, not a single-family structure. The French also "see" dates differently than we do, giving the day before the month before the year. To the French, this is a logical progression from the shortest period of time to the longest. We shouldn't view this as "wrong;" it's just different. To appreciate a French cultural perspective in the selection that follows, keep an eye on Marie-Claire's type of family, how they celebrate birthdays and how she expresses the date.

En famille

Marie-Claire va recevoir une jeune fille canadienne, Gilberte, pendant trois semaines en décembre. Gilberte fait partie d'un programme d'échanges. Voici la lettre de Marie-Claire à Gilberte.

12.7.07

日月年

Chère Gilberte,

Je suis très contente que tu viennes chez moi en décembre. J'ai 15 ans et je vais à l'école à Tours. Mes parents sont divorcés. J'habite dans une maison avec ma mère et mon beau-père. Ma mère est blonde aux yeux bleus. Demain c'est son anniversaire. Elle va avoir 42 ans. C'est aussi la fête de mon père. Quelle coïncidence, n'est-ce pas? Mon père est brun, grand et intelligent.

J'ai une sœur, Danielle. Elle a 21 ans. En ce moment, elle est à l'Université de Nantes. J'ai aussi un demi-frère. Il s'appelle Patrick et il a neuf ans.

J'adore les animaux. J'ai un chat, un chien et un canari chez ma belle-mère et mon père.

J'ai hâte de faire ta connaissance. Tu vas être comme un membre de la famille.

À bientôt,
Marie-Claire

12 ▸ En famille

Répondez aux questions.

1. When will Gilberte's visit take place?
2. How many pets does Marie-Claire have?
3. Where is Marie-Claire's sister? Why?
4. When did Marie-Claire write this letter?
5. Why is Marie-Claire writing to Gilberte?
6. What kind of a family does Marie-Claire have?
7. Marie-Claire is going to buy gifts for certain family members. Whom does she have in mind and why?

Nathalie et Raoul

To ask for information, use:

C'est toi? — *Is this you?*

Il est beau comme moi, — *He's handsome like I am,*
n'est-ce pas? — *isn't that so?*

To give information, use:

C'est Justin. — *It's Justin.*

To point out family members, use:

C'est mon père. — *This is my father.*
C'est ma mère. — *This is my mother.*
Ce sont mes parents. — *These are my parents.*
Milou **est un membre de la famille**. — *Milou is a member of the family.*

To ask how old someone is, use:

Tu as quel âge? — *How old are you?*

To tell how old someone is, use:

Il/Elle a quinze **an(s)**. — *He/She is fifteen years old.*

To describe physical traits, use:

J'ai les cheveux blonds. — *I have blond hair.*
J'ai les yeux bleus. — *I have blue eyes.*

To describe character, use:

Je suis généreux/généreuse. — *I'm generous.*

To express emotions, use:

Que je suis bête! — *How stupid I am!*

To ask what the date is, use:

C'est quelle date? — *What's the date?*

To tell what the date is, use:

Nous sommes le 25 avril. — *It's April 25.*
C'est le 1er août. — *It's August 1.*

To tell when someone's birthday is, use:

Son anniversaire est le vingt-six octobre. — *His/Her birthday is October 26.*

To explain something, use:

Parce que c'est ton anniversaire. — *Because it's your birthday.*

To tell location, use:

C'est **à** 7.000 **kilomètres de** Nantes. — *It's 7,000 kilometers from Nantes.*

Vocabulaire

l' **âge (m.)** age A
   Tu as quel âge? How old are you? A
un **an** year A
   J'ai... ans. I'm . . . years old. A
un **anniversaire** birthday C
   août August B
   avoir... ans to be . . . (years old) A
   avoir quel âge to be how old A
   avril April B

   bavard(e) talkative C
   beau, bel, belle beautiful, handsome A
un **beau-frère** stepbrother, brother-in-law A
un **beau-père** stepfather, father-in-law A
une **belle-mère** stepmother, mother-in-law A
une **belle-sœur** stepsister, sister-in-law A
   bête stupid, dumb C
   bleu(e) blue A
   blond(e) blond A
   brun(e) dark (hair), brown A

   c'est he is, she is A
un **cadeau** gift, present C
   ce sont they are, these are, those are A
un **chat** cat B
un **cheval** horse B
des **cheveux (m.)** hair A
un **chien** dog B
un(e) **cousin(e)** cousin A

une **date** date B
   décembre December B
un **demi-frère** half-brother A
une **demi-sœur** half-sister A
   diligent(e) hardworking C

   égoïste selfish C
   en on B
un(e) **enfant** child A
   être to be B
   Nous sommes le (+ date). It's the (+ date). B

une **famille** family A
une **femme** wife; woman A
   février February B
une **fille** daughter A
un **fils** son A
un **frère** brother A

   généreux, généreuse generous C
une **grand-mère** grandmother A
un **grand-père** grandfather A
   gris(e) gray A
la **Guadeloupe** Guadeloupe B

   intelligent(e) intelligent C

   janvier January B

   juillet July B
   juin June B
un **kilomètre** kilometer B
   leur their A
   mai May B
un **mari** husband A
   mars March B
la **Martinique** Martinique B
   méchant(e) mean C
un **membre** member B
une **mère** mother A
un **million** million B
un **mois** month B
   mon, ma; mes my A

   n'est-ce pas? isn't that so? A
   noir(e) black A
   notre; nos our A
   nous us B
   novembre November B

   octobre October B
un **oiseau** bird B
un **oncle** uncle A

   parce que because C
un **parent** parent; relative A
   paresseux, paresseuse lazy C
un **père** father A
une **photo** photo, picture A
un **poisson** fish B
   un poisson rouge goldfish B
   premier, première first B

   que how C
   Que je suis bête! How dumb I am! C

   ressembler à to look like, to resemble A
   rouge red B
   roux, rousse red (hair) A

   septembre September B
une **sœur** sister A
   son, sa; ses his, her, one's, its A
   sympa (sympathique) nice C

une **tante** aunt A
   timide timid, shy C
   ton, ta; tes your A
   tous les deux both A

les **vacances (f.)** vacation B
   vert(e) green A
   votre; vos your A

des **yeux (m.)** eyes A

Unité 6

Tu viens d'où?

In this unit you will be able to:

- greet someone
- identify nationalities
- ask and tell where someone is from
- identify professions
- ask for information
- give information
- explain something
- invite
- express emotions

www.emcp.com

Vocabulaire

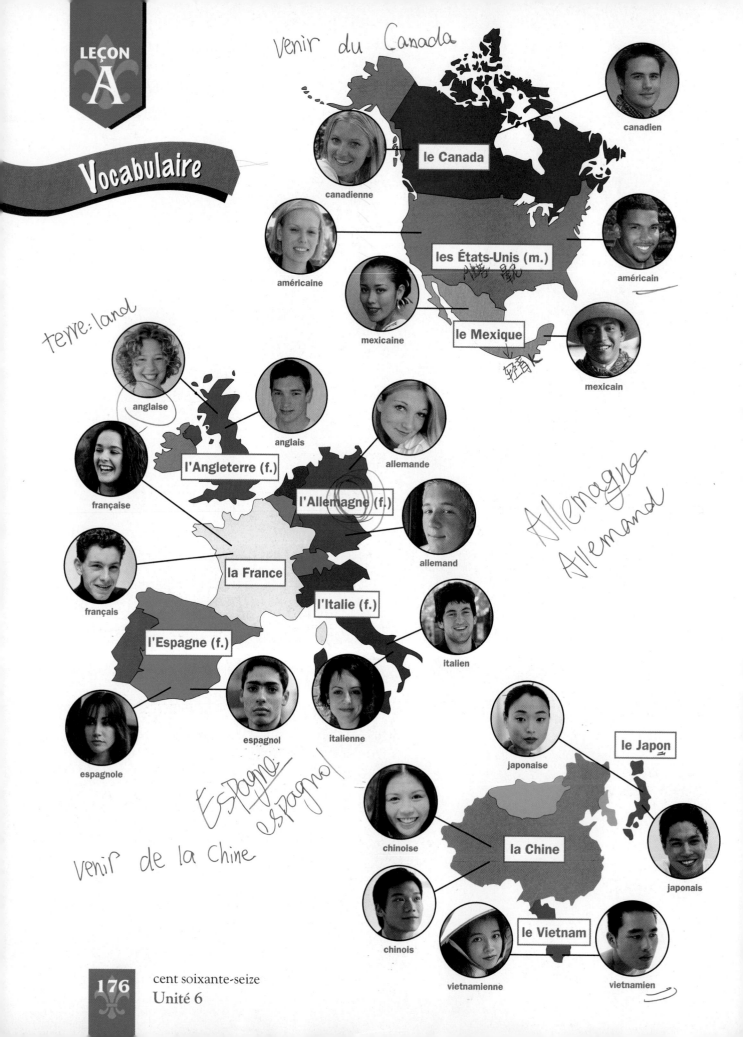

Venir du Canada

le Canada

canadienne

canadien

les États-Unis (m.)

américaine

américain

mexicaine

le Mexique

mexicain

terre: land

anglaise

anglais

allemande

l'Angleterre (f.)

l'Allemagne (f.)

française

allemand

français

la France

Allemagne
Allemand

l'Italie (f.)

l'Espagne (f.)

italien

espagnol

italienne

le Japon

espagnole

japonaise

Espagne
espagnol

chinoise

japonais

Venir de la Chine

chinois

la Chine

le Vietnam

vietnamienne

vietnamien

Sandy   José   Petra

It's the beginning of the school year in Tours. At a meeting of international exchange students, Petra, Sandy and José are showing each other pictures of their families.

[handwritten notes: ou: or / où: where / to come / Where are they from?]

Ils viennent d'où?

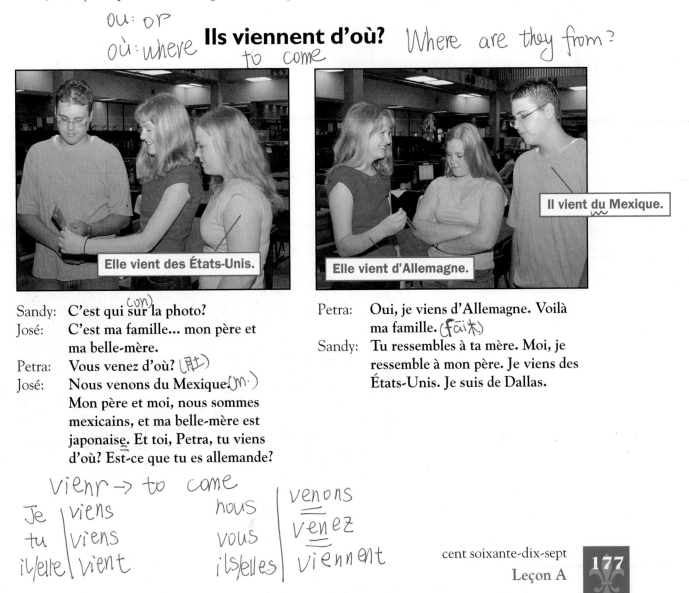

Elle vient des États-Unis.

Il vient du Mexique.

Elle vient d'Allemagne.

Sandy: C'est qui sur la photo? *(on)*

José: C'est ma famille... mon père et ma belle-mère.

Petra: Vous venez d'où? *(ai)*

José: Nous venons du Mexique. *(m.)* Mon père et moi, nous sommes mexicains, et ma belle-mère est japonaise. Et toi, Petra, tu viens d'où? Est-ce que tu es allemande?

Petra: Oui, je viens d'Allemagne. Voilà ma famille. *(faih)*

Sandy: Tu ressembles à ta mère. Moi, je ressemble à mon père. Je viens des États-Unis. Je suis de Dallas.

[handwritten conjugation table:
vienr → to come
Je viens   nous venons
tu viens   vous venez
il/elle vient   ils/elles viennent]

La vallée de la Loire

Situated in the Loire Valley, Tours is the capital of the Touraine region of France. The area around Tours has many beautiful castles, such as Chenonceaux and Chambord. The city's cultural and intellectual life centers around its university, which attracts students from all over the world. Many American teachers and students study in Tours.

The castle of Chenonceaux has formal gardens and a long gallery that crosses the river Cher.

Azay-le-Rideau, like the other Renaissance castles, was built in the sixteenth century.

Chambord is the largest of the Loire castles with 440 rooms.

Voyager en Europe

traveling in Europe

European teenagers have many opportunities to travel to other countries. Because of the relatively small size of the European continent, it doesn't take long by car or train to arrive in another country. Europeans often vacation in neighboring countries. Therefore, they find an immediate use for speaking a second language.

French tourists stroll through the streets of Brussels, Belgium, only one hour and 25 minutes from Paris by train.

---

1 Quel continent?

If the country whose name you hear is in North America, write "NA." If it's in Europe, write "E." If it's in Asia, write "A."

---

2 Ils viennent d'où?

Complétez les phrases avec la lettre qui correspond au mot convenable d'après le dialogue.

(Complete the sentences with the letter which corresponds to the appropriate word according to the dialogue.)

1. José vient du.... D
2. José et son père sont.... B G
3. La... de José est japonaise. E
4. Petra est.... B
5. Petra vient d'.... H
6. Petra ressemble à sa.... C
7. Sandy ressemble à son.... F
8. Sandy vient des.... A

A. États-Unis
B. allemande
C. mère
D. Mexique
E. belle-mère
F. père
G. mexicains
H. Allemagne

José vient du Mexi...

3 ▸ Quelle est sa nationalité?

Choisissez la lettre qui correspond à la nationalité de chaque personne.

1. Rolf vient d'Allemagne. F
2. Gina vient d'Italie. E
3. Tim vient des États-Unis. H
4. Francisco vient d'Espagne. A
5. Diana vient d'Angleterre. C
6. Liu vient de Chine. G
7. Sei vient du Japon. D
8. Yolanda vient du Mexique. B

A. Il est espagnol.
B. Elle est mexicaine.
C. Elle est anglaise.
D. Elle est japonaise.
E. Elle est italienne.
F. Il est allemand.
G. Il est chinois.
H. Il est américain.

Ly et Giang viennent du Vietnam; elles sont vietnamiennes.

4 ▸ C'est à toi!

Questions personnelles.

1. Tu viens d'où?
2. Tes parents, ils viennent d'où?
3. Tu ressembles à un membre de ta famille?
4. Tu étudies le français, l'espagnol ou l'allemand?
5. Ton professeur d'anglais, il/elle est américain(e)?

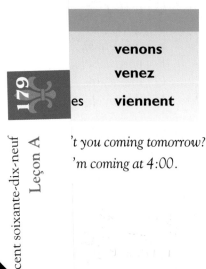

Guten Tag!   J'étudie l'allemand.

Jonny

Langue active

Present tense of the irregular verb *venir*

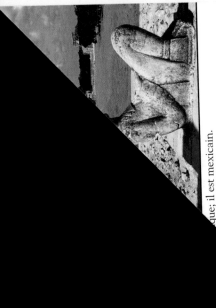

...que; il est mexicain.

venons

venez

179

...es   viennent

cent soixante-dix-neuf

Leçon A

't you coming tomorrow?

'm coming at 4:00.

Venez au festival!

Pratique

5 **Rendez-vous au café**

Dites qui vient ensemble au café.

Modèle:

Théo et Stéphanie/ensemble
Théo et Stéphanie viennent ensemble.

1. je/avec Charles
2. David et Renée/ensemble
3. Sandrine/avec Latifa
4. Charles et moi, nous/ensemble
5. tu/avec Delphine
6. Bruno/avec Louis
7. Françoise et Cécile/ensemble
8. Delphine et toi, vous/ensemble

Sabrina vient au café avec Myriam.

6 **Danse à l'école**

With a partner, take turns asking and telling who's coming to the school dance. Follow the models.

Modèles:

Clément/oui
A: **Clément vient?**
B: **Oui, il vient.**

Chloé et Alain/non
B: **Chloé et Alain viennent?**
A: **Non, ils ne viennent pas.**

1. Margarette/non
2. tu/oui
3. Daniel et toi, vous/oui
4. Abdou/non
5. Anne-Marie et Benjamin/non
6. Nathalie et moi, nous/oui
7. Béatrice et Karine/oui
8. le prof de français/non

De + definite articles

The preposition **de** (*of, from*) does not change before the definite articles **la** and **l'**.

C'est l'ordinateur **de la** fille.	*It's the girl's computer.*
Où est le cahier **de l'**élève?	*Where is the student's notebook?*

Before the definite articles **le** and **les**, however, **de** changes form. **De** combines with **le** and **les** as follows:

> **de + le = du**   *from (the), of (the)*
> **de + les = des** *from (the), of (the)*

Je viens **des** États-Unis.	*I'm from the United States.*
José vient **du** Mexique.	*José is from Mexico.*

To say that someone is from a country with a masculine name, use a form of **venir de** with the definite article: **Je viens du Canada. Elle vient des États-Unis.** To say that someone is from a country with a feminine name, do not use the definite article after **de** or **d'**: **Il vient de Chine. Elles viennent d'Angleterre.** (To say that someone is from a certain city or town, use a form of **être de**: **Je suis de Chicago.**)

7 Les animaux domestiques

Tell whom each pet belongs to in this French family.

Modèle:

Minou

C'est le chat de la mère.

1. Rex
2. Happy
3. Ouragan
4. Pompon
5. Roger
6. Sultan
7. Sylvestre

8 On vient d'où?

D'où vient chaque personne?

Modèle:

Ingrid vient d'Allemagne.

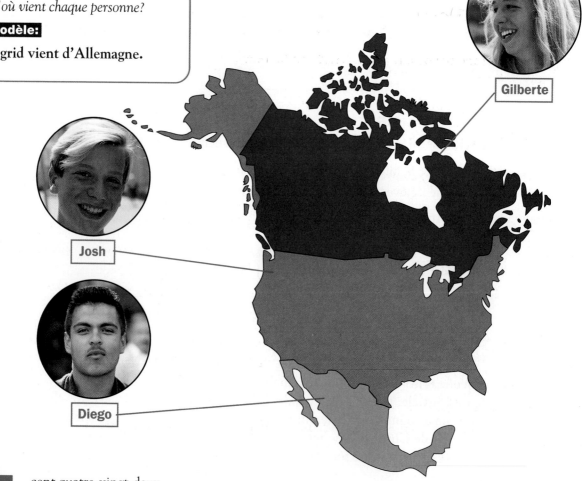

Forming questions

In spoken French there are three basic ways to ask a question that can be answered by "yes" or "no":

1. Make your tone of voice rise at the end of a sentence. (It rises at the end of all "yes" or "no" questions.)

    C'est ta famille sur la photo?   *Is this your family in the photo?*

2. Put the expression **est-ce que** right before the subject of the sentence. **Est-ce que** has no meaning by itself; it serves only to change a statement into a question. Before a word beginning with a vowel sound, **est-ce que** becomes **est-ce qu'**.

    Est-ce que Normand est canadien?   *Is Normand Canadian?*
    Est-ce qu'il est de Montréal?   *Is he from Montreal?*

3. Add the expression **n'est-ce pas** to the end of a sentence. **N'est-ce pas** basically means "isn't that so" and may be interpreted in various ways, depending on context.

    C'est ta sœur, **n'est-ce pas**?   *She's your sister, isn't she?*
    Vous venez du Mexique, **n'est-ce pas**? *You're from Mexico, aren't you?*

In spoken French you form a question that asks for information by using a specific question word followed by **est-ce que**, a subject and a verb. Some question words you have already seen are **comment, qui, pourquoi, combien** and **où**. where / how / who / why / how much

Où est-ce que tu vas?   *Where are you going?*
Avec **qui est-ce que** tu joues au tennis?   *With whom are you playing tennis?*

9 **Une enquête**

In order to conduct a survey about what teenagers do in their free time, prepare some questions.

Modèle:

skier

Est-ce que tu skies?

1. jouer au basket
2. nager
3. danser
4. aller au cinéma
5. manger au fast-food
6. regarder la télé
7. étudier
8. téléphoner

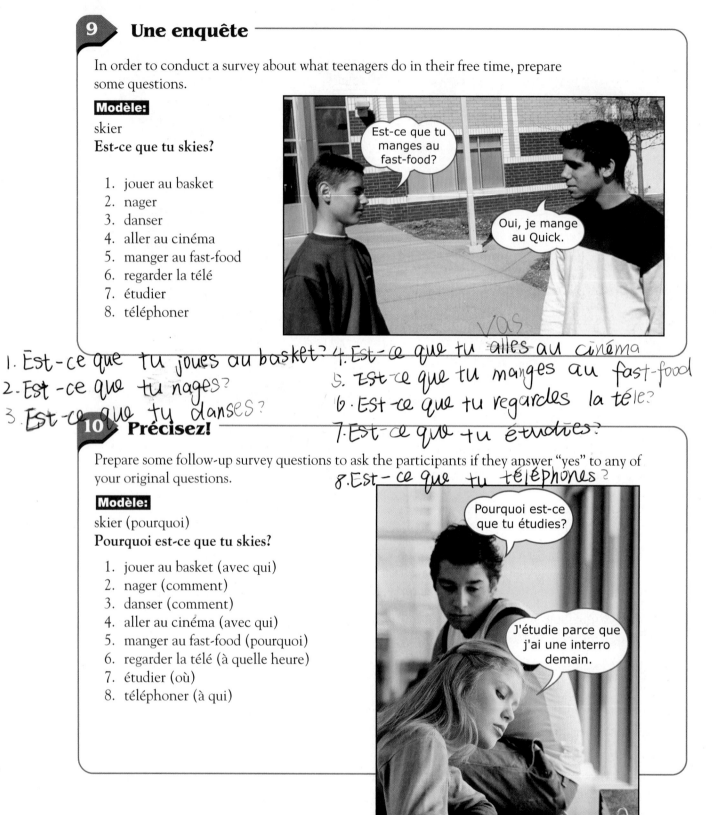

Est-ce que tu manges au fast-food?

Oui, je mange au Quick.

1. Est-ce que tu joues au basket? 4. Est-ce que tu vas alles au cinéma
2. Est-ce que tu nages? 5. Est-ce que tu manges au fast-food
3. Est-ce que tu danses? 6. Est-ce que tu regardes la télé?
7. Est-ce que tu étudies?

10 **Précisez!**

Prepare some follow-up survey questions to ask the participants if they answer "yes" to any of your original questions.

8. Est-ce que tu téléphones?

Modèle:

skier (pourquoi)

Pourquoi est-ce que tu skies?

1. jouer au basket (avec qui)
2. nager (comment)
3. danser (comment)
4. aller au cinéma (avec qui)
5. manger au fast-food (pourquoi)
6. regarder la télé (à quelle heure)
7. étudier (où)
8. téléphoner (à qui)

Pourquoi est-ce que tu étudies?

J'étudie parce que j'ai une interro demain.

Communication

11 ▶ Les étiquettes

You volunteered to introduce the French-speaking international students to your classmates. Practice your introductions by giving the appropriate information on each name tag.

Modèle:

Bonjour! Je m'appelle
Renée Tremblay
canadienne
Montréal

Voilà Renée Tremblay.
Elle vient du Canada.
Elle est de Montréal.

Bonjour! Je m'appelle
Jacques Delorme
français
Paris

Bonjour! Je m'appelle
Paola Malpezzi
italienne
Milan

Bonjour! Je m'appelle
Karl Kohl
allemand
Bonn

Bonjour! Je m'appelle
Jun An
chinoise
Beijing

Bonjour! Je m'appelle
Akio Kusumoto
japonais
Tokyo

Bonjour! Je m'appelle
María Herrera
mexicaine
Veracruz

Bonjour! Je m'appelle
Diego Botero
espagnol
Madrid

Bonjour! Je m'appelle
Loan Cao
vietnamienne
Hô Chi Minh-Ville

Bonjour! Je m'appelle
Margaret Tate
anglaise
Northampton

[handwritten notes:]

aller : to go
avoir : to have
être : to be
faire : to do/make
venir : to come
vouloir : to want

eg : Je ne veux pas
être grande.
Je ne veux pas que Nick
est grand.

vouloir → to want
Je veux   vous voulez
tu veux   ils veulent
il veut
nous voulons

Vocabulaire

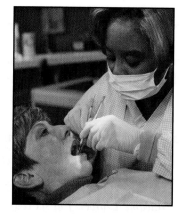

une dentiste

une fermière

un agent de police

un cuisinier

une femme d'affaires

un avocat

un homme au foyer

une journaliste

une infirmière

un médecin

une comptable

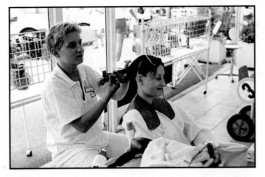

une coiffeuse

une informaticienne

un ingénieur
engineer

entraineur
= trainer/coach

蓝泽 "

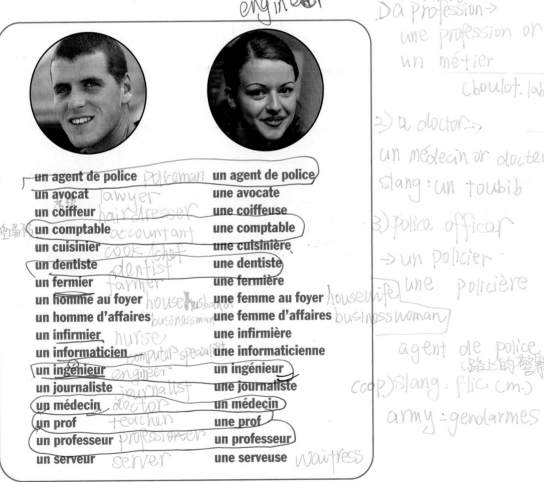

un agent de police Policeman	un agent de police
un avocat lawyer 律师	une avocate
un coiffeur hairdresser	une coiffeuse
un comptable accountant 空服员?	une comptable
un cuisinier cook/chef	une cuisinière
un dentiste dentist	une dentiste
un fermier farmer	une fermière
un homme au foyer househusband	une femme au foyer housewife
un homme d'affaires businessman	une femme d'affaires businesswoman
un infirmier nurse	une infirmière
un informaticien computer specialist	une informaticienne
un ingénieur engineer	un ingénieur
un journaliste journalist	une journaliste
un médecin doctor	un médecin
un prof teacher	une prof
un professeur professor	un professeur
un serveur server	une serveuse waitress

(intellectue. work)
1) Profession →
une profession or
un métier
(boulot. labour)

2) a doctor →
un médecin or docteur
slang: un toubib

3) police officer
→ un policier
une policière

agent de police
(路上的警察)
(cop) slang: flic (m.)
army = gendarmes

Petra

José

Sandy

Petra, Sandy and José continue to exchange information about their families.

Quelle est la profession de tes parents?

Mon père est prof de français.

Petra: **Mon père, il est homme d'affaires. Il voyage beaucoup. Ma mère travaille beaucoup aussi. Elle est femme au foyer. Et tes parents, José?**

José: **Mon père est informaticien et ma belle-mère est dentiste. Sandy, quelle est la profession de tes parents?**

Sandy: **Je n'ai pas de mère. Mon père est prof de français.** French teacher

Petra: **Tiens, c'est pourquoi tu parles si bien le français!** That's why you speak a lot French

Le travail

By law teenagers under the age of 18 may not hold a regular full-time job. But sometimes younger students may find temporary, part-time work, for example, camp counseling or working at a market or on a farm. The official work week in France is 35 hours, but naturally the actual number of hours spent working depends on the specific job and worker. In offices and stores, the work day typically begins around 8:00 A.M. or 9:00 A.M. and finishes between 5:00 P.M. and 7:00 P.M. All people who are salaried for 12 months are given six weeks of vacation. Many people take up to four weeks of vacation in the summer; the other weeks must be taken at a different time of the year. In addition, employers must pay salaried employees for 11 holidays each year.

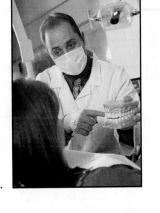

Employees at this store work from 9:30 to 7:00, with an hour and a half for lunch.

---

1 ▶ **Quelle profession?**

Write the letter of the person's profession that you hear.

A.   B.   C.

D.   E.   F.

Les professions

Répondez par "vrai" ou "faux" d'après le dialogue.

1. Le père de Petra est informaticien.
2. La mère de Petra voyage beaucoup.
3. La belle-mère de José n'est pas femme au foyer.
4. Le père de José est dentiste.
5. Le père de Sandy est professeur de français.
6. Sandy ne parle pas très bien le français.

3 **Quelle est sa profession?**

Répondez à la question.

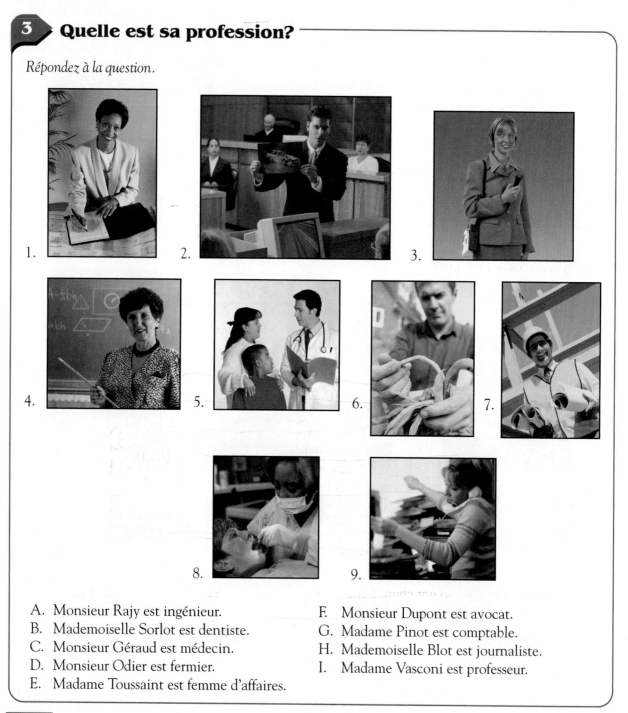

1. 2. 3. 4. 5. 6. 7. 8. 9.

A. Monsieur Rajy est ingénieur.
B. Mademoiselle Sorlot est dentiste.
C. Monsieur Géraud est médecin.
D. Monsieur Odier est fermier.
E. Madame Toussaint est femme d'affaires.

F. Monsieur Dupont est avocat.
G. Madame Pinot est comptable.
H. Mademoiselle Blot est journaliste.
I. Madame Vasconi est professeur.

4 C'est à toi!

Questions personnelles.

1. Quelle est la profession de tes parents?
2. Est-ce que tu préfères être journaliste ou comptable?
3. Est-ce que tu préfères être agent de police ou médecin?
4. Est-ce que tu voyages beaucoup?
5. Dans la salle de classe, qui parle bien le français?

Les Français voyagent beaucoup. Et toi? (Saint-Barthélemy)

Indefinite articles in negative sentences

The indefinite articles **un**, **une** and **des** become **de** or **d'** (*a, an, any*) in a negative sentence.

Tu as **un** frère?	Non, je n'ai pas **de** frère.
Est-ce que Marcel a **une** tante?	Non, il n'a pas **de** tante.
M. Rondeau a **des** enfants?	Non, il n'a pas **d'**enfants.

Il n'y a pas de serveuse aujourd'hui.

However, **un**, **une** and **des** do not change after a form of the verb **être** in a negative sentence.

Ce sont des photos de mes parents; ce ne sont pas **des** photos de mes profs.

These are pictures of my parents; they're not pictures of my teachers.

11 ▶ Les cours à l'école

For your top five career choices in activity 10, list what three classes in high school you might need to take in order to prepare for each profession.

12 ▶ Un sondage

Read a French newspaper article that reports the results of a survey in which 200 students were asked about their parents' occupations. Then make two bar graphs on a separate sheet of paper that show how many people are in each profession. In the first one, graph the occupations of the men; in the second one, graph the occupations of the women.

Bourges, le 23 septembre

Deux cents élèves ont participé à un sondage hier pour indiquer les professions et les métiers de leurs parents. Cent élèves de lycée technique, 50 élèves de collège et 50 élèves d'école primaire ont rempli ce sondage. Voilà les résultats.

Les Hommes

Il y a beaucoup de médecins et d'informaticiens parmi les hommes. Il y a 34 informaticiens et 28 médecins. Vingt de ces hommes sont dentistes, 10 sont avocats, six sont professeurs et cinq sont ingénieurs. Dans ce groupe il y a neuf journalistes, trois infirmiers, sept agents de police et 14 comptables. Quinze hommes travaillent comme cuisiniers et huit sont fermiers. Cinq travaillent à la maison comme hommes au foyer et 13 ne travaillent pas.

Les Femmes

Les femmes ont aussi beaucoup de professions différentes. Les professions les plus populaires pour les femmes sont médecin, professeur et ingénieur. Vingt-deux de ces femmes sont médecins, 21 sont professeurs et 20 sont ingénieurs. Dans ce groupe il y a 12 infirmières, 12 dentistes et sept journalistes. Il y a aussi 13 coiffeuses, 15 serveuses, sept comptables, deux fermières et neuf cuisinières. Dix-sept sont femmes au foyer et 16 ne travaillent pas.

13 ▶ Les petites annonces

Study the employment ads from a newspaper in Nice and answer the questions.

A. Clinique Nice cherche infirmier, service chirurgie, temps plein, poste à pourvoir à partir du 26 août. Tél. 04.93.13.65.20 de 9 à 16 heures.

B. Cherche serveuse. Se présenter RESTAURANT DE PARIS, 28 rue d'Angleterre, Nice, ce jour à partir de 18h.

C. Hôtel 4 étoiles recherche secrétaire réception, expérience, anglais courant, libre de suite pour saison, tél. 04.93.50.02.02. Vence.

D. Cherche apprenti(e) coiffeur(euse). 1ère année et 3ème année. Tél. 04.93.31.12.65.

E. CNRS pour laboratoire de recherche Sophia-Antipolis recrute sur concours, un assistant ingénieur en Biologie, ayant bonnes connaissances en biologie moléculaire, culture de cellules, biologie et physiologie cellulaires (DUT ou équivalence). 04.93.95.77.05.

F. INTERNATIONAL HOUSE, 90 écoles de langues dans 20 pays, recrute en septembre pour son centre de Nice, secrétaire commerciale bilingue confirmée. Ecrire 22 boulevard Dubouchage, Nice.

G. Restaurant poissons Cagnes-Sur-Mer, cherche cuisinier ou commis de cuisine qualifié, de langue maternelle française, pour saison, libre de suite, bien rémunéré. Tél. pour rendez-vous, au 04.93.07.36.59 le matin avant 12h00.

H. Clinique Nice cherche un infirmier psychiatrique ou DE, jour, temps complet. Tél. 04.93.13.65.00.

I. Restaurant cherche jeune cuisinier, connaissances pâtisserie, sérieuses références contrôlables. Tél. 04.93.67.14.06.

1. Which ads are for cooking positions? G·I
2. Which ads are for secretarial positions? C
3. Which ad is for an apprentice hair stylist? D
4. Which ad is for an organization looking for a biological engineer? E
5. Which ad is for a waitressing job? B
6. Which ad is for a surgical nurse? A
7. Which other ad is for a nurse? H
8. Which ads are for jobs that require a knowledge of English? F

La France et ses voisins

Rugged coastlines, sunlit beaches, snowcapped mountains and fields of lavender: this is the landscape of France. In the shape of a hexagon, France is bordered on three sides by water and on three sides by land. This diverse country, slightly smaller than the state of Texas, contains a variety of picturesque scenery.

To the north of France lies the English Channel, called **la Manche** by the French because it narrows from the Atlantic Ocean to the North Sea much like a shirt sleeve. The coastal cities of Saint-Malo, Étretat and Deauville attract thousands of tourists each year. A 31-mile-long tunnel under the English Channel now joins Folkestone, England, with Calais, France. The French wanted an easy way to cross the Channel for hundreds of years, but it was only recently that the English agreed to be joined "by land" to the continent. The sleek Eurostar bullet train makes the trip between London and Paris in just under four hours.

During the Hundred Years War (1337-1453), the English were going to destroy the city of Calais, but six men volunteered to be killed to save it. The Queen later intervened on their behalf and they were never killed. Rodin's life-size statue, *les Bourgeois de Calais*, honors their memory. (Calais)

Business travelers take the Eurostar from Waterloo Station in London to the *gare du Nord* in Paris.

England, France and many of their neighbors have joined to form the European Union, an organization which promotes the economic growth of its members. Most of the barriers to the movement of money, goods, people and services among EU members have been removed, forming the largest single market in the world. Citizens of the 25 EU countries may travel to other member nations without passports, may work in other EU countries and are not required to pay import or export taxes on products purchased in other member countries.

Françoise, a French university student, doesn't need a passport when she goes to England to work during her summer break.

The highest mountains in western Europe, the Alps extend from France into Switzerland, Italy and Austria.

Belgium, Luxembourg, Germany, Switzerland and Italy border France on the east. French is spoken in France, Belgium, Luxembourg and Switzerland. Three mountain ranges, **les Vosges** (between France and Germany), **le Jura** (between France and Switzerland) and **les Alpes** (between France and Italy) form natural boundaries between France and its neighbors. Skiing and mountain climbing are popular hobbies in these regions.

To the south of France lie the Mediterranean Sea, the tiny principality of Monaco and the island of Corsica. The beaches of the French Riviera, stretching from near the city of Toulon to the Italian border, appeal to vacationers from all over the world. Colors seem brighter in the south of France and even the food, spiced with olive oil, garlic and tomatoes, has a unique flavor. Monaco is an independent country where citizens speak French. Napoléon Bonaparte was born in Corsica, a department of France.

The mountains called **les Pyrénées** form a natural boundary between France and Spain on the west. The resort city of Biarritz and the port city of Bordeaux, famous for its vineyards, are on the Atlantic Ocean.

There are several important rivers in France. **La Seine** divides the capital city of Paris in half before it meanders north to the city of Le Havre on the English Channel. Along the tranquil banks of **la Loire**, the longest river in France,

La Seine divides Paris into the Right Bank and the Left Bank.

deux cent un
Leçon B

201

kings had beautiful châteaux built during the Renaissance. **Le Rhône** empties into the Mediterranean Sea near the city of Marseille, the largest French port. Two other important rivers in France are **la Garonne**, near Bordeaux, and **le Rhin**, which forms a border between France and Germany.

The Gulf Stream from the Atlantic Ocean keeps the climate of France quite mild throughout the year. However, **le mistral**, a powerful wind, blows dry air through the mountains of **le Massif Central** in central France during the spring and summer.

France used to be divided into provinces; people still maintain pride in the food, wine, architecture, art, dialects and traditional costumes associated with these provinces. Several of the more well-known French provinces are Brittany and Normandy to the north, Provence to the south, Aquitaine to the west, and Alsace and Lorraine to the east. Alsace and Lorraine have belonged to either Germany or France at various times throughout history; many of the people in these provinces speak both German and French, as well as local dialects.

Do you prefer the architecture of Normandy…

… or Alsace?

Today France is divided into smaller **départements** for governmental purposes. You can tell what department people are from by the last two numbers of their license plates and also by the first two numbers of their zip codes.

A combination of the traditional and the contemporary, beautiful countryside and bustling cities, France, the largest country in western Europe, is rightly called **la Belle France**.

14 La France et ses voisins

Répondez aux questions.

1. France is in the shape of what geometrical figure? *hexagon* — *it shows narrows from the Atlantic Ocean...*
2. Why do the French call the English Channel **la Manche**?
3. What is the purpose of the European Union? *promotes the*
4. What are three European countries, other than France, where citizens speak French? *Belgium. Luxembourg. Swizerland*
5. What three mountain ranges are located in the eastern part of France? *Les Vosges, Le Jura. Les Alpes*
6. What is the name of the small principality located in the southern part of France?
7. How is the food in the southern part of France unique? *Mediterranean Sea* *spiced with olive oil, garlic & tomatoes*
8. What river divides the city of Paris in half? *La Seine*
9. What two cities are important French ports? *Le Garonne, Le Rhin*
10. What is responsible for France's moderate climate? *The Gulf Stream*
11. Why are the French proud to be associated with the former provinces? *⎛[ ]*
12. How is France divided for governmental purposes today? *départements*
13. What is France often called? *La Belle France*

Monaco, ruled by Prince Albert, is smaller than Central Park in New York City.

15 La météo

Répondez aux questions sur le bulletin de météo (weather forecast) pour le 30 octobre.

1. All temperatures in this weather report are given in Celsius degrees (°C). What five French cities had temperatures of 10°C? *Paris, Nantes, Brest*
2. With the exception of Bastia on the island of Corsica, which city had the warmest temperature? *Nice*
3. What was the temperature in Biarritz? *13*
4. For soccer players was the weather better in Rennes or Bordeaux? *Rennes*
5. It was 9°C in Dijon. What else can you say about the weather there? *It's in the east*
6. What city is located on the Rhône River between Lyon and Marseille? What was the temperature in this city? *Valence* *13*
7. What city is located near the border between France and Belgium? What was the weather like there?
8. In what two mountain ranges did it snow?

Vocabulaire

le printemps
spring

Printemps

l'été (m.)
Summer

l'automne (m.)
{ autumn
{ fall   automme

l'hiver (m.) winter

Quel temps fait-il?
What's the temperature today?

Il fait beau.

Il fait chaud.
hot

Il fait froid.
cold

Il fait frais.

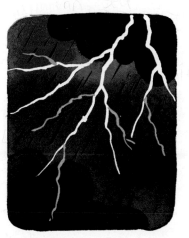

Il fait mauvais.
bad weather

Il fait du soleil.
sunny

Il neige.
snowing

Il fait du vent.
windy

Il pleut.
rainy

Sandy

José

Petra

Petra, Sandy and José are talking about how they spend their free time.

On fait un tour ensemble?

Sandy: **Il fait beau à Tours en automne. Après les cours je fais souvent du vélo.**

José: **Moi aussi. Et quand il fait mauvais, je joue aux jeux vidéo.**

Petra: **J'aime aussi faire du vélo. Mais je n'ai pas de vélo ici.**

José: **Ma famille a un autre vélo.**

Sandy: **Alors, on fait un tour ensemble aujourd'hui?**

Petra: **D'accord. Quelle chance! J'ai déjà deux amis à Tours.**

Les températures

Temperatures (**les températures**) in all French-speaking countries and most other countries in the world are calculated on the basis of the Celsius scale. Like all scales in the metric system, the Celsius scale is based on a division of measurements into hundredths or thousandths. Water freezes at 0° Celsius and boils at 100° Celsius. (It freezes at 32° Fahrenheit and boils at 212° Fahrenheit.)

Les scooters

Bicycles (**les vélos**) and scooters (**les scooters**) are popular ways to get around in France. **Les scooters** get through traffic easily and relatively quickly. Teenagers find them to be economical, easy to park and simple to operate. People over the age of 14 may operate **un scooter** if they have a special license and a license plate.

Daniel finds that *un scooter* offers him freedom and independence.

1

Quelle saison?

Write the letter of the season that you hear.

A.

B.

C.

D.

2 Températures et transports

Répondez aux questions.

1. At what temperature (Celsius) does water boil? 100°C
2. What are two advantages of driving a **scooter**? get through traffic easily & relatively quickly
3. How old must a person be to drive a **scooter**? 14
4. Do you need a license to drive **a scooter**? Yes.

3 Le temps libre

Répondez en français.

1. Sandy, José et Petra, ils sont où? France / Ils sont à tours
2. Quel temps fait-il à Tours en automne? José — Il fait beau à Tours en automne
3. Est-ce que Sandy fait souvent du vélo? Après — Oui (often)
4. Qui joue aux jeux vidéo quand il fait mauvais? José (bad)
5. Qui n'a pas de vélo à Tours? Petra
6. Quand est-ce qu'on fait un tour ensemble? D'accord.
7. Qui sont les deux amis de Petra à Tours? Petra (to)

3. Oui, Sandy fait souvent du vélo
6. On fait un tour ensemble ~~et~~ aujourd'hui. when

4 Quel temps fait-il?

Répondez à la question.

Il fait...

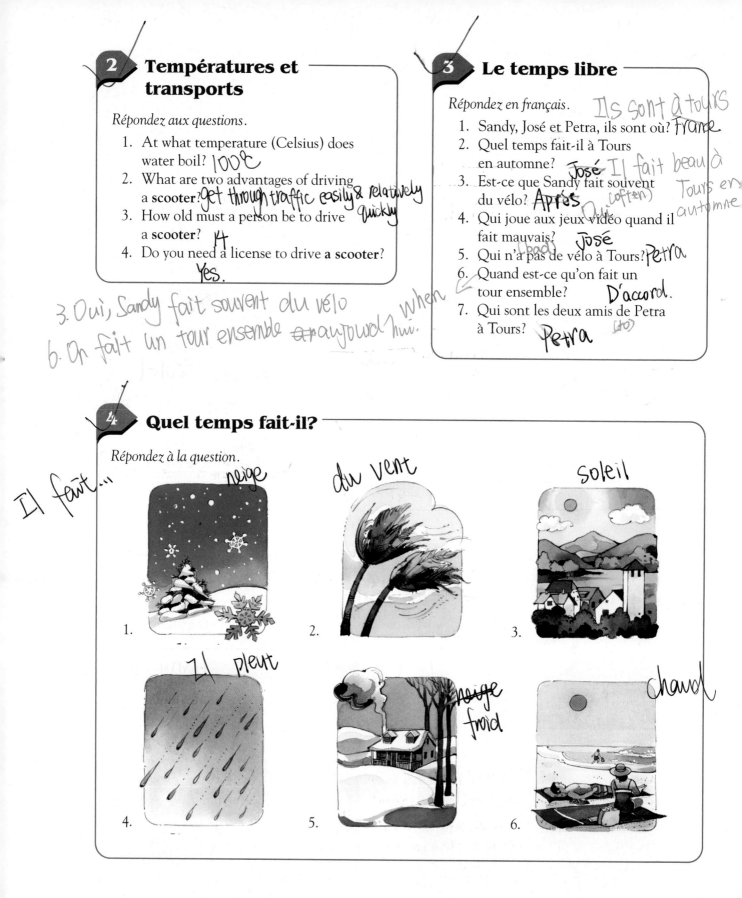

1. neige
2. du vent
3. soleil
4. Il pleut
5. ~~neige~~ froid
6. chaud

5. Une rencontre

Complétez le dialogue suivant.

Fred: Tu... d'où?   *[viens]*
Maria: Je viens.... Je suis.... Et toi?   *[la Chine, chinoise]*
Fred: Je viens.... Je suis....   *[la France, français]*
Maria   Quel temps fait-il chez toi en...?   *[la chine]*
Fred: Il fait.... Moi, j'aime.... Qu'est-ce
        que tu aimes faire en...?   *[soleil, l'été, ~~nage~~]*
Maria: Moi, j'aime... en....   *[nage prêté été]*

6. C'est à toi!

Questions personnelles.

1. Est-ce que tu préfères l'automne ou le
   printemps? Pourquoi?   *[l'auto~~mne~~ cause it's windy le printemps. It's big]*
2. Qu'est-ce que tu aimes faire en été?   *[nage]*
3. Qu'est-ce que tu aimes faire en hiver?   *[stay at home]*
4. Tu as un vélo?   *[Oui]*
5. Est-ce que tu aimes jouer aux jeux vidéo?   *[I don't like to play video game]*
6. Est-ce que tu travailles après les cours?   *[Watch TV]*

En hiver j'aime skier dans les Alpes.

Langue active

Present tense of the irregular verb *faire*

The basic meaning of the irregular verb **faire** is "to do" or "to make," but it has other meanings as well.

faire			
je	**fais**	nous	**faisons**
tu	**fais**	vous	**faites**
il/elle/on	**fait**	ils/elles	**font**

Qu'est-ce que tu **fais**?	*What are you doing?*
Nous **faisons** des omelettes.	*We're making omelettes.*

Like the irregular verbs **aller** and **avoir**, **faire** is used in many expressions where a different verb is used in English, for example, when talking about participating in various activities, prices and what the weather's like.

Tu **fais** du footing?	*Are you going running?*
Ça **fait** combien?	*How much is it/that?*
Il **fait** chaud.	*It's (The weather's) hot/warm.*

Il fait beau au printemps. (Normandie)

Reading Speeds and Predicting

Reading is made up of three main speeds: skimming, scanning and digesting. Skimming–reading very quickly–is a high-speed technique used to figure out context. Scanning–hunting for precise information–is a medium-speed technique used to search for specifics. Digesting–reading very thoroughly to accomplish a task–is a low-speed technique used to assimilate important, detailed information. As you read the selection below, skim to find out the names of the characters in the dialogue. Then use digesting to read the entire selection. Scan when you look for the answers to the questions.

Predicting is a skill that successful readers use to make an educated guess about what is going to happen next, based on what they already know. As you read the dialogue that follows, try to predict how Olivier will comment on his father's party at the end of the evening, considering what he says to his father and the questions he asks.

La Soirée de Papa

Chez les Piedbois. Paul Piedbois, le père d'Olivier, ouvre la porte.

M. Piedbois: Bonsoir, Charles!

M. Théron: Salut, Paul!

M. Piedbois: Entre! Tu préfères un coca, une limonade ou un café?

M. Théron: Une limonade, s'il te plaît. Tiens, qui est ce beau garçon, Paul?

M. Piedbois: C'est mon fils.

Olivier: Bonsoir, Monsieur. Je m'appelle Olivier. Et vous?

M. Théron: Je m'appelle Charles Théron.

M. Piedbois: Monsieur Théron est musicien professionel.

Olivier: Musicien? C'est super génial! Papa, tu peux me présenter aux autres invités?

M. Piedbois: D'accord. Ah, Martin! Je te présente mon fils, Olivier. Il s'intéresse beaucoup aux professions de mes amis.

M. Nanteuil: Martin Nanteuil. Enchanté de faire ta connaissance, Olivier. Je suis dentiste.

Olivier: Enchanté!

M. Piedbois: Et voilà Fernando Ortiz. Il est ingénieur.

Olivier: Il est français?

M. Piedbois: Non, mexicain. Tu vois la femme brune?

Olivier: Oui.

M. Piedbois: C'est Danielle Graedel. On l'appelle "Dana." Elle vient de Suisse.

Olivier: Quelle est sa profession?

M. Piedbois: C'est une interprète. Elle parle français, italien, allemand, japonais et russe. Et là-bas, l'homme aux yeux noirs, c'est Marco Casati. Il est de Florence. Il assiste à une conférence de pharmaciens demain. Voilà Cathy Collins, une Anglaise. Mademoiselle Collins désire être prof de français à Londres, mais pour le moment elle est serveuse.

Olivier: Et la femme blonde?

M. Piedbois: C'est Astrid Schiller, une copine de Cathy. C'est une cuisinière. *[Betriff]*

Olivier: Elle est anglaise aussi?

M. Piedbois: Non, elle est allemande. Et voilà Hisatake Tanaka. Il vient du Japon. C'est un pilote pour Air France. À côté il y a Mercedes Pizano, une Espagnole. Elle est comptable.

Olivier: C'est une soirée internationale, papa! Tu as des copains intéressants!

16 ▸ La Soirée de Papa

Répondez aux questions.

1. Where is Fernando Ortiz from? *Mexico* Where is Cathy Collins from? *England*
2. Who has a nickname? What is it? *Danielle → Dana*
3. What is Danielle Graedel's profession? *interprète* Which guests could she talk to in their native language?
4. Who is Italian? Who is Swiss? Who is Japanese? *# Astrid Schiller (German)*
5. Cathy Collins and Astrid Schiller are friends. How might they know each other? *both workin reste restaurant yesterfor*
6. How does Olivier evaluate his father's party? *C'est une soirée internationale*
7. What do you think Paul Piedbois does for a living? *Teacher in school*

Nathalie et Raoul

Évaluation

✓ Évaluation culturelle

Decide if each statement is **vrai** or **faux**.

In Switzerland 20 percent of the people speak French.

1. Chenonceaux and Chambord are two of the many beautiful castles located in the Loire Valley.
2. Teenagers in Europe frequently vacation in neighboring countries and therefore find it practical to speak a second language.
3. All people who receive a salary for 12 months are entitled to six weeks of vacation each year.
4. France is bordered on three sides by water: the English Channel, the Atlantic Ocean and the Mediterranean Sea.
5. The European Union is a new underwater tunnel that connects France and England.
6. French is spoken in four European countries: France, Belgium, Luxembourg and Switzerland.
7. The three mountain ranges in France are **les Vosges, le Jura** and **le Rhône.**
8. Today France is divided into provinces for governmental purposes.
9. Temperatures are measured in degrees Fahrenheit in most European countries.
10. You must be at least 16 years old to operate a **scooter** in France.

✓ Évaluation orale

To be prepared for an upcoming visit to your school from businesspeople representing various countries, have a conversation with your partner about these guests.

M. Jouffret - France	Mme Chatton - France
Mlle Castillo - Mexico	M. Alonso - Mexico
Mlle DiPiazza - Italy	Mlle Ounsworth - England
M. Kraft - Germany	Mme Liu - China
Mme Paquette - Canada	M. Pagnucci - Italy
M. Cortés - Spain	Mlle Peltier - Canada

Take turns naming at least eight different visitors. Tell their names, what countries and cities they are from, their professions, the languages they speak and the family members, if any, who are coming along with them. Follow the model.

Modèle:

A: **M. Jouffret vient de France. Il est de Marseille. Il parle français et anglais. Il vient ici avec sa femme et son fils.**

B: **Quelle est sa profession?**

A: **M. Jouffret est informaticien.**

✔ Évaluation écrite

Write a note to your teacher telling him or her who all the international visitors from the previous activity are. Include what cities and countries they are from, what languages they speak, what their professions are and what family members, if any, are coming with them.

✔ Évaluation visuelle

 Working with a partner, write a dialogue for each scene. Two foreign exchange students meet and exchange information in French about where they're from and their parents' occupations. (You may want to refer to the *Révision de fonctions* on page 218 and the *Vocabulaire* on page 219.)

Révision de fonctions

Can you do all of the following tasks in French?

- I can tell someone's nationality.
- I can ask and tell what country and what city someone is from.
- I can identify someone's profession.
- I can ask for and give information about various topics, including the weather.
- I can explain why.
- I can invite someone to do something.
- I can express emotions.

Quelle est la profession de Mme Nguyen?

To identify someone's nationality, use:

Il est français.

C'est un Français.   He is French.

Elle est japonaise.

C'est une Japonaise.   She is Japanese.

To ask where someone is from, use:

Tu viens/Vous venez d'où?   Where are you from?

To tell where someone is from, use:

Il/Elle est de New York.   He/She is from New York.

Il/Elle vient du Canada.   He/She is from Canada.

Il/Elle vient de Chine.   He/She is from China.

Il/Elle vient d'Angleterre.   He/She is from England.

Il/Elle vient des États-Unis.   He/She is from the United States.

Juanita María est mexicaine.

To identify someone's profession, use:

Il est avocat.

C'est un avocat.   He's a lawyer.

Elle est journaliste.

C'est une journaliste.   She's a journalist.

To ask for information, use:

C'est qui?   Who is it?

Quelle est la profession de Monsieur Desmarais?   What is Mr. Desmarais' occupation?

Il fait beau, **n'est-ce pas?**   It's nice, isn't it?

Est-ce que tu es allemande?   Are you German?

Quand viens-tu?   When are you coming?

Nathalie est de Paris. C'est une élève.

To give information, use:

Il voyage beaucoup.   He travels a lot.

Elle travaille beaucoup.   She works a lot.

Je n'ai pas de mère.   I don't have a mother.

Il fait beau en automne.   It's nice in autumn.

Il fait mauvais en hiver.   The weather's bad in the winter.

To explain something, use:

C'est pourquoi tu parles si bien le français!   That's why you speak French so well!

To invite someone to do something, use:

On fait un tour **ensemble?**   Do you want to take a trip together?

To express emotions, use:

Quelle chance!   What luck!

Vocabulaire

请以我单词表君" 时时~

	à in C
un	**agent de police** police officer B
l'	**Allemagne (f.)** Germany A
	allemand(e) German A
	américain(e) American A
un(e)	**ami(e)** friend C
	anglais(e) English A
l'	**Angleterre (f.)** England A
	après after C
	au in (the) B
	aujourd'hui today C
l'	**automne (m.)** autumn, fall C
	autre other C
	un(e) autre another C
un(e)	**avocat(e)** lawyer B

c'est that's A

le	**Canada** Canada A
	canadien, canadienne Canadian A
la	**chance** luck C
	chaud(e) warm, hot C
la	**Chine** China A
	chinois(e) Chinese A
un	**coiffeur, une coiffeuse** hairdresser B
un(e)	**comptable** accountant B
un	**cuisinier, une cuisinière** cook B

de (d') a, an, any B

un(e)	**dentiste** dentist B
	des from (the), of (the) A
	du from (the), of (the) A

en in C

l'	**Espagne (f.)** Spain A
	espagnol(e) Spanish A
	est-ce que? (phrase introducing a question) A
les	**États-Unis (m.)** United States A
l'	**été (m.)** summer C

faire un tour to go for a ride C
Quel temps fait-il? What's the weather like? How's the weather? C
Il fait beau. It's (The weather's) beautiful/nice. C
Il fait chaud. It's (The weather's) hot/warm. C
Il fait du soleil. It's sunny. C
Il fait du vent. It's windy. C
Il fait frais. It's (The weather's) cool. C
Il fait froid. It's (The weather's) cold. C
Il fait mauvais. It's (The weather's) bad. C

une	**femme au foyer** housewife B
une	**femme d'affaires** businesswoman B

un	**fermier, une fermière** farmer B
	frais, fraîche cool, fresh C
	français(e) French A
la	**France** France A
	froid(e) cold C
l'	**hiver (m.)** winter C
un	**homme** man B
	un homme au foyer househusband B
	un homme d'affaires businessman B
	ici here C
un	**infirmier, une infirmière** nurse B
un	**informaticien, une informaticienne** computer specialist B
un	**ingénieur** engineer B
l'	**Italie (f.)** Italy A
	italien, italienne Italian A
le	**Japon** Japan A
	japonais(e) Japanese A
un(e)	**journaliste** journalist B
	mauvais(e) bad C
un	**médecin** doctor B
	mexicain(e) Mexican A
le	**Mexique** Mexico A
	neiger: Il neige. It's snowing. C
	parler to speak, to talk B
	pleuvoir: Il pleut. It's raining. C
le	**printemps** spring C
une	**profession** occupation B
	quand when C
	si so B
le	**soleil** sun C
	souvent often C
	sur in A
le	**temps** weather C
	Quel temps fait-il? What's the weather like? How's the weather? C
un	**tour** trip C
	travailler to work B
	venir to come A
le	**vent** wind C
le	**Vietnam** Vietnam A
	vietnamien, vietnamienne Vietnamese A
	voyager to travel B

Unité 7

On fait les magasins.

In this unit you will be able to:

- express likes and dislikes
- agree and disagree
- express need
- express intentions
- invite
- inquire about and compare prices
- ask for information
- give information
- ask someone to repeat
- choose and purchase items

www.emcp.com

Vocabulaire

les vêtements (m.)

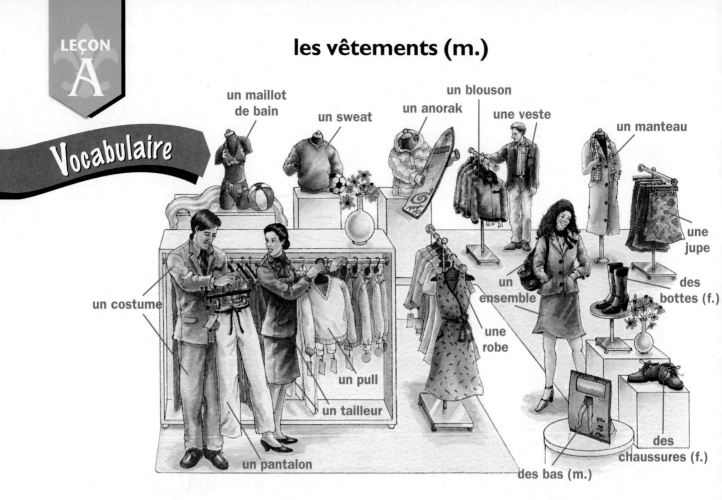

un maillot de bain

un sweat

un anorak

un blouson

une veste

un manteau

un costume

un ensemble

une jupe

des bottes (f.)

une robe

un pull

un tailleur

un pantalon

des bas (m.)

des chaussures (f.)

les magasins (m.)

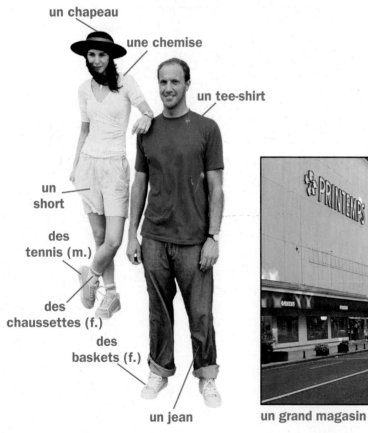

un chapeau

une chemise

un tee-shirt

un short

des tennis (m.)

des chaussettes (f.)

des baskets (f.)

un jean

un grand magasin

une boutique

un centre commercial

Isabelle

Ariane

Isabelle and Ariane are talking about what they're going to wear to a party.

Isabelle: **Je vais aller au centre commercial pour chercher un jean et un tee-shirt pour samedi soir. Et toi, qu'est-ce que tu vas porter à la boum?**

Ariane: **Moi, j'ai un pull mais j'ai besoin d'une jupe.**

Isabelle: **Allons ensemble au grand magasin! On va peut-être trouver quelque chose là-bas.**

Ariane: **D'accord. J'aime bien faire les magasins!**

Les magasins

There are huge shopping malls in France but fewer than in the United States. However, small specialized stores still do a brisk business. Just as in the United States, you can go to **le pressing** or **la teinturerie** (*dry cleaner's*) to have your clothes dry-cleaned, **le tailleur** (*tailor*) to have your clothes altered and **la cordonnerie** (*shoe repair shop*) to have your shoes repaired.

La mode

In general, the French place more importance on having quality clothing that is the latest style than on having many different outfits.

Le pressing 5àSec has 400 stores in France.

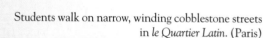

Students walk on narrow, winding cobblestone streets in *le Quartier Latin*. (Paris)

Le Quartier latin

Le Quartier latin, near the University of Paris, is an area where students often find clothes, international restaurants and entertainment which appeal to their contemporary tastes.

Le marché aux puces

At **le marché aux puces** (*flea market*) you can purchase a variety of items ranging from antique lamps to secondhand clothing. At such outdoor markets buyers often try bargaining with vendors to get a reduced price.

Les marchés aux puces are set up on public streets or squares. (Bruxelles)

1 Quels vêtements?

Write the letter of the clothing item that you hear.

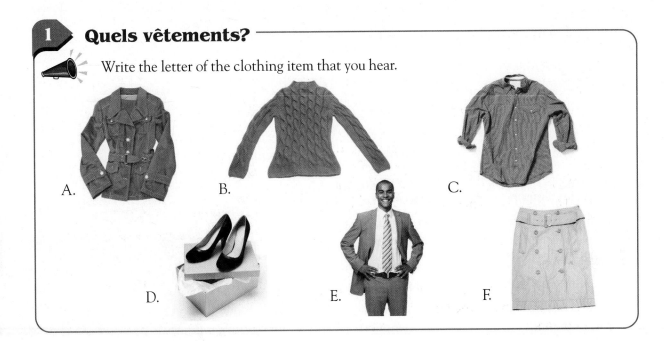

A.   B.   C.

D.   E.   F.

2 Qu'est-ce qu'elles vont porter?

Répondez en français.

1. Qui va faire les magasins?
2. Qu'est-ce qu'Isabelle va porter à la boum?
3. La boum, c'est quand?
4. Qu'est-ce qu'Ariane a déjà pour la boum?
5. De quoi Ariane a-t-elle besoin?
6. Ariane et Isabelle, est-ce qu'elles vont au grand magasin ou à la boutique?

3 Les vêtements

Identifiez.

Modèle:

Ce sont des bas.

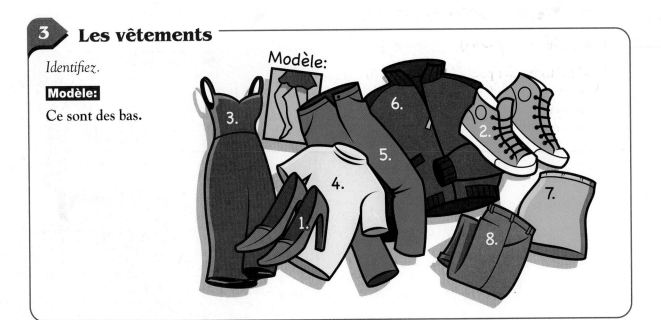

4 ▸ Qu'est-ce qu'on porte?

Complétez les phrases.

1. Sabrina skie. Elle porte....
   A. une jupe   B. un anorak   C. une robe

2. Mamadou nage. Il porte....
   A. une veste   B. des baskets   C. un maillot de bain

3. Michèle joue au volley. Elle porte....
   A. un blouson   B. des bas   C. un short

4. Nadia porte des tennis. Elle porte aussi....
   A. des chaussettes   B. des bottes   C. des bas

5. Il fait froid. Catherine porte une robe et aussi....
   A. un ensemble   B. un sweat   C. un manteau

6. Sylvie porte une jupe et aussi....
   A. un pull   B. un pantalon   C. un costume

7. Diana voyage beaucoup. Elle porte un ensemble: des chaussures, un tailleur et....
   A. des tennis   B. un chapeau   C. un tee-shirt

8. Édouard va au café avec ses parents. Il porte un pantalon et....
   A. une chemise   B. un jean   C. un tailleur

Édouard va au centre commercial.
Il porte un tee-shirt, un pull, un jean
et des chaussures. (Saint-Jean-de-Luz)

5 ▸ C'est à toi!

Questions personnelles.

1. Est-ce que tu aimes faire les magasins?
2. Où est-ce que tu préfères faire les magasins, au centre commercial, au grand magasin ou à une boutique?
3. Qu'est-ce que tu portes aujourd'hui?
4. Qu'est-ce que ton ami(e) porte aujourd'hui?
5. Qu'est-ce que tu portes quand tu vas à une boum?
6. Qu'est-ce que tu portes en été?

> J'aime faire les magasins. Et toi?

Aller + infinitive

One way to express what you are going to do in the near future is to use the present tense form of **aller** that agrees with the subject plus an infinitive.

Je **vais faire** les magasins.   *I'm going to go shopping.*

Qu'est-ce que tu **vas chercher**?   *What are you going to look for?*

To make a negative sentence, put **ne (n')** before the form of **aller** and **pas** after it.

André **ne** va **pas** porter son costume noir.   *André's not going to wear his black suit.*

Chloé et Paul vont faire du roller.

Pratique

6 **Les activités**

Qu'est-ce qu'on va faire après les cours?

Modèle:

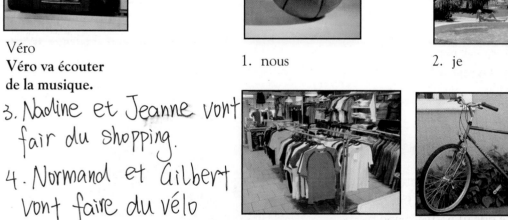

Véro

Véro va écouter de la musique.

Nous allons jouer au basket

1. nous

Je vais nager.

2. je

3. *Nadine et Jeanne vont fair du shopping.*

4. *Normand et Gilbert vont faire du vélo*

3. Nadine et Jeanne

4. Normand et Gilbert

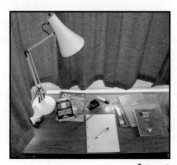

5. tu *Vas lire les magasins.*

6. Vincent *va étudier.*

7. vous *alez regarder la télé.*

7 ▸ La tempête

According to the weather forecast, everyone will be stranded at home tomorrow because of a storm. Tell whether or not the following people are going to do what they had planned.

Modèles:

M. Martin/écouter de la musique
Monsieur Martin va écouter de la musique.

les filles/faire les magasins
Les filles ne vont pas faire les magasins.

1. Antonine et Marie/téléphoner à leurs amis
2. nous/étudier
3. vous/skier
4. Mme Delacroix/dormir
5. je/faire des crêpes
6. Étienne/sortir avec Sara
7. Emmanuel et Fabrice/manger au café
8. tu/aller à la boum de Monique

8 ▸ En partenaires

Demandez (Ask) à votre partenaire s'il ou elle va faire les activités suivantes pendant (during) les vacances. Répondez aux questions et puis (then) alternez. Suivez le modèle.

Modèles:

nager
A: **Est-ce que tu vas nager?**
B: **Oui, je vais nager. Et toi, est-ce que tu vas nager?**
A: **Non, je ne vais pas nager.**

1. skier
2. aller au centre commercial
3. voyager
4. jouer au foot
5. faire les devoirs
6. regarder la télé
7. travailler

À + definite articles

The preposition **à** (*to, at, in*) does not change before the definite articles **la** and **l'**.

Allons ensemble **à la** boutique!	*Let's go to the boutique together!*
Pas possible. Je finis mes devoirs **à l'**école.	*Not possible. I'm finishing my homework at school.*

Before the definite articles **le** and **les**, however, **à** changes form. **À** combines with **le** and **les** as follows:

> **à + le = au**   *to (the), at (the), in (the)*
> **à + les = aux**   *to (the), at (the), in (the)*

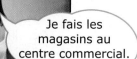

Je fais les magasins au centre commercial.

Qui va **au** centre commercial?	*Who is going to the mall?*
Jean et moi, nous allons **aux** grands magasins.	*Jean and I are going to the department stores.*

Au and **aux** are used before countries with masculine names.

Tu vas **aux** États-Unis ou **au** Canada?	*Are you going to the United States or to Canada?*

Pratique

9 ▸ Où va-t-on?

Dites où vont vos amis. Suivez le modèle.

la boum de Marc	la boutique	le cinéma	l'école
le Mexique	le fast-food	les États-Unis	

Modèle:

Ariane va parler espagnol.
Elle va au Mexique.

1. Béatrice et Éric vont danser samedi soir.
2. Catherine et Florence ont faim.
3. Salim va parler anglais.
4. Yasmine a besoin de chercher un jean et un tee-shirt.
5. Magali et Patrick désirent regarder un film de Spielberg.
6. Thomas a besoin de parler avec le prof d'informatique.

10 ▸ Vente de charité

Dites quels objets vous allez donner aux personnes suivantes.

Modèle:

le frère de Stéphanie
Je vais donner le blouson au frère de Stéphanie.

1. les profs de français
2. la prof de musique
3. le fils de la prof de biologie
4. l'informaticien de l'école
5. le prof de géographie
6. la sœur de David

Communication

11 ▸ Une liste de vêtements

Qu'est-ce que les élèves américains portent quand ils font les activités suivantes? Faites une liste de quatre vêtements qu'on porte selon (according to) la situation.

jouer au basket
aller à l'école
aller à une boum
aller au café avec les parents

12 ▸ Faisons les valises!

According to the weather report from each French-speaking vacation spot, select at least three clothing items for male travelers and three clothing items for female travelers to take along.

1. À Québec, au Canada, il fait très froid et il neige beaucoup en hiver. Il fait -15° C.
2. À Fort-de-France, à la Martinique, il fait du soleil et il fait très chaud en hiver. Il fait 28° C.
3. À la Nouvelle-Orléans, aux États-Unis, il fait beau et il fait chaud au printemps. Il fait 24° C.
4. À Paris, en France, il fait frais et il pleut au printemps. Il fait 12° C.

Au printemps à la Nouvelle-Orléans, les hommes portent un short, un tee-shirt et des tennis.

Have a phone conversation with a partner about going shopping.

Say you need to go to the mall and what you would like to buy.

Say that you would like to go to the mall also and what you need to buy.

Suggest a time to go.

Agree and say good-bye.

Prononciation

The sound [ɔ]

The sound [ɔ], or "open o," is just one of the sounds corresponding to the letter **o** in French. It is called "open **o**" because your mouth must be more open than closed to form it. Say each of these words:

    robe   anorak   short   costume   botte   porter

The sound [ɔ̃]

The sound [ɔ̃] is an open nasal sound. It is represented by the letters **on** and **om**. In either case, the **n** or **m** is not pronounced and the sound [ɔ̃] comes out through your nose. Say each of these words:

    pantal**on**   all**ons**   blous**on**   Jap**on**   c**om**bien   c**om**ptable

les couleurs (f.)

Vocabulaire

brown
marron

orange

vert(e)

beige

violet, violette

rose

rouge

noir(e)

blanc, blanche

bleu(e)
补勤

jaune

gris(e)

Il est grand.

Il est petit.
short

Elle est courte.
short

Elle est longue.

Elle est moche.
ugly
呜嘘

Elle est belle.
Elle est jolie.

SOLDES

$160.00

$32.99

Il est cher. expensive

Il est vieux.
old

Il est nouveau.

Il est bon marché.
cheap

bon marché
marron
orange   校渡 m./f./pl.

petit	petite
grand	grande
joli	jolie
beau	belle
moche	moche
nouveau	nouvelle
vieux	vieille
court	courte
long	longue
cher	chère
bon marché	bon marché

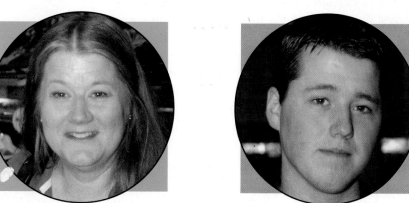

Madame Desrosiers   Jean

Madame Desrosiers is shopping with her son Jean at a store in Montreal, Canada

Mme Desrosiers: J'adore la chemise marron
　　　　　　　　et noire! Et elle est
　　　　　　　　bon marché. Elle
　　　　　　　　coûte 18 dollars.
Jean:　　　　　　Beurk! Je ne vais pas
　　　　　　　　acheter ça! Elle est
　　　　　　　　moche. Mais j'ai besoin
　　　　　　　　d'une nouvelle chemise.

Mme Desrosiers: Il y a beaucoup de belles
　　　　　　　　chemises ici-noires,
　　　　　　　　blanches, vertes....
Jean:　　　　　　C'est vrai. Tiens, j'aime la
　　　　　　　　grande chemise noire.
Mme Desrosiers: C'est combien? C'est
　　　　　　　　en solde?
Jean:　　　　　　Non, elle est assez
　　　　　　　　chère... 40 dollars.

SOLDES → on sale

À Montréal

There are many opportunities for shopping in Montreal, the second largest French-speaking city in the world. Beneath Montreal's busy streets in the midtown area, and literally carved from the rock that supports them, lies the world's largest subterranean city. Shopping, strolling, eating, doing business and finding entertainment are easy at any time of the day or night, with no worries about the cold Canadian winters. Department stores, hotels, restaurants, movie theaters and many businesses are located in and around large squares, such as the **Place Ville-Marie** and the **Place Bonaventure**. The four-line **métro** (*subway*) system and a series of walkways, stairways and elevators connect this underground complex. Decorations, such as stained glass windows, murals and ceramic artworks, beautify the modern **métro** stations, each designed by a different architect. Aboveground, concrete and glass skyscrapers top the subterranean complex.

In underground Montreal, shops are on multiple levels.

Looking at Montreal's cityscape, it is not evident that underground lies another complete city.

Soldes

When items are **en solde** (*on sale*) in French shops, they are sometimes displayed on the sidewalk in front of the store marked with the sign **Soldes** to attract customers.

Every Parisian walking by can tell there are sales at the Galeries Lafayette, one of the premier department stores in Paris.

1 Quelle couleur?

Write the letter of the color that you hear.

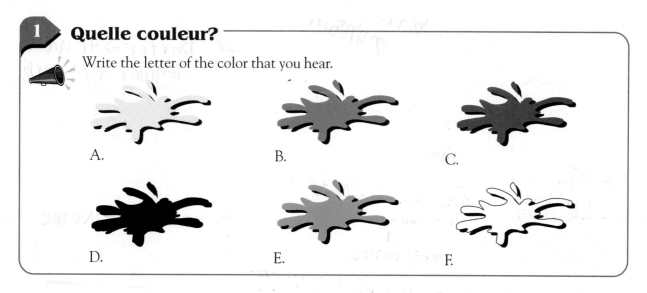

A.

B.

C.

D.

E.

F.

2 Au magasin

Répondez en français.

1. Qui fait les magasins?
2. Qui aime la chemise marron et noire?
3. La chemise marron et noire, est-elle chère ou bon marché?
4. Est-ce que Jean aime la chemise marron et noire?
5. Pourquoi est-ce que Jean ne va pas acheter la chemise marron et noire?
6. La chemise noire, est-elle grande ou petite?
7. Combien coûte la chemise noire?

3 Qui est-ce?

Identifiez la personne décrite (described).

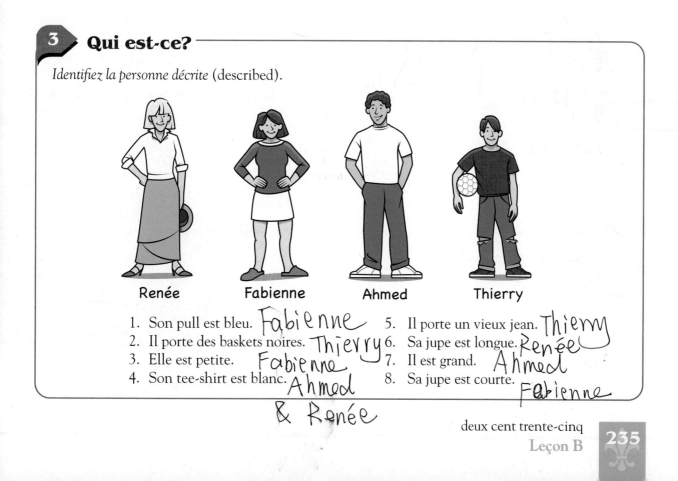

Renée   Fabienne   Ahmed   Thierry

1. Son pull est bleu. *Fabienne*
2. Il porte des baskets noires. *Thierry*
3. Elle est petite. *Fabienne*
4. Son tee-shirt est blanc. *Ahmed & Renée*
5. Il porte un vieux jean. *Thierry*
6. Sa jupe est longue. *Renée*
7. Il est grand. *Ahmed*
8. Sa jupe est courte. *Fabienne*

4 · C'est à toi!

Questions personnelles.

1. Avec qui fais-tu souvent les magasins?
2. Où vas-tu pour acheter des vêtements?
3. Est-ce que tu aimes acheter des vêtements en solde?
4. Qui porte un tee-shirt aujourd'hui?
5. Qui porte un jean aujourd'hui? Est-il nouveau ou vieux?
6. Qu'est-ce que tu portes aujourd'hui?

(Handwritten annotations:)

开店 do shopping 下面的方法

with open Store

wear door Porter → to wear (regular "er" verb)

wear

Cloths buy Sale new

Qu'est-ce que → 什么
Est-ce que → 就是个疑问词

1. Je fais souvent les magasins avec mes amies.
2. Je vais pour acheter / (J'acheter) des vêtements à Khols.
   (Je n'achète pas ...) 没
3. Oui.
4.
5. Personne. → No one
6.

Langue active

Irregular adjectives

You already know that most feminine adjectives are formed by adding an **e** to masculine adjectives.

gris	gris**e**
bleu	bleu**e**

You also know that if a masculine adjective ends in **-e**, the feminine adjective is identical.

rouge	rouge
moche	moche

Some irregular adjectives never change form, even in the plural.

orange	orange
marron	marron
super	super
sympa	sympa
bon marché	bon marché

Some feminine adjectives are formed by doubling the final consonant of a masculine adjective and adding an **e.**

bon	bon**ne**
quel	quel**le**
violet	violet**te**
italien	italien**ne**

nouve**ll**e co**ll**ection

La jupe est bon marché.

deux cent trente-six
Unité 7

To form a feminine adjective from a masculine adjective that ends in **-er**, change the ending to **-ère**.

cher	ch**è**re
premier	premi**è**re

Some other masculine adjectives also have irregular feminine forms.

blanc	**blanche**
frais	**fraîche**
long	**longue**

The adjectives **nouveau** and **vieux,** like the adjective **beau,** have irregular feminine forms as well as irregular forms before a masculine noun beginning with a vowel sound.

Masculine Singular before a Consonant Sound	Masculine Singular before a Vowel Sound	Feminine Singular
un **beau** magasin	un **bel** homme	une **belle** affiche
un **nouveau** pantalon	un **nouvel** ami	une **nouvelle** robe
un **vieux** costume	un **vieil** anorak	une **vieille** photo

The irregular masculine plural forms of these adjectives are **beaux, nouveaux** and **vieux.**

les **beaux** vêtements   les **nouveaux** élèves   les **vieux** pulls
[z]

Pratique

{ mettre = to put on (regular "è")
{ s'habiller = to dress oneself

5   **En boîte**

Sophie et Jérémy vont en boîte. Qu'est-ce qu'ils vont porter?

Modèle: *She is going to wear...*
Sophie va porter un pull noir....

Jérémy va Porter une veste, un tee-shirt, un jean, des baskets blanches tennis basket (m.) et un des chaussettes (f.) violettes
② (violette)
① (violet) ③ (bleu)
(blanc)

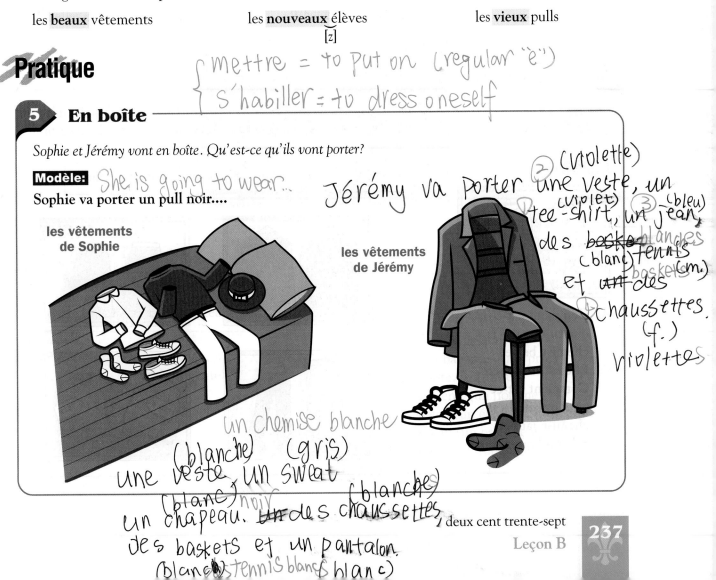

les vêtements de Sophie

les vêtements de Jérémy

un chemise blanche
une veste, un sweat
(blanche) (gris)
(blanc) noir
un chapeau. un des chaussettes,
(blanche)
des baskets et un pantalon.
(blanc) tennis blancs (blanc)

deux cent trente-sept

Haute couture designer Paco Rabanne shows off some of his creations in his workshop.

Models prepare to walk down the runway at a fashion show by designe Christian Lacroix.

The entire world looks to French fashion houses, such as Cardin, Dior, Lacroix, Chanel, Saint Laurent and Nina Ricci, for the latest styles. Fashion shows twice a year in Paris attract buyers from all around the globe to see the **défilés** (*showings*). Most designers also create **prêt-à-porter** (*ready-to-wear*) clothing which is more affordable for the average customer. If you can't get a ticket to a fashion show, you can always go to Angelina. In the spring and fall, you can get a seat near the window of this tea salon on the **rue de Rivoli** and watch models and designers rushing off to exhibit the latest collections.

But French teenagers are interested in more than high fashion. For school, casual clothing is the usual attire; many students wear jeans to class. On weekends and for parties, students have a chance to show off their own personal style. Some prefer an upscale, conservative look called **B.C.B.G.** Others favor a more radical style. For French teenagers, tastes in **fringues** (slang for *clothes*) vary just as they do in the rest of the world.

15 ▸ Les vêtements

Répondez aux questions.

1. Where do teenagers often go in Paris to find secondhand clothing? *marché aux purces*
2. Along what street in Paris are the boutiques of the leading fashion designers located? *haute couture rues piétoons*
3. What is the French term for streets reserved only for pedestrians? *rues piétonnes*
4. Why do some people prefer to shop in a small boutique? *les grands magains*
5. In a small boutique is it the customer or the salesperson who takes clothing from racks and shelves? *salesperson*
6. What are the names of two French department stores? *les grands surfaces & hypermarchés*
7. In what country did the concept of a department store originate? *France*
8. If you are invited to eat at a French person's home, what is it customary to bring? *fringues*
9. What are the names of two famous French designers? *Paco Rabanne & Christian Lacroix*
10. What are the initials used to describe a rather expensive, conservative style of clothing? *BCBG*

16 ▸ Au Vieux Campeur

Au Vieux Campeur *est un magasin qui vend (sells) des articles de sport. Chaque magasin se spécialise dans quelque chose de particulier. Choisissez la lettre du magasin qui correspond aux intérêts de chaque personne.*

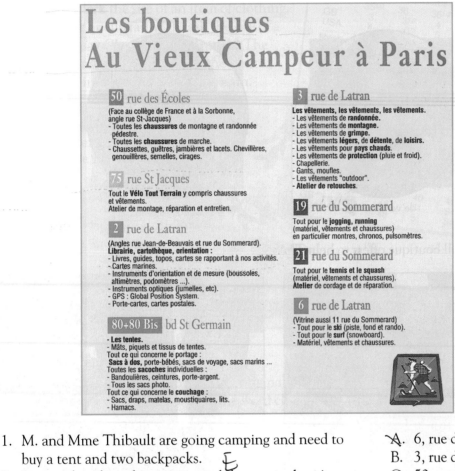

Les boutiques
Au Vieux Campeur à Paris

50 rue des Écoles

(Face au collège de France et à la Sorbonne, angle rue St-Jacques)
- Toutes les **chaussures** de montagne et randonnée pédestre.
- Toutes les **chaussures** de marche.
- Chaussettes, guêtres, jambières et lacets. Chevillères, genouillères, semelles, cirages.

75 rue St Jacques

Tout le **Vélo Tout Terrain** y compris chaussures et vêtements.
Atelier de montage, réparation et entretien.

2 rue de Latran

(Angles rue Jean-de-Beauvais et rue du Sommerard).
Librairie, cartothèque, orientation :
- Livres, guides, topos, cartes se rapportant à nos activités.
- Cartes marines.
- Instruments d'orientation et de mesure (boussoles, altimètres, podomètres ...).
- Instruments optiques (jumelles, etc).
- GPS : Global Position System.
- Porte-cartes, cartes postales.

80+80 Bis bd St Germain

- **Les tentes.**
- Mâts, piquets et tissus de tentes.
Tout ce qui concerne le portage :
Sacs à dos, porte-bébés, sacs de voyage, sacs marins ...
Toutes les **sacoches** individuelles :
- Bandoulières, ceintures, porte-argent.
- Tous les sacs photo.
Tout ce qui concerne le **couchage :**
- Sacs, draps, matelas, moustiquaires, lits.
- Hamacs.

3 rue de Latran

Les vêtements, les vêtements, les vêtements.
- Les vêtements de **randonnée.**
- Les vêtements de **montagne.**
- Les vêtements de **grimpe.**
- Les vêtements **légers,** de **détente,** de **loisirs.**
- Les vêtements pour **pays chauds.**
- Les vêtements de **protection** (pluie et froid).
- Chapellerie.
- Gants, moufles.
- Les vêtements "outdoor".
- **Atelier de retouches.**

19 rue du Sommerard

Tout pour le **jogging, running**
(matériel, vêtements et chaussures)
en particulier montres, chronos, pulsomètres.

21 rue du Sommerard

Tout pour le **tennis et le squash**
(matériel, vêtements et chaussures).
Atelier de cordage et de réparation.

6 rue de Latran

(Vitrine aussi 11 rue du Sommerard)
- Tout pour le **ski** (piste, fond et rando).
- Tout pour le **surf** (snowboard).
- Matériel, vêtements et chaussures.

1. M. and Mme Thibault are going camping and need to buy a tent and two backpacks. *E*
2. Issa needs to have her mountain bike repaired. *H*
3. Mlle Bernier needs to have her tennis racket restrung. *D G*
4. Fabrice wants to buy some new ski poles. *A*
5. M. Martin wants to buy some running shoes and a windbreaker. *D*
6. The Dubois family is planning a trip to Normandy and wants to find some guidebooks and maps of the region. *B*
7. Jean-Philippe is spending the month of January in Montreal and needs to buy some new winter clothing, including a coat and some gloves. *F*
8. Martine is going hiking and needs to buy some thick socks. *C*

A. 6, rue de Latran
B. 3, rue de Latran
C. 50, rue des Écoles
D. 19, rue du Sommerard
E. 80 + 80 bis, boulevard Saint-Germain
F. 2, rue de Latran
G. 21, rue du Sommerard
H. 75, rue Saint-Jacques

Critical Reading

If a store advertisement claims that a shirt is stylish and will make you popular, you, the reader, need to evaluate this statement. Do you like the style of the shirt? You may not. Can a shirt really guarantee popularity? It's doubtful. Evaluating what you read is called critical reading. It will help you separate fact from opinion and form your own ideas. Using critical reading will help you develop more advanced thinking skills so that you will become a better reader.

The reading below is part of an article from a back-to-school issue of a French magazine. Read critically the three clothing descriptions.

Bon chic, bon genre au masculin, c'est LA BLANCHE PORTE. Aucun problème avec le proviseur, ton succès est assuré !
Veste en maille côtelée sur une chemise en coton rayé et jean (27,14 €, 24,24 € et 22,71 €). Chaussures La Blanche Porte.

À prévoir dans la penderie, la tenue BASIC... souhaitable pour un examen ou un premier entretien professionnel !
Veste en lainage à col tailleur et poches plaquées (76,07 €, Tissaïa) sur un petit pull chaussette à encolure polo en laine mélangée. Pantalon de forme cigarette en coton strech (82,32 € chacun, Bensimon). Écharpe et chaussettes Soki. Bottines Un Matin d'Été.

Dans la mode
c'est déjà
la rentrée!

Chassez le naturel... En disciple de l'écologie, PRISUNIC le rattrape au galop ! Fausse fourrure, laine rustique et motifs ethniques pour le confort...
Parka molletonné avec capuche bordée de fausse fourrure sur un pull irlandais en laine rustique et une minijupe portefeuille en lainage (64,79 €, 49,55 € et 34,91 €). Collant Pingouin. Bottes Un Matin d'Été.

10 ▸ La mode

Répondez aux questions.

1. You know that the French word for "boot" is **botte**. What is the French word for "short boot"?
2. Which of the three outfits is the most expensive? Which is the least expensive?
3. Is the fur on the parka from Prisunic real or fake? Why does the retailer mention this?
4. According to the article, wearing the outfit from La Blanche Porte guarantees that you won't have any problems with your school principal. What assumption is this claim based on?
5. How would you describe the **bon chic bon genre** look in English?
6. Which outfits, if any, are appropriate to wear...
   A. to school?
   B. to a job interview?
   C. to a party?
   D. at home while watching TV?
7. Does one of these outfits reflect your own personal style? Why or why not?

Nathalie et Raoul

To say what you like, use:

J'aime bien faire les magasins.

J'adore la chemise bleue.

To say what you dislike, use:

Beurk!

To agree with someone, use:

C'est vrai.

To say you need something, use:

J'ai besoin d'un pull.

J'ai besoin d'une chemise.

To express intentions, use:

Je vais aller au centre commercial.

To invite someone to do something, use:

Allons ensemble au grand magasin!

To inquire about prices, use:

C'est combien?

C'est en solde?

To compare prices, use:

Il/Elle est assez cher/chère.

Il/Elle est bon marché.

To ask for information, use:

Quelle taille?

Est-ce que **vous vendez** aussi
des chaussures?

To give information, use:

Je fais du 42.

To ask someone to repeat, use:

Excusez-moi?

To choose and purchase an item, use:

Je cherche un pantalon gris.

I really like to go shopping.
I love the blue shirt.

Yuk!

This is/It's/That's true.

I need a sweater.
I need a shirt.

I'm going to go to the mall.

*Let's go to the department
store together!*

How much is it?
Is it on sale?

It's rather expensive.
It's cheap.

What size?
Do you also sell shoes?

I wear size 42.

Excuse me?

I'm looking for gray pants.

Vocabulaire

acheter to buy B
adorer to love B
un **anorak** ski jacket A
assez rather, quite B
aux to (the), at (the), in (the) A

des **bas (m.)** (panty) hose A
des **baskets (f.)** hightops A
beige beige B
Beurk! Yuk! B
blanc, blanche white B
un **blouson** jacket (outdoor) A
bon marché cheap B
une **botte** boot A
une **boum** party A
une **boutique** shop, boutique A

un **centre commercial** shopping center, mall A
un **chapeau** hat A
une **chaussette** sock A
une **chaussure** shoe A
une **chemise** shirt A
cher, chère expensive B
chercher to look for A
une **chose** thing A
    quelque chose something A
un **costume** man's suit A
une **couleur** color B
court(e) short B

un **dollar** dollar B

en solde on sale B
un **ensemble** outfit A
excusez-moi excuse me C

faire du (+ *number*) to wear size (+ number) C
faire les magasins to go shopping A

grand(e) tall, big, large B

il y a there is, there are B

jaune yellow B
un **jean** (pair of) jeans A
joli(e) pretty B
une **jupe** skirt A

là-bas over there A
long, longue long B

un **magasin** store A
    un grand magasin department store A
un **maillot de bain** swimsuit A
un **manteau** coat A
marron brown B
moche ugly B

nouveau, nouvel, nouvelle new B

orange orange B

un **pantalon** (pair of) pants A
petit(e) short, little, small B
peut-être maybe A
porter to wear A
pour (in order) to A
un **pull** sweater A

quelque chose something A

une **robe** dress A
rose pink B

un **short** (pair of) shorts A
un **soir** evening A
des **soldes (f.)** sale(s) B
un **sweat** sweatshirt A

une **taille** size C
un **tailleur** woman's suit A
un **tee-shirt** T-shirt A
des **tennis (m.)** tennis shoes A
trouver to find A

un **vendeur, une vendeuse** salesperson C
vendre to sell C
une **veste** (sport) jacket A
des **vêtements (m.)** clothes A
vieux, vieil, vieille old B
violet, violette purple B
voici here is/are C
vrai(e) true B

Unité

8

On fait les courses.

In this unit you will be able to:
- ask for information
- give information
- express likes and dislikes
- agree and disagree
- identify objects
- ask for permission
- ask for a price
- state prices
- inquire about and compare prices
- make a complaint
- insist
- negotiate
- choose and purchase items

www.emcp.com

Vocabulaire

les crabes (m.)

les crevettes (f.)

les poissons (m.)

Vegetable   Shirmp   fish

les légumes (m.)

les carottes (f.)

les petits pois (m.)

les haricots verts (m.)

les pommes de terre (f.)

les oignons (m.)

les tomates (f.)

les champignons (m.)

Madame Laurier   Madeleine

beautiful port city

Madame Laurier and her daughter Madeleine are at the supermarket in Marseille.

Mme Laurier: Qu'est-ce que tu veux manger
              ce soir?
Madeleine: Euh... tu peux faire
              une bouillabaisse?
Mme Laurier: OK, je vais acheter ces tomates
              et cet oignon pour la soupe.
              Maintenant on va chercher les
              crabes et les poissons.

Madeleine: Nous pouvons acheter des
              oranges aussi?
Mme Laurier: Oui, ton père veut toujours un
              fruit après le repas.

soup: tomato, onion

meal

À Marseille

Marseille is France's largest seaport and oldest city. Tourists often visit **le Vieux Port**, a small port near the center of the city filled with recreational and fishing boats, and **la Canebière**, the main commercial street lined with many shops. Ships from all over the world dock at the modern, international port nearby. One of the well-known churches of the city, **Notre-Dame-de-la-Garde**, has a golden statue of the Virgin Mary on its steeple. This statue still guides sailors safely to the port, since it can be seen far out into the Mediterranean Sea. The French national anthem, the "Marseillaise," received its name from the city of Marseille.

Early in the morning, people head to *le Vieux Port* to buy fresh fish. (Marseille)

Les spécialités régionales

Each region in France has its own culinary specialty. **Bouillabaisse, a fish soup**, is a specialty of Marseille. **Pâté de foie gras**, a pork and goose liver pâté, comes from the city of Strasbourg. **Cassoulet**, from the southwestern part of France, is a stew made from duck, goose or sausage and white beans. **Quiche lorraine**, a quiche containing bacon, onions and cheese, was created in the province of Lorraine. **Bœuf bourguignon**, a meat stew cooked in red wine, originated in the Burgundy region.

The origins of *cassoulet* date from the fourteenth century.

1 Quels légumes?

Faites correspondre la lettre au légume que vous entendez (hear).

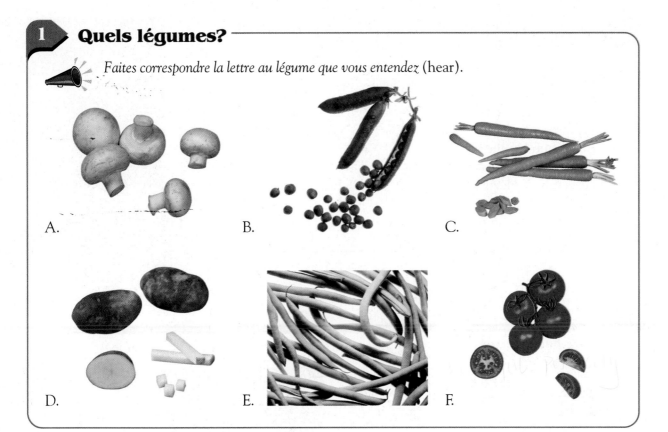

A.

B.

C.

D.

E.

F.

2 Au supermarché

Répondez aux questions.

1. Qu'est-ce que Mme Laurier va faire ce soir?
2. La bouillabaisse, c'est un dessert?
3. Quels légumes est-ce qu'il y a dans une bouillabaisse?
4. Qu'est-ce qu'il y a aussi dans une bouillabaisse?
5. Quel fruit est-ce que Mme Laurier et Madeleine vont acheter?
6. Qu'est-ce que les Français mangent souvent après le repas?

La bouillabaisse est une soupe aux poissons.

3 ▸ Complétez!

Choisissez la bonne réponse.

1. Les... sont des légumes longs.
2. Les... sont des fruits.
3. Les... sont des légumes orange.
4. L'... est un légume blanc.
5. Les... sont des légumes blancs.
6. Les... sont des légumes rouges.
7. Les frites sont des....
8. On trouve les... dans la Méditerranée.

A. tomates
B. oignon
C. haricots verts
D. crabes
E. carottes
F. oranges
G. champignons
H. pommes de terre

Est-ce que ces crabes sont frais?

4 ▸ Beaucoup, un peu ou pas du tout?

*Choisissez **J'aime beaucoup**, **J'aime un peu** ou **Je n'aime pas**.*

1. les petits pois
2. les crevettes
3. les légumes
4. les champignons
5. les poissons
6. les oignons
7. les fruits

J'aime beaucoup les champignons.

Est-ce que tu manges beaucoup de carottes?

5 ▸ C'est à toi!

Questions personnelles.

1. Est-ce que tu manges beaucoup de légumes?
2. Quels légumes aimes-tu?
3. Est-ce que tu préfères le poisson ou le steak?
4. Quand est-ce que tu aimes manger de la soupe, en été ou en hiver?
5. Dans ta famille, qui aime les oranges?
6. Qu'est-ce que tu vas manger ce soir?

Handwritten note at top:

pouvoir: to be able to

je peux	nous pouvons
tu peux	vous pouvez
il peut	ils peuvent

...egular verb *vouloir*

je	**veux**	nous	**voulons**
tu	**veux**	vous	**voulez**
il/elle/on	**veut**	ils/elles	**veulent**

| Où **voulez**-vous manger? | *Where do you want to eat?* |
| Je **veux** manger au fast-food. | *I want to eat at the fast-food restaurant.* |

You already know one form of the verb **vouloir** that you use when you ask for something: **Je voudrais....** (*I would like . . . .*) The French often use this form, which is more polite than **je veux**.

Tu veux manger une pizza?

Pratique

6 **Au café ou au fast-food?**

Dites si les personnes suivantes veulent manger au café ou au fast-food.

Modèles:

Clément
Clément veut manger au fast-food.

Luc et Marie-Alix
Luc et Marie-Alix veulent manger au café.

1. Christine

2. nous

3. Jamila et Latifa

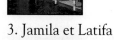

4. tu

5. David

6. je

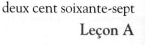

7. Laurent et Philippe

8. vous

7 ▶ On veut manger ou boire?

Choisissez ce que (what) *les personnes suivantes veulent, selon la description. Suivez les modèles.*

Modèles:

Patricia a soif. (un dessert/un coca)
Elle veut un coca.

M. et Mme Lavigne ont faim. (des frites/un jus
de raisin)
Ils veulent des frites.

1. Édouard a soif. (une eau minérale/
   une crêpe)
2. J'ai soif. (une orange/un café)
3. Mme Pinetti et son fils ont faim. (des jus
   d'orange/des légumes)
4. Tu as faim. (des crevettes/un jus
   de pomme)
5. Nous avons soif. (des pommes de terre/
   des limonades)
6. Vous avez faim. (des fruits/des boissons)

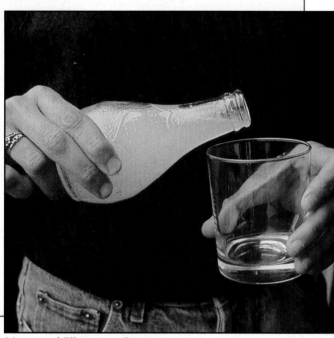

Marie a soif. Elle veut un Orangina.

Present tense of the irregular verb *pouvoir*

The verb **pouvoir** (*to be able to*) is irregular. In the following examples
note the different meanings of **pouvoir** in English.

pouvoir			
je	**peux**	nous	**pouvons**
tu	**peux**	vous	**pouvez**
il/elle/on	**peut**	ils/elles	**peuvent**

Pouvez-vous venir demain?   *Are you able to come tomorrow?*

Non, je ne **peux** pas.   *No, I can't.*

Tu peux faire une soupe à l'oignon?

Handwritten (top):
5. Mme. Wolff peut acheter le sac à dos ~~chapeau~~
6. Les soeurs de Nicolas peuvent le ~~chau~~ chapeau
7. Nous Pouvons acheter ~~une~~ le cheval.
8. Tu peu~~x~~ acheter ~~la~~ le stylo.

Pratique

8 ▸ En solde

Selon l'argent disponible (available money), qu'est-ce qu'on peut acheter? Suivez le modèle.

Modèle:

Abdou (quinze euros)
Abdou peut acheter le sac à dos.

Handwritten:
1. M. Prat peut acheter ~~une~~ le ordinateur
2. Vous pouvez acheter ~~la~~ le pantalon
3. Thibault et son frère peuvent acheter ~~le~~ CD
4. Je peux acheter ~~la~~ le ordinateur.

1. M. Prat (sept cent soixante-dix euros)
2. vous (cent sept euros)
3. Thibault et son frère (vingt et un euros)
4. je (soixante-dix euros)
5. Mme Wolff (trente euros)
6. les sœurs de Nicolas (trente-huit euros)
7. nous (six cent dix euros)
8. tu (cinq euros)

Handwritten label: le oiseau

94,52 €

22,87 €

34,91 €

14,89 €

67,08 €

553,57 €

19,06 €

686,02 €

4,42 €

Vocabulaire

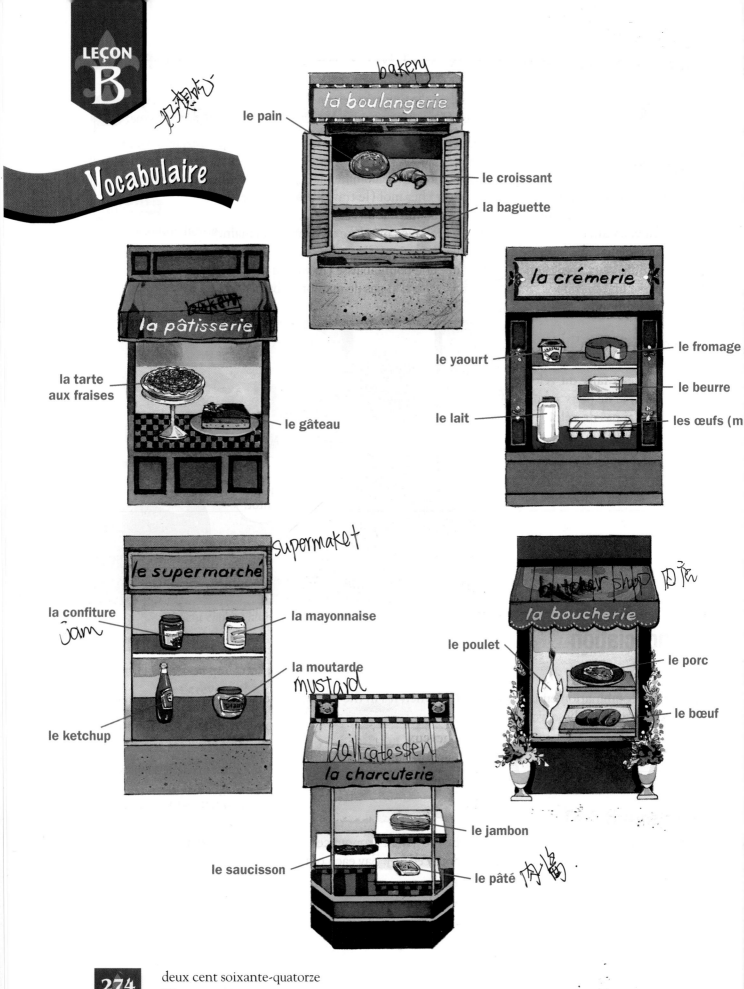

bakery
la boulangerie

le pain

le croissant

la baguette

la pâtisserie

la tarte aux fraises

le gâteau

la crémerie

le yaourt

le fromage

le beurre

le lait

les œufs (m

supermaket
le supermarché

la confiture
jam

la mayonnaise

la moutarde
mustard

le ketchup

la boucherie

butcher shop

le poulet

le porc

le bœuf

delicatessen
la charcuterie

le jambon

le saucisson

le pâté

Combien de confiture as-tu?

J'ai trop de confiture.

too much

J'ai beaucoup de confiture.

a lot

J'ai assez de confiture.

enough [第二种 enough 好吗]

J'ai un peu de confiture.

a little bit

une tranche
de jambon

slice

une boîte de
petits pois

can

un pot de
moutarde

un morceau
de fromage

piece

un kilo → kg
de tomates

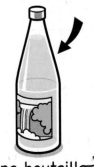

une bouteille → *bottle*
d'eau minérale

Madame Rousseau

Benjamin

Madame Rousseau and her son Benjamin are talking about grocery shopping.

Benjamin: Où est-ce qu'on va faire les courses, maman?

Mme Rousseau: D'abord, on va aller à la boulangerie acheter du pain et des croissants.

Benjamin: Ouais! J'aime bien les croissants le matin.

Mme Rousseau: Puis, on va acheter des yaourts et un peu de fromage, peut-être du camembert, à la crémerie.

Benjamin: Moi, j'aime aussi le pâté. On ne va pas acheter de pâté?

Mme Rousseau: Si, si, mais attends! Nous pouvons aussi aller à la charcuterie.

Le pain et la pâtisserie

The expression **Repas sans pain, repas de rien** ("A meal without bread is nothing") shows the importance of bread in the French diet. Although French bread comes in many shapes and sizes, the most common type, the **baguette**, is a long, thin loaf of bread with a crisp crust. This hard crust keeps the bread fresh without being wrapped; people can be seen carrying **baguettes** tucked under their arms or nibbling on the ends of them as they walk home from the **boulangerie**. The bread has such a good taste that the French usually don't butter it, except for breakfast. Other sweeter types of bakery products are just as delicious. A **pain au chocolat** tastes like a **croissant** and has a piece of chocolate in the center. Children often eat them for snacks. **Un éclair** is a cream-filled pastry, **un chausson aux pommes** resembles an apple turnover and **une brioche** is a soft, round roll.

Unlike Americans, the French don't wrap their bread in plastic bags. (Quimper)

In 1962, President Charles de Gaulle said "How can you be expected to govern a country that has 246 different kinds of cheese?"

Le fromage

Cheese, another staple in the French diet, is often served as dessert at the end of a meal. Today most regions of France produce their own special cheese, with some 360 different kinds in all to choose from. Camembert, Pont-l'Évêque and Neufchâtel are three of the many famous types of cheese from the northern province of Normandy. Brie, the most famous of all French cheeses, comes from the Parisian area. Roquefort, one of the better-known blue cheeses from the Massif Central, is made from sheep's milk.

Le yaourt

Instead of cheese, the French often eat yogurt for dessert. French yogurt is generally thinner than the custard-type yogurt found in the United States. In general, French teenagers drink less milk than American teens but consume more cheese and yogurt. They generally eat their yogurt plain, but sometimes sweeten it with a little sugar, honey, jam or jelly.

This yogurt is flavored with strawberries.

1 ▸ **Quel magasin?**

Écrivez "P" si vous achetez l'aliment à la pâtisserie; "B" à la boucherie; "C" à la crémerie.

2 ▸ **Un sommaire**

Écrivez un paragraphe de quatre phrases. Dites ce que Mme Rousseau et Benjamin font. Puis mentionnez ce qu'ils vont acheter à la boulangerie et à la crémerie. Enfin, dites ce que Benjamin aime.

3 ▸ **Un pique-nique**

Demandez à votre partenaire quels aliments il ou elle préfère. Répondez aux questions et puis alternez. Suivez le modèle.

Modèle:

1.
2.
3.
4.
5.
6.
7.
8.

Thomas: **Tu préfères le lait ou le jus d'orange?**

Amina: **Moi, je préfère le jus d'orange.**

Complétez!

Choisissez la lettre de l'aliment qui complète l'expression de quantité.

C 1. un pot de... ~~moutarde~~ A. eau minérale

E 2. une tranche de... ~~jambon~~ B. tomates

B 3. une boîte de... ~~petits pois~~ C. confiture

A 4. une bouteille d'... ~~eau minérale~~ D. camembert

D 5. un morceau de... ~~fromage~~ E. jambon

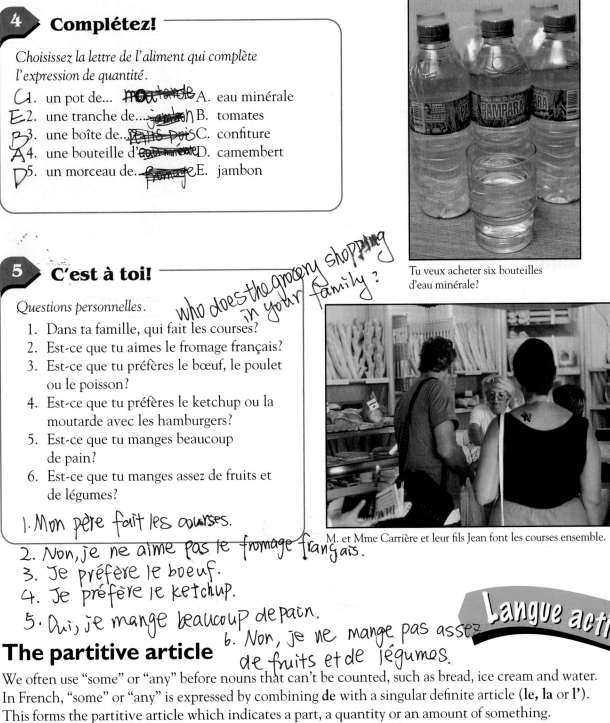

Tu veux acheter six bouteilles d'eau minérale?

5

C'est à toi!

Questions personnelles.

who does the grocery shopping in your family?

1. Dans ta famille, qui fait les courses?
2. Est-ce que tu aimes le fromage français?
3. Est-ce que tu préfères le bœuf, le poulet ou le poisson?
4. Est-ce que tu préfères le ketchup ou la moutarde avec les hamburgers?
5. Est-ce que tu manges beaucoup de pain?
6. Est-ce que tu manges assez de fruits et de légumes?

1. Mon père fait les courses.

M. et Mme Carrière et leur fils Jean font les courses ensemble.

2. Non, je ne aime pas le fromage français.
3. Je préfère le bœuf.
4. Je préfère le ketchup.
5. Oui, je mange beaucoup de pain.
6. Non, je ne mange pas assez de fruits et de légumes.

The partitive article

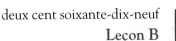

We often use "some" or "any" before nouns that can't be counted, such as bread, ice cream and water. In French, "some" or "any" is expressed by combining **de** with a singular definite article (**le, la** or **l'**). This forms the partitive article which indicates a part, a quantity or an amount of something.

Masculine before a Consonant Sound	Feminine before a Consonant Sound	Masculine or Feminine before a Vowel Sound
du café	**de la** soupe	**de l'**eau minérale

On va acheter **du** pain.   *We're going to buy (some) bread.*

Vous avez **de la** glace?   *Do you have (any) ice cream?*

Je voudrais **de l'**eau minérale.   *I would like (some) mineral water.*

The partitive article in negative sentences

You've already learned that in negative sentences, **des** becomes **de** or **d'**.

Je ne veux pas **de** pommes de terre.   *I don't want (any) potatoes.*

The partitive articles **du, de la** and **de l'** also change to **de** or **d'** in negative sentences.

On ne va pas acheter **de** fromage.   *We're not going to buy (any) cheese.*
Il n'y a pas **d'**eau minérale.   *There isn't any mineral water.*

Pratique

10 ▶ Un végétarien

Olivier est végétarien. Dites s'il mange ou non les aliments suivants.

Modèles:

frites
Il mange des frites.

saucisson
Il ne mange pas de saucisson.

1. porc
2. steak
3. pâté
4. pain
5. légumes
6. fruits
7. jambon
8. camembert
9. glace
10. bœuf

Olivier mange du camembert.

11 ▶ En partenaires

Demandez à votre partenaire ce qu'il y a dans le frigo (refrigerator). Répondez aux questions et puis alternez. Suivez le modèle.

Modèle:

salade/beurre
A: **Il y a de la salade?**
B: **Oui, il y a de la salade.**
   Il y a du beurre?
A: **Non, il n'y a pas de beurre.**

1. moutarde/ketchup
2. lait/jus d'orange
3. fromage/œufs
4. eau/coca
5. pommes de terre/ tomates
6. crevettes/poisson
7. pâté/bœuf

Expressions of quantity

To ask "how many" or "how much," use the expression **combien de** before a noun.

Combien de croissants est-ce que tu veux?   *How many croissants do you want?*

Il y a **combien d'œufs** dans cette omelette?   *How many eggs are there in this omelette?*

To tell "how many" or "how much," use one of these general expressions of quantity before a noun:

assez de	*enough*
beaucoup de	*a lot of, many*
(un) peu de	*(a) little, few*
trop de	*too much, too many*

Je voudrais **un peu de** fromage.   *I would like a little cheese.*

Non, merci, j'ai **assez d'**eau.   *No thanks, I have enough water.*

Certain nouns express a specific quantity. They are followed by **de** and a noun.

un morceau de	*a piece of*
une tranche de	*a slice of*
un pot de	*a jar of*
une boîte de	*a can of*
une bouteille de	*a bottle of*
un kilo de	*a kilogram of*

Donnez-moi **une tranche de** jambon.   *Give me a slice of ham.*

Je veux acheter **un kilo d'**oranges.   *I want to buy one kilo of oranges.*

Vous voulez un morceau de fromage?

Pratique

12 Les restes

Demandez à votre partenaire combien de chaque aliment reste (remains) sur la table. Répondez aux questions et puis alternez. Suivez le modèle.

Modèle:

salades/quiches

A: **Il y a combien de salades?**

B: **Il y a quatre salades.**
   Il y a combien de quiches?

A: **Il y a une quiche.**

1. omelettes/sandwichs
2. croissants/crevettes
3. poissons/oranges
4. gâteaux/tartes

13 Un inventaire

*Vous travaillez au marché. Dites combien de chaque fruit ou légume vous avez. Utilisez **trop de**, **assez de** ou **peu de**. Suivez le modèle.*

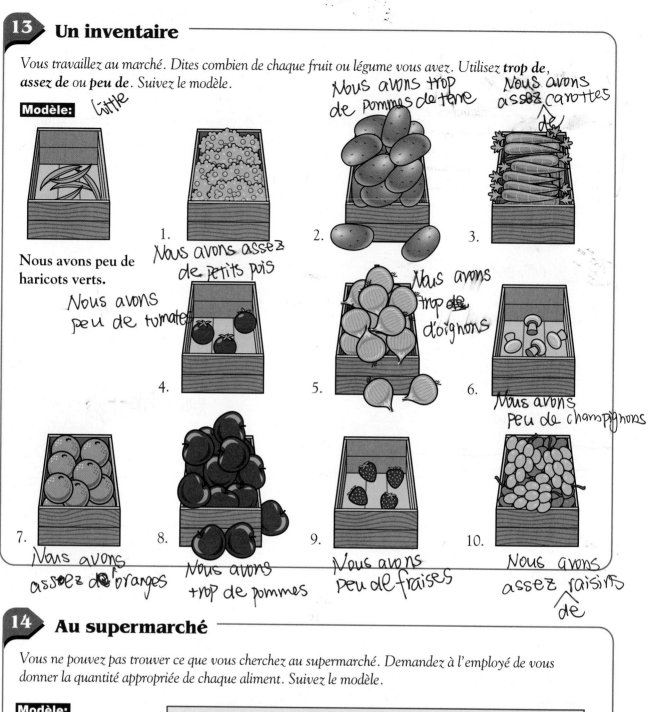

Modèle: little

Nous avons peu de haricots verts.

1. *Nous avons assez de petits pois*

2. *Nous avons trop de pommes de terre*

3. *Nous avons assez carottes de*

4. *Nous avons peu de tomates*

5. *Nous avons trop de d'oignons*

6. *Nous avons peu de champignons*

7. *Nous avons assez d'oranges*

8. *Nous avons trop de pommes*

9. *Nous avons peu de fraises*

10. *Nous avons assez raisins de*

14 Au supermarché

Vous ne pouvez pas trouver ce que vous cherchez au supermarché. Demandez à l'employé de vous donner la quantité appropriée de chaque aliment. Suivez le modèle.

Modèle:

café
Donnez-moi un kilo de café, s'il vous plaît.

un pot de	une tranche de	une boîte de
un kilo de	une bouteille de	

1. pommes de terre
2. jus de pomme
3. mayonnaise
4. jambon

5. confiture
6. petits pois
7. coca
8. pâté

Communication

15 Piqueniquons ensemble!

Votre classe va piqueniquer ensemble demain.
Faites une liste d'aliments que vous allez acheter:
sandwichs, fruits, fromages, desserts et boissons.
Dites la quantité de chaque aliment, par exemple,
10 tranches de jambon, **7 baguettes**, **4**
bouteilles de coca, *etc.*

16 Catégorisez!

Avec un(e) partenaire, catégorisez ce
que vous allez acheter pour le pique-
nique. D'abord, écrivez **crémerie**, **pâtisserie**,
boulangerie, **charcuterie**, **marché** *et*
supermarché. *Puis écrivez chaque aliment que*
vous allez acheter sous le magasin approprié.

17 À vous de jouer!

Avec un(e) partenaire, jouez les rôles d'un(e) client(e) et un(e) employé(e) au supermarché.
Le (La) client(e) fait les courses pour le pique-nique.

Dites "Bonjour!"

Dites la quantité de chaque aliment que vous allez acheter.

Dites que vous avez ou pas chaque aliment. Si vous n'avez pas un certain aliment, suggérez quelque chose d'autre.

Demandez "Ça fait combien?"

Dites le total.

Dites "Au revoir."

Les courses

France is known throughout the world for its good food. However, it may be difficult deciding where to shop. From open-air markets to specialty food shops, from corner grocery stores to large supermarkets, choices are everywhere.

Casino is a popular supermarket chain in France.

Open-air markets generally offer the freshest food, with farmers bringing their products directly to the customer. Along with the fresh produce, reasonable prices also attract customers, who sometimes bargain to get an even better buy. Merchants set up stands of regional specialties as well as seasonal fruits, vegetables, meat, seafood and cheese. Few of the products are refrigerated, not even the meat. Often located on a public square, markets open early in the morning. Shoppers arrive with their shopping basket (**un sac à provisions**) in hand, as shopping bags are usually not provided.

Markets in other French-speaking countries reflect the local character. In Senegal, Morocco and Algeria, the smell of exotic spices, the shouts of the merchants tempting customers to their stalls and the bright colors of the merchandise itself all offer a lively shopping experience. Markets on the Caribbean islands of Guadeloupe and Martinique sell tuna, lobster, clams and other products from the sea, as well as bananas, papayas, mangoes, avocados, guavas and yams.

Specialty shops are popular with people who live nearby and who appreciate their individualized service. To buy bakery products, such as bread and rolls, let your nose guide you to **la boulangerie.** For special pastries, as well as cakes,

A Moroccan merchant sells fruits, vegetables and eggs in the *souk,* a market in the old part of town.

pies and cookies, head for **la pâtisserie**. For most meat products, stop in **la boucherie** where the butcher will be happy to advise you on the appropriate cut of meat for a certain recipe and will cut and wrap it for you. **La boucherie chevaline**, a specialized butcher shop, offers only horse meat. For prepared pork products or deli food, including salads and cold meat dishes, go to **la charcuterie**. Convenient corner grocery stores (**les épiceries**) stock many different products. Sidewalk stands in front of these stores sell fruits and vegetables to passersby.

Shoppers at supermarkets like Monoprix, Uniprix and Prisunic usually pay a small deposit to rent a shopping cart (**un chariot**) which they fill at different departments before paying at the check-out (**la caisse**). One French supermarket chain, Carrefour, is so large that some supervisors wear roller skates to move quickly back and forth to help cashiers in the many checkout lines. In some ways French supermarkets differ from their counterparts in the United States. For example, the long rows of bottled water, the large cheese section and the limited variety of cold cereal and snack food reflect traditional French shopping habits. Frozen foods (**les produits surgelés**) have become increasingly popular as busy lifestyles limit the time spent on meal preparation.

Whether customers pick a place to shop based on fresh products, a large selection, individualized help or convenience, they will find a place to buy good food close to home.

Organizations such as *La Fondation Brigitte Bardot,* which are concerned with animal rights, are convincing more and more people to stop buying horse meat.

Shoppers go to the basement of Monoprix to find *le supermarché*. (Colmar)

18 Les courses

Répondez aux questions.

1. Where can a French-speaking shopper bargain for a lower price, at an open-air market, a specialty shop, a corner grocery store or a supermarket? *open-air market*
2. Are products at an open-air market refrigerated? *few of them*
3. Where are markets often located? *on a public square*
4. Why do shoppers often bring their own **sac à provisions** with them? *shopping bags are not usually provided*
5. How would you describe a typical African market? *smell of exotic spices*
6. What are three kinds of food that can be found in Caribbean markets? *tuna, lobster, clam*
7. What is the difference between a **boucherie** and a **charcuterie**? *charcuterie is prepared*
8. What are the names of two supermarket chains in France? *Carrefour*
9. Where do you go to pay for your purchases at a supermarket? *la caisse*
10. What section of a French supermarket is larger than its American counterpart? What section is smaller? *cheese, bottled water, limited variety of cold cereal & snack*

19 Les reçus

Voici un reçu (receipt) de Monoprix et un autre de Prisunic. Répondez aux questions.

At Monoprix:

1. What brand of mineral water did the customer buy? *Evian*
2. How much did the bread cost? *0.61€*
3. How many grams did the Babybel cheese weigh? *200G*
4. What was the date of the customer's purchase? *5/7, 2007*
5. In what city is this Monoprix? *Paris*

At Prisunic:

1. How many packages of Lavazza coffee did the customer purchase? *2*
2. How much was the customer's bill? *6.2*
3. How many euros did the customer give the cashier? *7.2*
4. How many euros did the customer receive in change? *1*
5. At what time did the customer check out? *14=52*

```
SOLDES! SOLDES! SOLDES! SOLDES! SOLDES
! SOLDES! SOLDES! SOLDES! SOLDES! SOLD
                                   0,45
  EVIAN BTLLE 50          0,61
  PAIN PARISIE            3,23
  CAFE SOLUBLE            1,52
  BABYBEL 200G            0,82
  FRUITERIE         TOT   6,63
****                      7,00
   ESPECES                0,37
   A RENDRE
5.07.07 19:21 0160103 0538 17
*** MERCI D'AVOIR CHOISI MONOPRIX! ***
     99 FG ST-ANTOINE 75011 PARIS
```

```
***    PRISUNIC CAUMARTIN     ***

2x2,21 LAVAZZA EXPRESSO
     FRUITS ET LEGUMES      4,42
        **** TOTAL          1,78
                            6,20
   ESPECES
                            7,20
   A RENDRE
                            1,00
7.08.07 14:52 1119201 0248 210
***
       HERCI DE VOTRE VISITE    ***
```

les fruits (m.)

Vocabulaire

les cerises (f.)

les pêches (f.)

les fraises (f.)

les pommes (f.)

1,52 €
le kilo

les melons (m.)

1,52 €
le kilo

les pastèques (f.)

les poires (f.)

les raisins (m.)

les oranges (f.)

2,29 €
le kilo

les bananes (f.)

Les bananes sont plus chères que les pastèques.
Les melons sont aussi chers que les pastèques.
Les melons sont moins chers que les bananes.

le marchand   M. Gagnon

Monsieur Gagnon is shopping for fruit at an open-air market in Guadeloupe.

Le marchand: **Bonjour, Monsieur. Vous désirez?**

M. Gagnon: **Combien coûtent les melons, s'il vous plaît?**

Le marchand: **Les melons... euh... 1,52 euros le kilo.**

M. Gagnon: **Mais ils sont déjà mûrs. Je trouve que c'est trop cher. Est-ce que je peux acheter deux kilos pour 2,50 euros?**

Le marchand: **D'accord, Monsieur.**

M. Gagnon: **Et les bananes, combien coûtent-elles?**

Le marchand: **Les bananes sont plus chères que les melons. Elles coûtent 2,29 euros le kilo.**

M. Gagnon: **Bon, alors je vais aussi acheter deux kilos de bananes.**

La Guadeloupe

The Caribbean island of Guadeloupe, made up of two main islands and some smaller ones, is one of France's overseas departments in the West Indies (**les Antilles**). Its tropical climate encourages the growth of many fruits and vegetables. Some of the island's other exports are cocoa, coffee and sugar cane.

Banana plantations in Guadeloupe grow fruit for customers at home and abroad.

Au marché guadeloupéen

Since most people in Guadeloupe have fruit trees and gardens near their homes, they need to shop for only some of their fruits and vegetables. When they go shopping at an open-air

A merchant at a *marché* in Pointe-à-Pitre sells fresh fruit and exotic flowers. (Guadeloupe)

market, they usually bargain with the merchants. Fruit prices in the Caribbean vary according to the season and the type of fruit. In the metric system, **un kilogramme (un kilo)** equals 2.2 U.S. pounds. **Une livre** (*metric pound*) is the equivalent of half a kilogram or 500 grams.

---

1 **Quels fruits?**

Faites correspondre la lettre au fruit que vous entendez.

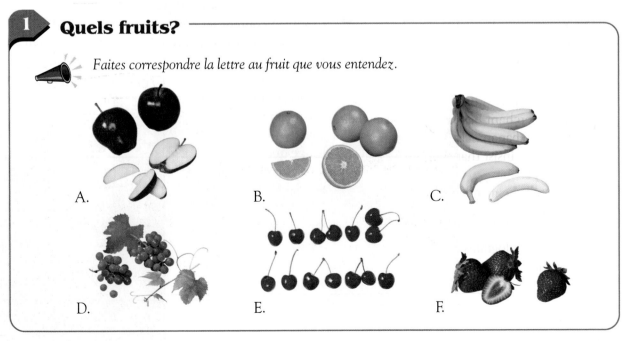

A.

B.

C.

D.

E.

F.

Predicting

If you were reading a list of classroom rules, you might expect to see sentences beginning with "Do" and "Don't." Sometimes predicting means more than just guessing what happens next. When you can predict what to expect in different types of readings, you will become a more effective reader.

What can you predict in reading a recipe? First, you will need to understand what ingredients are needed. Second, you will need to know the quantities of each ingredient. (Remember that French measurements are given in the metric system.) Third, you will need to understand the verbs that tell you what to do, such as **mélangez** ("mix") and **hachez** ("chop"). Note that these verbs are in the command form.

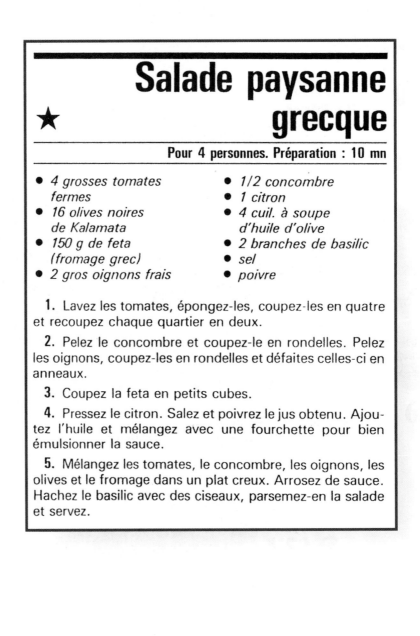

Salade paysanne grecque

★

Pour 4 personnes. Préparation : 10 mn

- 4 grosses tomates fermes
- 16 olives noires de Kalamata
- 150 g de feta (fromage grec)
- 2 gros oignons frais
- 1/2 concombre
- 1 citron
- 4 cuil. à soupe d'huile d'olive
- 2 branches de basilic
- sel
- poivre

1. Lavez les tomates, épongez-les, coupez-les en quatre et recoupez chaque quartier en deux.

2. Pelez le concombre et coupez-le en rondelles. Pelez les oignons, coupez-les en rondelles et défaites celles-ci en anneaux.

3. Coupez la feta en petits cubes.

4. Pressez le citron. Salez et poivrez le jus obtenu. Ajoutez l'huile et mélangez avec une fourchette pour bien émulsionner la sauce.

5. Mélangez les tomates, le concombre, les oignons, les olives et le fromage dans un plat creux. Arrosez de sauce. Hachez le basilic avec des ciseaux, parsemez-en la salade et servez.

11 ▸ La recette

Répondez aux questions.

1. How long does it take to make this salad?
2. Should you buy green or black olives?
3. Do you need French cheese?
4. Which ingredients could you buy at the **marché**? Which could you buy at the **crémerie**?
5. After you wash and dry the tomatoes, how should you cut them?
6. Should you grate the cheese?
7. What part of the lemon do you use?
8. What does this salad look like? Draw a picture or describe it to a classmate.
9. Does this salad appeal to you? Why or why not?

Nathalie et Raoul

✓ Évaluation culturelle

Decide if each statement is **vrai** or **faux**.

1. Marseille is France's oldest city and largest seaport.
2. Some well-known French foods are named after the provinces they come from: **quiche lorraine** comes from Lorraine and **bœuf bourguignon** is from Burgundy.
3. Regional specialties, such as **bouillabaisse** and **pâté de foie gras**, can be purchased in French grocery stores and ordered in restaurants.
4. The long, thin loaf of bread with the crisp crust that we often call "French bread" is called a **croissant** in French.
5. Camembert, Brie and Roquefort are three of the more than 300 different kinds of yogurt produced in France.
6. French teenagers drink as much milk as American teens do.
7. French people now do all of their grocery shopping in large supermarkets instead of going to small shops and markets.
8. French supermarkets sell more bottled water and usually have a smaller variety of cold cereal than American supermarkets.
9. Because of its climate, Guadeloupe must buy most of its fresh fruits and vegetables from France.

Because of its tropical climate, Guadeloupe doesn't need to import a lot of fruits and vegetables. (Pointe-à-Pitre)

 With a partner, play the roles of a student who is planning a party to celebrate a friend's birthday and a grocer. The student orders food and beverages by phone

Phone the grocery store, saying the numbers out loud in pairs.

Say hello and identify the store.

Say you need to buy some meat, cheese, fruits, vegetables, desserts and beverages for a party.

Ask what day the party is.

Give the date of the party and then ask for the prices of specific items.

Give the prices.

Order a specific amount of meat, cheese, fruits, vegetables, desserts and beverages.

Give the price of each item and the total.

Thank the grocer and say good-bye.

✓ Évaluation écrite

You are giving a party to celebrate a special event. Design and write an invitation to send to your guests. Say that you're having a party, what event you're celebrating, what day and where the party is, and at what time. Also include the foods and beverages you'll be serving. Add RSVP, your name and phone number at the end of the invitation.

✓ Évaluation visuelle

With a partner, write a dialogue between a shopper and a vendor at an open-air market. In your dialogue, ask and give information about the produce, ask and give prices, compare prices and finally purchase some fruits and vegetables. (You may want to refer to the *Révision de fonctions* on pages 303-4 and the *Vocabulaire* on page 305.)

Vincent veut faire du vélo. (Saint-Tropez)

Révision de fonctions

Can you do all of the following tasks in French?
- I can ask for and give information about what someone can and wants to do.
- I can tell what I like.
- I can agree with someone.
- I can point out specific things.
- I can ask for permission.
- I can ask for, state and compare prices.
- I can make a complaint.
- I can insist on something.
- I can negotiate prices.
- I can choose and purchase various things.

To ask for information, use:

Qu'est-ce que tu veux manger ce soir?　　What do you want to eat tonight?
Tu peux faire une bouillabaisse?　　Can you make fish soup?

Qu'est-ce que tu veux acheter?

Je veux acheter du saucisson.

To give information, use:

Il veut toujours un fruit après le repas.　　He always wants (a piece of) fruit after a meal.
Nous pouvons aussi aller à la charcuterie.　　We can also go to the delicatessen.

To say what you like, use:

Moi, j'aime aussi le pâté.　　Me, I like pâté, too.

To agree with someone, use:

OK.　　OK.
Ouais.　　Yeah.

To identify objects, use:

Je vais acheter **ces** tomates et **cet** oignon pour la soupe.　　I'm going to buy these tomatoes and this onion for the soup.

To ask for permission, use:

Nous pouvons acheter des oranges aussi?　　Can we buy oranges, too?

To ask for a price, use:

Combien coûte la pastèque?　　How much does the watermelon cost?
Combien coûtent les melons?　　How much do the melons cost?

Combien coûtent les tomates?

To state prices, use:

Ils/Elles coûtent 2,29 **euros** le kilo.   *They cost 2,29 euros per kilo.*

Le poulet que Mme Deguil achète? Il coûte sept euros.

To compare prices, use:

Le fromage est **plus cher que** le beurre.   *Cheese is more expensive than butter.*
Les raisins sont **aussi chers que** les pastèques.   *Grapes are as expensive as watermelons.*
Les pommes sont **moins chères que** les cerises.   *Apples are less expensive than cherries.*

To make a complaint, use:

Les melons sont **déjà mûrs**.   *The melons are already ripe.*
Je trouve que c'est trop cher.   *I think it's too expensive.*

To insist on something, use:

Si!   *Yes!*

To negotiate a price, use:

Est-ce que je peux acheter deux   *May I buy two kilos of melons*
kilos de melons **pour** 2,29 euros?   *for 2,29 euros?*

To choose and purchase items, use:

Je vais acheter trois kilos de bananes.   *I am going to buy three kilos of bananas.*

Vocabulaire

assez de enough *B*
attendre to wait (for) *B*
aussi as *C*

une **baguette** long, thin loaf of bread *B*
une **banane** banana *C*
beaucoup de a lot of, many *B*
le **beurre** butter *B*
le **bœuf** beef *B*
une **boîte** can *B*
une **boucherie** butcher shop *B*
une **bouillabaisse** fish soup *A*
une **boulangerie** bakery *B*
une **bouteille** bottle *B*

le **camembert** Camembert cheese *B*
une **carotte** carrot *A*
ce, cet, cette; ces this, that; these, those *A*
une **cerise** cherry *C*
un **champignon** mushroom *A*
une **charcuterie** delicatessen *B*
combien de how much, how many *B*
la **confiture** jam *B*
les **courses: faire les courses** to go grocery shopping *A*
un **crabe** crab *A*
une **crémerie** dairy store *B*
une **crevette** shrimp *A*
un **croissant** croissant *B*

d'abord first *B*
des any *A*
du some, any *B*

euh uhm *A*

faire les courses to go grocery shopping *A*
une **fraise** strawberry *B*
un **fruit** fruit *A*

un **gâteau** cake *B*

des **haricots verts (m.)** green beans *A*

le **ketchup** ketchup *B*
un **kilogramme (kilo)** kilogram *B*

le **lait** milk *B*
un **légume** vegetable *A*

maintenant now *A*
maman (f.) Mom *B*
un(e) **marchand(e)** merchant *C*
un **marché** market *C*

le **matin** in the morning *B*
un **matin** morning *B*
la **mayonnaise** mayonnaise *B*
un **melon** melon *C*
moins less *C*
un **morceau** piece *B*
la **moutarde** mustard *B*
mûr(e) ripe *C*

un **œuf** egg *B*
un **oignon** onion *A*
OK OK *A*
ouais yeah *B*

le **pain** bread *B*
une **pastèque** watermelon *C*
le **pâté** pâté *B*
une **pâtisserie** pastry store *B*
une **pêche** peach *C*
des **petits pois (m.)** peas *A*
(un) **peu de** (a) little, few *B*
plus more *C*
une **poire** pear *C*
les **pois (m.): des petits pois (m.)** peas *A*
une **pomme de terre** potato *A*
le **porc** pork *B*
un **pot** jar *B*
un **poulet** chicken *B*
pouvoir to be able to *A*
puis then *B*

que than, as, that *C*

un **repas** meal *A*

le **saucisson** salami *B*
ce **soir** tonight *A*
la **soupe** soup *A*
un **supermarché** supermarket *B*

une **tarte (aux fraises)** (strawberry) pie *B*
la **terre: une pomme de terre** potato *A*
une **tomate** tomato *A*
toujours always *A*
une **tranche** slice *B*
trop too *B*
trop de too much, too many *B*

vouloir to want *A*

le **yaourt** yogurt *B*

Unité 9

À la maison

In this unit you will be able to:
- invite
- accept and refuse an invitation
- greet someone
- greet guests
- introduce someone else
- offer and accept a gift
- identify objects
- describe daily routines
- tell location
- express intentions
- agree and disagree
- offer food and beverages
- excuse yourself

www.emcp.com

un appartement

un balcon

un immeuble

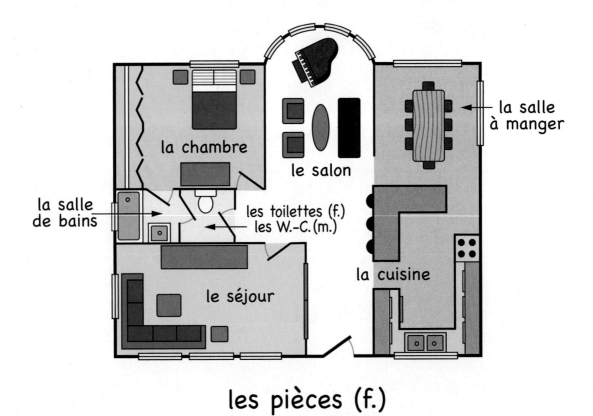

la chambre

le salon

la salle
à manger

la salle
de bains

les toilettes (f.)
les W.-C. (m.)

la cuisine

le séjour

les pièces (f.)

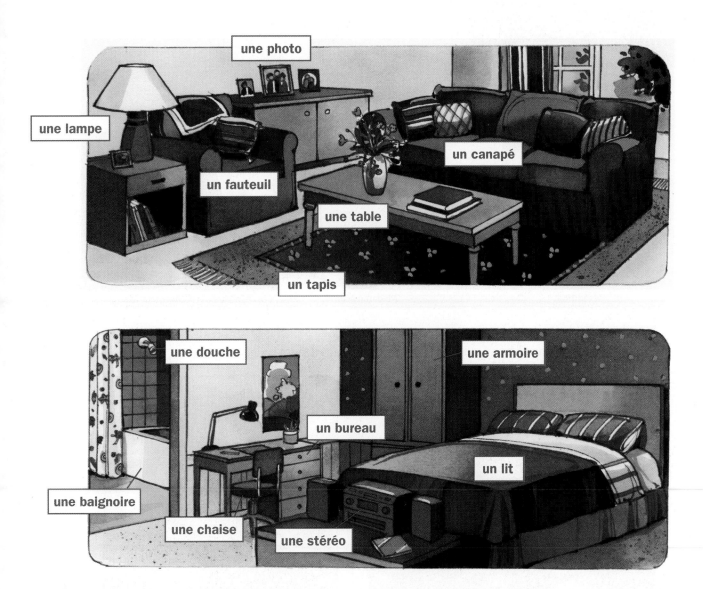

une photo

une lampe

un fauteuil

un canapé

une table

un tapis

une douche

une armoire

un bureau

un lit

une baignoire

une chaise

une stéréo

un micro-onde

un évier

une cuisinière

un frigo

un placard

un four

Nadine

Madame Mairet

Monsieur Mairet

Nadine Mairet is giving her parents a tour of her new apartment.

Nadine: **Vous voulez faire le tour de mon appartement maintenant? Voici le salon. J'ai toujours votre vieux canapé, mais j'ai de nouveaux fauteuils.**

Mme Mairet: **Tu as aussi de belles photos de ton voyage en Espagne.**

Nadine: **Et voici la cuisine. J'ai même un micro-onde.**

M. Mairet: **Avec la chambre, la salle de bains et les W.-C., cet appartement est assez grand. Tu aimes bien habiter ici?**

Nadine: **Oui, pour moi, ça va bien.**

Les appartements

It usually costs more to live in **le centre-ville** (*downtown*) of a French city than in **la banlieue** (*suburbs*). Many people reside in apartment buildings which surround **une cour** (*central courtyard*). They frequently purchase, rather than rent, their apartments. Single people often prefer living in a studio apartment, consisting of only a kitchenette, a main room and a bathroom. Even for a small studio apartment in the heart of a large city, the cost is high since rent is based on the apartment's location, not on its facilities. To enter the building, residents often use a numbered security system rather than a key. They punch in a code number in a box which is installed near the front door.

Living in *le centre-ville* usally costs more than living in *la banlieue*. (Paris)

Une armoire

Although some bedrooms have closets, many French people keep their clothes in a tall, freestanding piece of furniture called **une armoire**.

Only 24% of French teenagers have a computer in their bedroom.

Dans la chambre

French teens generally have smaller bedrooms than American teens. In France most students have a desk, a TV, CD and DVD players, video games, books and posters in their rooms. Since rugby, soccer, martial arts, in-line skating and volleyball are also popular, teens may store sports equipment in their rooms as well.

Les repas

The French enjoy well-prepared food served on a beautifully set table and observe dining customs that have been handed down from generation to generation.

For breakfast, the French drink their *chocolat chaud* or *café au lait* in *un bol*.

Breakfast (**le petit déjeuner**) is often a light meal. At home, adults usually have coffee, coffee with milk (**le café au lait**) or tea (**le thé**). Children drink fruit juices or hot chocolate (**le chocolat chaud**). Although some French people choose to eat a bowl of cereal in the morning, most of them prefer to cut crusty **baguettes** into thick slices and cover them with butter and jam. Other choices include dry toast (**les biscottes**) and toasted bread (**le pain grillé**). Occasionally, perhaps on Sunday mornings, one member of the family goes to the bakery for fresh **croissants**. Since warm beverages are usually served in large, deep bowls, many people like to dip their bread in their coffee or hot chocolate when they are at home. The usual hotel breakfast consists of part of a **baguette**, a **croissant**, butter, jam and a beverage.

Lunch (**le déjeuner**) is still the largest meal of the day when families are able to get together. However, many women work outside of the home, students eat at school or at cafés, and businesses in urban areas remain open over the noon hour. Therefore, families usually reserve long lunches for weekends and special occasions. Since the French usually don't eat dinner until 7:30 or 8:00 P.M., students often enjoy a small snack (**le goûter**) after school. Teenagers often stop for something sweet at a **pâtisserie** or sit down at home or at a café for a bite to eat and a beverage.

Families often spend time during the evening meal, **le dîner**, discussing what they did during the day. A typical main meal, either lunch or dinner, may last several hours and consists of various courses. First of all comes an **hors-d'œuvre**, such as soup, **crudités** or **pâté**, or an **entrée**, such as a small slice of quiche. Then the main dish (**le plat principal**), usually meat and vegetables, is served. A salad of lettuce mixed with vinegar and oil dressing (**vinaigrette**) usually follows the main

Snails, *les escargots*, are a popular entrée.

course, although sometimes the salad may be served before or with the main course. Different kinds of cheeses are offered next; each person takes just a small portion of his or her favorites. A dessert, such as fruit, ice cream or pastries, tops off the meal.

A bottle of water or mineral water accompanies most meals. Children sometimes drink fruit juices or soft drinks; adults often drink wine. Coffee is served at the end of the meal.

Fresh bread accompanies every meal. Instead of being sliced, bread is usually broken into individual pieces and served in a basket. Bread plates are generally used only in elegant restaurants; at home, each person puts his or her bread right on the table.

Diners at Maxim's, a famous restaurant in Paris, appreciate its traditional table setting.

A beautiful table setting enhances the presentation of the food. Fresh flowers often serve as a centerpiece. Most families use cloth napkins. Each family member has his or her own napkin which may be kept in a napkin ring or a cloth holder.

French families have adopted certain eating habits and traditions that have been passed on from one generation to the next. They set the table differently in France than in the United States. Teaspoons or dessert forks go horizontally above the plate, and forks and spoons are turned face down. French silverware is slightly larger and heavier than American silverware. For formal meals the French use different dishes for each course. They usually cut and eat each piece of meat separately, keeping the fork, tines down, in the left hand. They even scoop up vegetables, such as peas, on the fork. Instead of leaving one hand in their lap, they keep both hands above or resting on the table during the meal. At the end of the meal, they place the fork and knife horizontally across the plate.

Guillaume demonstrates French table manners, keeping the fork in his left hand and the knife in his right hand.

French cooking is famous throughout the world, and the presentation of the food and the chance to maintain family traditions are as important to the French as a well-prepared meal.

15 ▸ Les repas

Répondez aux questions.

1. What is a typical French breakfast for an adult?
2. When French people eat breakfast at home, how do they serve warm beverages?
3. What is a typical French breakfast served at a hotel?
4. When is lunch still the largest meal of the day?
5. At what time do most French people eat their evening meal?
6. At a French dinner, what might be served as an hors-d'œuvre?
7. What is the French expression for the main course of a meal?
8. What are two desserts that might be served in France?
9. What kind of napkins do the French use?
10. How is a French table setting different from a table setting in the United States?
11. Do the French switch the fork from one hand to the other while eating?
12. How can you tell that someone has finished eating in France?

A typical French breakfast served at a hotel consists of part of a *baguette*; a croissant; butter; jam and a beverage, such as *café au lait*.

16 ▸ Les menus

Voici des menus d'un vol (flight) international entre (between) les États-Unis et la France. Répondez aux questions.

1. Which is the larger of the two meals that are served on this flight?
2. Based on the order in which the two meals are served, at approximately what time of day does this flight arrive in Paris?

In the first meal:
1. What is the first course?
2. What are the two choices for the main course?
3. What is served with either main course?
4. What is the dessert?

In the second meal:
1. What beverages are offered?
2. What accompanies the pastries?

DÎNER

Salade verte de saison
avec sauce "Caesar"

•

Plats Principaux

Filet mignon
sauce chutney à la mangue

Crevettes à la créole
avec jalapeno et riz à la coriandre

Servis avec des légumes sélectionnés

•

Glace

PETIT-DÉJEUNER

Avant votre arrivée nous avons le plaisir
de vous offrir des jus de fruits rafraîchis,
la pâtisserie du jour, confiture et beurre.

le couvert

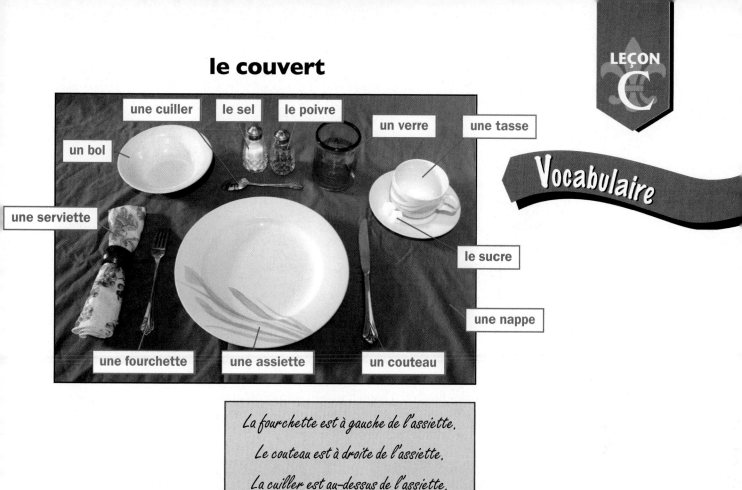

une cuiller • le sel • le poivre • un verre • une tasse • un bol • une serviette • le sucre • une nappe • une fourchette • une assiette • un couteau

La fourchette est à gauche de l'assiette.

Le couteau est à droite de l'assiette.

La cuiller est au-dessus de l'assiette.

le petit déjeuner

le déjeuner

le goûter

le dîner

Djamel

Arabéa

Arabéa Mamoudi and her younger brother, Djamel, live in Rabat, Morocco. They are helping their parents get ready to entertain luncheon guests to celebrate the end of Ramadan. Djamel is going to set the dining room table while Arabéa finishes preparing the meal.

Djamel: **Qu'est-ce que j'ai besoin de mettre sur la table pour le déjeuner?**

Arabéa: **On va manger du couscous. Mets les verres, les serviettes et les cuillers, s'il te plaît.**

Djamel: **Je mets aussi les assiettes pour le fruit?**

Arabéa: **Bien sûr.**

Le Maghreb

Le Maroc (*Morocco*), l'Algérie (*Algeria*) and la Tunisie (*Tunisia*) make up a region in North Africa called **le Maghreb**. Each year thousands of tourists flock to this sunlit area. They explore the markets and the Muslim sections (**les médinas**) of the cities in **le Maghreb**, admire the artwork, stone-cuttings and ancient fortresses of the region and relax at its beaches on the Mediterranean Sea.

These Moroccans, who are performing at a coronation feast, live in *le Maghreb*.

Le Maroc

Morocco's two largest cities are Casablanca and the capital, Rabat. They both lie on the Atlantic Ocean. The country gained its independence from France in 1956. Arabic is the official language of Morocco, yet many people also speak French and Spanish.

Le Ramadan

Ramadan is the ninth month of the Islamic year. During this sacred month, Muslims don't eat or drink from sunrise to sunset. On the day after the end of Ramadan, **l'Aïd el-Fitr**, people celebrate by eating from morning until night. The noon meal often consists of **couscous**, which is served in a large bowl placed in the middle of the table.

Eating *couscous* marks the end of Ramadan. (La Rochelle)

Everyone eats out of the same bowl with spoons. For dessert, people have fruit, often watermelon. In the afternoon, young people visit their friends and relatives. Even if they stay for only a few minutes, they have time to enjoy mint tea, the national beverage of Morocco, and cookies, cakes or baklava, a honey and nut pastry.

Baklava is a sweet made of thin pastry, honey and nuts. (Morocco)

1 Vrai ou faux?

*Écrivez "V" si la phrase est vraie;
écrivez "F" si la phrase est fausse.*

2 À Rabat

*Choisissez la bonne réponse d'après le dialogue et les **Aperçus culturels**.*

1. Qui parle?
   A. une femme et son mari
   B. une sœur et son frère
   C. deux amis

2. Où habite la famille Mamoudi?
   A. en France
   B. à Casablanca
   C. à Rabat

3. Quelle heure est-il?
   A. 11h30
   B. 15h00
   C. 20h00

4. Où est-ce que Djamel travaille?
   A. dans le séjour
   B. dans la salle à manger
   C. dans la salle de bains

5. Où est-ce qu'Arabéa travaille?
   A. dans le salon
   B. dans la cuisine
   C. dans le grenier

6. Comment est-ce qu'on mange du couscous?
   A. avec les cuillers
   B. avec les verres
   C. avec les serviettes

7. Le dessert, c'est quoi?
   A. du fromage
   B. de la glace
   C. de la pastèque

3 De quoi a-t-on besoin?

Dites ce que vous utilisez quand vous prenez les aliments suivants. Suivez le modèle.

Modèle:

le steak

une assiette; une fourchette, un couteau

1. le jambon
2. le couscous
3. le café
4. les haricots verts
5. la pizza
6. le lait
7. la glace

Pour manger une salade, on a besoin d'une assiette et d'une fourchette.

4 ▸ **C'est à toi!**

Questions personnelles.

1. Qu'est-ce que tu prends au petit déjeuner?
2. Est-ce que tu préfères un grand déjeuner ou un grand dîner?
3. Où est-ce que tu prends le goûter?
4. À quelle heure est-ce que tu prends le dîner?
5. Est-ce que tu mets souvent la table?
6. Est-ce que tu veux manger du couscous?

Des amis prennent le goûter ensemble.

Present tense of the irregular verb *mettre*

The verb **mettre** (*to put, to put on, to set*) is irregular.

mettre			
je	**mets**	nous	**mettons**
tu	**mets**	vous	**mettez**
il/elle/on	**met**	ils/elles	**mettent**

Où **mets**-tu les cuillers?
Je **mets** les cuillers avec les couteaux.

Where are you putting the spoons?
I'm putting the spoons with the knives.

En automne, Patricia met un pull et un jean quand elle va à l'école.

5 ▸ On met la table.

Pour célébrer l'anniversaire de Claude, dites qui met les objets suivants sur la table.

Modèle:

la grand-mère de Claude
La grand-mère de Claude met la nappe.

1. M. Garnier

2. je

3. nous

4. les sœurs de Claude

5. vous

6. Mme Garnier et Daniel

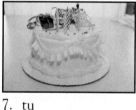

7. tu

Le serveur met les couteaux et les fourchettes.

6 ▸ Dans le frigo ou dans le placard?

Dites si les personnes suivantes mettent les aliments indiqués dans le frigo ou dans le placard.

Modèles:

Mme Surprenant/le lait
Madame Surprenant met le lait dans le frigo.

Daniel et Alain/le sel
Daniel et Alain mettent le sel dans le placard.

1. Zakia et Karima/les yaourts
2. nous/les boîtes de petits pois
3. je/les œufs
4. M. Baribeau/le steak
5. tu/le poulet
6. Diane/le poivre
7. M. et Mme Charpentier/le fromage
8. vous/les chips

7 ▶ En partenaires

Demandez à votre partenaire où dans la maison vous mettez les objets suivants: dans le salon, dans la cuisine ou dans la chambre. Répondez aux questions et puis alternez. Suivez le modèle.

Modèle:

le lit/la stéréo

A: **Où est-ce que je mets le lit?**

B: **Mets le lit dans la chambre. Où est-ce que je mets la stéréo?**

A: **Mets la stéréo dans le salon.**

1. le bureau/l'armoire
2. la table/le fauteuil
3. le canapé/le micro-onde
4. la lampe/le tapis
5. les chaises/la télé

Communication

8 ▶ Mettons la table!

Imaginez que vous et votre partenaire allez mettre la table pour huit personnes. Avec votre partenaire, parlez de ce dont (what) vous avez besoin. Faites une liste de chaque objet et sa quantité. Suivez le modèle.

Modèle:

A: **On a besoin de combien de fourchettes?**

B: **On a besoin de 16 fourchettes.**

9 ▶ Dessinez!

Faites un dessin d'une assiette. Puis demandez à votre partenaire où il ou elle met un autre objet en relation à l'assiette. Quand votre partenaire répond, ajoutez (add) l'objet à votre dessin. Enfin, alternez avec votre partenaire. Suivez le modèle.

Modèle:

A: **Où est-ce que je mets les deux fourchettes?**

B: **Mets les deux fourchettes à gauche de l'assiette.**

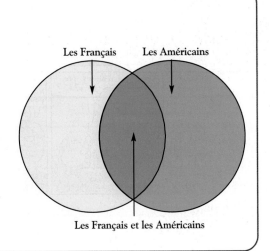

10 ▶ Comparez!

Regardez les pages 328-29 sur les repas. Avec quatre ou cinq élèves, faites une liste d'habitudes de manger (eating habits) françaises et une autre liste d'habitudes de manger américaines. Par exemple, "À la maison les Français prennent le café ou le chocolat dans un bol" et "Les Américains prennent le café ou le chocolat dans une tasse." Puis faites deux cercles intersectés. Écrivez les phrases qui décrivent (describe) seulement les Français à gauche; écrivez les phrases qui décrivent seulement les Américains à droite. Au centre écrivez les phrases qui décrivent les Français et les Américains.

Les Français   Les Américains

Les Français et les Américains

Inference

You're going to read some information from a brochure on vacation housing. The underlined words are ones you probably haven't seen before. The rest are either words you already know or obvious cognates. As you read the passage, practice the technique of inference – that is, use the context of the words you *do* know to help you decipher the ones you *don't* know.

Le logement

Cent appartements <u>répartis</u> dans 13 chalets sur 2 ou 3 étages sont regroupés <u>autour</u> du <u>pavillon</u> central. Vous <u>serez logé</u> dans un trois-pièces pour 5 ou 6 personnes.

<u>Chaque</u> <u>logement</u> <u>comprend</u>: une salle de séjour-chambre des parents <u>meublée</u> de 2 lits ou d'un canapé-lit, d'une table et de chaises; une chambre d'enfants avec 2 lits <u>superposés</u>; un <u>coin</u>-cuisine équipé d'un bloc-évier-réfrigérateur-<u>plaque</u> 2 <u>feux</u> incorporés et placard de <u>rangement</u> du matériel de cuisine; une salle d'eau avec w.-c. séparé.

11 **Le logement**

Faites un plan de cet appartement et utilisez le contexte des mots que vous savez (know) pour déterminer le sens (meaning) des mots que vous ne savez pas.

Nathalie et Raoul

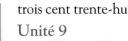

✓ Évaluation culturelle

Decide if each statement is **vrai** or **faux**.

1. Many people in France live in apartment buildings and often buy their apartments.
2. Most French homes and apartments have two different types of bathrooms.
3. To ask to use the bathroom in French, you say **Où est la salle de bains, s'il vous plaît**?
4. The style of houses in France differs from region to region depending on construction materials.
5. The second floor of a French building is called **le premier étage**.
6. If you are invited to a French home for a meal, it's appropriate to bring or send chrysanthemums to your hosts.
7. A typical French breakfast consists of eggs, bacon, pancakes and fruit juice.
8. The French often serve the salad and cheese courses after their main course.
9. **Le Maghreb** is a region in North Africa that includes **le Maroc**, **l'Algérie** and **la Tunisie**.
10. Muslims celebrate the month of Ramadan by eating **couscous**, fruit and desserts for their noon meal.

In *le Maroc* hides are tanned traditionally with saffron, poppies, indigo and other natural colors.

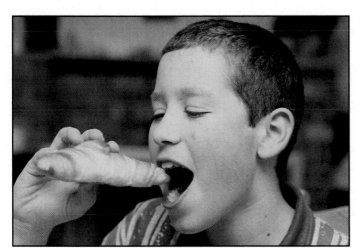

The French eat a *croissant* for breakfast on special occasions.

The apartment buildings that the French rent or buy usually have at least one *balcon*.

✓ Évaluation orale

With a partner, play the roles of an American host student and a French-speaking exchange student who has just arrived in the U.S.

Greet the exchange student and welcome him or her to the U.S.

Ask questions about your room and what's in it.

Answer the questions with specific information.

✓ Évaluation écrite

Imagine that Abdel-Cader Mamoude, a French-speaking Moroccan exchange student, is coming to live with your family for the year. He has written you asking what his room in your home is like. Answer his letter, describing his room, and saying where each piece of furniture and electronic appliance is in relation to something else. Also enclose a floor plan of his room.

✓ Évaluation visuelle

Write a paragraph that describes everything you see in the living room. Then do the same for the dining room. Identify as many objects as possible in the table setting by saying where they are in relation to other things. (You may want to refer to the *Révision de fonctions* on pages 341-42 and the *Vocabulaire* on page 343.)

Révision de fonctions

Can you do all of the following tasks in French?

- I can invite someone to do something.
- I can accept an invitation.
- I can greet someone by saying good evening.
- I can welcome guests.
- I can introduce people to each other.
- I can offer and accept a gift.
- I can identify objects, including types of housing, rooms, pieces of furniture and appliances.
- I can describe daily routines.
- I can tell where things are located, such as items in a place setting.
- I can say what someone is going to do.
- I can agree with someone.
- I can offer someone something to eat and drink.
- I can excuse myself.

Bonsoir, Adèle! Bienvenue!

To invite someone to do something, use:

Vous voulez faire le tour de mon appartement?

Entrez donc!

Allons au salon.

To accept an invitation, use:

Oui, je veux bien.

Do you want to take a tour of my apartment?

Then come in!

Let's go to the living room.

Yes, I'm willing.

Tu veux venir chez moi?

Oui, je veux bien.

To greet someone, use:

Bonsoir!

To greet guests, use:

Bienvenue!

To introduce someone else, use:

Je vous présente....

Raymond, Anne-Marie.

To offer a gift, use:

Voici des fleurs, Madame.

To accept a gift, use:

Oh, que vous êtes gentil!

Good evening!

Welcome!

Let me introduce you to . . . .

Raymond, this is Anne-Marie.

Here are some flowers, Ma'am.

Oh, how nice you are!

Voici la chambre des parents.

To identify objects, use:

    Voici la cuisine.   *Here's the kitchen.*

To describe daily routines, use:

    Je mets les verres, les serviettes   *I'm putting the glasses, napkins and plates*
    et les assiettes.   *on (the table).*

Le weekend on met des vêtements confortables.

To tell location, use:

    La fourchette est **à gauche** de l'assiette.   *The fork is (to the) left of the plate.*
    Le couteau est **à droite** de l'assiette.   *The knife is (to the) right of the plate.*

To express intentions, use:

    On va manger du couscous.   *We're going to eat couscous.*

To agree, use:

    Bien sûr.   *Of course.*

To offer food, use:

    Prenez des chips.   *Have some snacks.*

To offer a beverage, use:

    Vous voulez un jus de fruit?   *Do you want fruit juice?*

To excuse yourself, use:

    Pardon, j'ai encore quelques   *Excuse me, I still have some things to do.*
    choses à faire.

Vocabulaire

à **droite** to (on) the right C
à **gauche** to (on) the left C
un **appartement** apartment A
un **arbre** tree B
une **armoire** wardrobe A
une **assiette** plate C
au-dessus de above C

une **baignoire** bathtub A
un **bain: une salle de bains** bathroom A
un **balcon** balcony A
bien: bien sûr of course B
Bienvenue! Welcome! B
un **bol** bowl C
bonsoir good evening B

un **canapé** couch, sofa A
une **chambre** bedroom A
des **chips (m.)** snacks B
le **couscous** couscous C
un **couteau** knife C
un **couvert** table setting C
une **cuiller** spoon C
une **cuisine** kitchen A
une **cuisinière** stove A

de (d') some A
le **déjeuner** lunch C
  le **petit déjeuner** breakfast C
dessus: au-dessus de above C
le **dîner** dinner, supper C
donc so, then B
une **douche** shower A
la **droite: à droite** to (on) the right C

enchanté(e) delighted B
encore still B
une **entrée** entrance B
entrer to enter, to come in B
un **escalier** stairs, staircase B
un **étage** floor, story B
un **évier** sink A

faire le tour to take a tour A
un **fauteuil** armchair A
une **fleur** flower B
un **four** oven A
une **fourchette** fork C
un **frigo** refrigerator A

un **garage** garage B
la **gauche: à gauche** to (on) the left C
gentil, gentille nice B
le **goûter** afternoon snack C
un **grenier** attic B

habiter to live A
un **immeuble** apartment building A
un **jardin** garden, lawn B
le **jus de fruit** fruit juice B
une **lampe** lamp A
un **lit** bed A
une **maison** house A
manger: une salle à manger dining room A
même even A
mettre to put (on), to set C
un **micro-onde** microwave A
une **nappe** tablecloth C
le **petit déjeuner** breakfast C
une **pièce** room A
un **placard** cupboard A
le **poivre** pepper C
prendre to take, to have (food or drink) B
que: Que vous êtes gentils! How nice
  you are! B
quelques some B
le **rez-de-chaussée** ground floor B
s'il te plaît please B
une **salle à manger** dining room A
une **salle de bains** bathroom A
un **salon** living room A
un **séjour** family room A
le **sel** salt C
une **serviette** napkin C
un **sous-sol** basement B
le **sucre** sugar C
sûr: bien sûr of course B
une **table** table A
un **tapis** rug A
une **tasse** cup C
les **toilettes (f.)** toilet A
toujours still A
le **tour** tour A
un **vase** vase B
un **verre** glass C
une **voiture** car B
vouloir bien to be willing B
vous to you B
un **voyage** trip A
les **W.-C. (m.)** toilet A

Unité 10

La santé

In this unit you will be able to:
- **express astonishment and disbelief**
- **express emotions**
- **point out something**
- **make a complaint**
- **explain a problem**
- **congratulate and commiserate**
- **express concern**
- **express need and necessity**
- **give advice**
- **express reassurance**
- **make a prediction**
- **make an appointment**
- **state exact and approximate time**
- **give information**

www.emcp.com

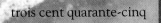

Chamonix

The French capital of mountain climbing and a popular international winter sports resort, Chamonix is situated in **les Alpes** in the eastern part of the country. From Chamonix, the highest cable car (**le téléphérique**) in the Alps carries people several thousand meters up the slopes of the **Aiguille du Midi**, one of the highest peaks in **les Alpes**, to ski, hike and enjoy the spectacular view.

Le Mont Blanc

Le Mont Blanc, the highest mountain in **les Alpes**, rises over 15,000 feet and stands on the border of France, Switzerland and Italy. This mountain received its name (in English, "White Mountain") because its peak remains snow covered the entire year.

Frequent *téléphériques* allow skiers to get quickly back on the slope. (La Haute-Savoie)

Many mountain peaks in France are named *aiguilles* because they resemble needles. (Chamonix)

Le ski

When French schools are closed for a week during winter vacation in February, many students go skiing in **les Alpes** and **les Pyrénées**. During the regular school year some schools offer organized excursions, such as **les classes de neige**, where students have academic classes in the morning and ski in the afternoon. Most teenagers in France would rather downhill ski (**le ski de piste** or **le ski alpin**) than cross-country ski (**le ski de fond**). Skiing is also a popular winter sport in Switzerland, the site of many world-class ski slopes.

Proverbe

The French proverb **Mains froides, cœur chaud** means "Cold hands, warm heart." This proverb suggests that you may be cold on the outside but still have a warm and friendly personality.

Mains froides, cœur chaud.

Les écoles de ski offer courses in downhill skiing.

1 ▸ Quelle partie du corps?

📢 *Écrivez la lettre de la partie du corps que vous entendez.*

2 ▸ Une leçon de ski

Répondez par "vrai" ou "faux" d'après le dialogue.

1. Francis et Sébastien sont à Paris.
2. Chamonix est en Italie.
3. Sébastien a froid.
4. Sébastien a peur.
5. Francis trouve que skier, c'est facile.
6. Il faut prendre les bâtons dans les mains.
7. Il faut beaucoup baisser la tête.

3 ▸ Complétez!

Choisissez la lettre de l'objet qui est associé à chaque partie du corps.

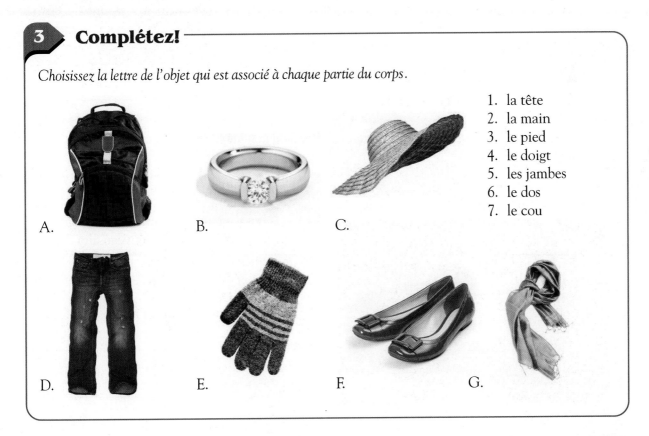

A. B. C.

D. E. F. G.

1. la tête
2. la main
3. le pied
4. le doigt
5. les jambes
6. le dos
7. le cou

4 ▶ C'est à toi!

Questions personnelles.

1. Tu trouves qu'il est facile de skier?
2. Est-ce que tu skies bien ou mal?
3. Qu'est-ce que tu portes quand tu skies?
4. Quand est-ce que tu as peur?
5. Est-ce que tu as chaud ou froid maintenant?
6. Est-ce que tu étudies trop?
7. Est-ce que tu manges de la pizza avec les doigts ou avec une fourchette?

Je trouve qu'il n'est pas facile de skier.

Langue active

Present tense of the irregular verb *falloir*

The verb **falloir** (*to be necessary, to have to*) has only one present tense form. **Il faut** means "it is necessary," "one has to/must" or "we/you have to/must." **Il faut** usually is followed by an infinitive.

Il faut garder les jambes solides.   *You have to keep your legs steady.*

Il ne **faut** pas baisser la tête.   *You must not lower your head.*

Il faut bien manger à midi.

Pratique

5 ▶ Qu'est-ce qu'il faut faire?

Après chaque affirmation (statement) *d'Ariane, dites ce qu'il faut faire. Suivez le modèle.*

Modèle:

J'ai soif.
Il faut prendre une boisson.

1. J'ai faim.
2. Je voudrais faire une quiche.
3. Il n'y a pas de légumes dans le frigo.
4. Je veux regarder le nouveau film de Gérard Depardieu.
5. J'ai besoin de nouvelles chaussures.
6. Il fait très froid.
7. J'ai une interro demain.

Il faut aller au magasin de chaussures.

6 En partenaires

Avec un(e) partenaire, demandez s'il faut certains aliments pour faire certaines choses. Répondez à la question et puis alternez. Suivez les modèles.

Modèles:

des œufs/une omelette

A: **Est-ce qu'il faut des œufs pour faire une omelette?**

B: **Oui. Pour faire une omelette, il faut des œufs.**

de la confiture/une salade

B: **Est-ce qu'il faut de la confiture pour faire une salade?**

A: **Non. Pour faire une salade, il ne faut pas de confiture.**

1. de la mayonnaise/une pizza
2. des pommes de terre/des frites
3. des raisins/du jus d'orange
4. de la moutarde/un gâteau
5. du pain/un sandwich
6. du poisson/une bouillabaisse
7. des pêches/une tarte aux fraises
8. de l'eau/du café

Pour faire une salade niçoise, il faut des tomates.

Communication

7 Une chanson, un rap ou un poème

Avec un(e) partenaire, créez une chanson (song), un rap ou un poème sur les parties du corps. Puis présentez votre chanson/rap/poème à la classe et indiquez chaque partie du corps que vous mentionnez.

la réceptionniste   Madame Graedel

It's Thursday morning. Madame Graedel wants to make an appointment with her dentist in Lausanne, Switzerland.

La réceptionniste:	**Allô? Cabinet du docteur Odermatt.**
Mme Graedel:	**Bonjour, Madame. Je voudrais prendre rendez-vous avec Monsieur Odermatt, s'il vous plaît.**
La réceptionniste:	**Oui, Madame. Quand est-ce que vous voulez venir?**
Mme Graedel:	**Aussitôt que possible. J'ai mal aux dents.**

La réceptionniste:	**Je regrette, mais nous n'avons rien ce matin.**
Mme Graedel:	**Alors, cet après-midi?**
La réceptionniste:	**Monsieur Odermatt n'est jamais ici le jeudi après-midi. Est-ce que vous pouvez venir demain matin à 9h30?**
Mme Graedel:	**Bien sûr.**

La Suisse

The city of Lausanne sits on the hills overlooking the north shore of Lake Geneva in Switzerland. Of glacial origin, beautiful Lake Geneva attracts many tourists. Also called **le lac Léman**, Lake Geneva is approximately 70 kilometers long. On the western side of the lake, close to France, lies the city of Geneva (Genève). Many organizations, such as the Red Cross, the World Health Organization and the European headquarters of the United Nations, have their main offices here.

The waterspout in Lake Geneva shoots 130 meters into the air. (Genève)

Les langues en Suisse

Switzerland has four official languages. About 20 percent of the Swiss speak French; most of these people live in western Switzerland near the French border. German is the language of the majority of people in northern Switzerland. Almost all of those in the south of the country speak Italian, while a small portion of the population in the eastern part of the country uses Romansch.

Even though Switzerland is not a member of the United Nations, its *Palais des Nations* is the seat of the UN in Europe. (Genève)

L'économie suisse

In addition to its spectacular scenery, Switzerland is famous for its watch industry, its delicious chocolates and its stable banking system.

Laurent, Michel, Thibault and Benjamin—who live in Lausanne, Switzerland—speak French.

Écrivez la lettre de la partie de la figure que vous entendez.

2 **Un sommaire**

Écrivez un paragraphe de cinq phrases sur la conversation de Mme Graedel. Dites le nom de son dentiste et pourquoi elle a besoin de prendre rendez-vous avec lui. Puis dites pourquoi elle ne peut pas venir ce matin et cet après-midi. Enfin, dites quand elle peut prendre rendez-vous avec le dentiste.

3 **Complétez!**

Choisissez le mot convenable qui complète chaque phrase.

tête	oreilles	jambes	dents	yeux	bouche	doigts	pieds

1. On écoute avec les....
2. On porte un chapeau sur la....
3. On parle avec la....
4. On regarde la télé avec les....
5. On fait du footing avec les... et les....
6. On joue aux jeux vidéo avec les....
7. On téléphone au dentiste quand on a mal aux....

On joue au volley avec les mains.

4 ▸ C'est à toi!

Questions personnelles.

1. Quand est-ce que tu prends rendez-vous avec le/la dentiste?
2. Est-ce que tu as souvent mal aux dents?
3. Est-ce que tu as peur de prendre rendez-vous avec le/la dentiste?
4. Ton/ta dentiste, il/elle s'appelle comment?
5. De quelle couleur sont tes yeux?
6. Quand il n'y a plus de place dans un café, est-ce que tu attends ou est-ce que tu vas à un autre café?

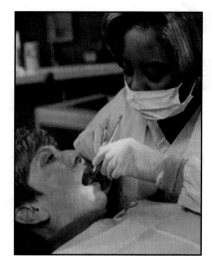

Mme Broquedis prend rendez-vous avec la dentiste quand elle a mal aux dents.

Verbs + infinitives

Many French verbs may be followed directly by an infinitive.

adorer	**J'adore faire** du shopping.
aimer	**Aimez**-vous **prendre** rendez-vous avec le dentiste?
aller	Maman **va téléphoner** à la réceptionniste.
désirer	Nous **désirons finir** aussitôt que possible.
falloir	Il ne **faut** pas **baisser** la tête.
pouvoir	Est-ce que vous **pouvez venir** demain matin?
préférer	Mes amis **préfèrent faire** du roller.
venir	Mes cousins **viennent regarder** mes photos.
vouloir	Qu'est-ce que tu **veux faire** maintenant?

Mme Charras préfère acheter des légumes frais au marché.

Pratique

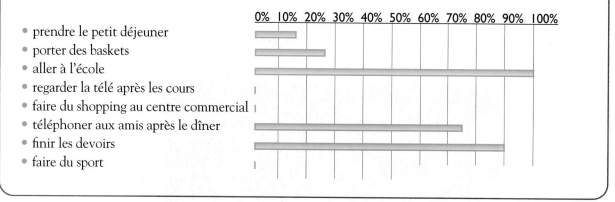

7 ▸ **Les activités d'Élodie**

Le graphique suivant montre quand Élodie a fait certaines choses. Pour chaque activité, écrivez une phrase qui utilise **toujours**, **souvent**, **ne (n')… pas souvent** *ou* **ne (n')… jamais**.

Modèle:

Élodie ne prend pas souvent le petit déjeuner.

0% 10% 20% 30% 40% 50% 60% 70% 80% 90% 100%

- prendre le petit déjeuner
- porter des baskets
- aller à l'école
- regarder la télé après les cours
- faire du shopping au centre commercial
- téléphoner aux amis après le dîner
- finir les devoirs
- faire du sport

8 ▸ **À vous de jouer!**

Le magasin Pied-à-terre va fermer (to close). Avec un(e) partenaire, jouez les rôles d'un(e) client(e) et d'un(e) employé(e) du magasin.

Demandez si le magasin a toujours chaque chose dans la liste.

Répondez aux questions. Dites que vous avez seulement les articles de sport et la vaisselle (dinnerware).

Modèles:

A: **Vous avez toujours des stéréos?**
B: **Non, je regrette, nous n'avons plus de stéréos.**

A: **Vous avez toujours des assiettes?**
B: **Oui, nous avons toujours des assiettes.**

9 ▶ De mauvaise humeur

*Répondez aux questions à la forme négative. Utilisez **ne (n')... rien** ou **ne (n')... personne**.*

Modèles:

Tu manges quelque chose?
Non, je ne mange rien.

Tu attends quelqu'un?
Non, je n'attends personne.

1. Tu cherches quelque chose dans le grenier?
2. Tu veux quelque chose?
3. Tu achètes quelque chose au supermarché?
4. Tu invites quelqu'un à la boum?
5. Tu fais quelque chose ce soir?
6. Tu présentes quelqu'un à tes parents?
7. Tu ressembles à quelqu'un dans ta famille?
8. Tu étudies avec quelqu'un?

Communication

10 ▶ Un monstre

Faites un dessin d'un monstre avec des parties du corps bizarres, par exemple, trois petites têtes, une jambe très longue, cinq yeux, etc. Puis écrivez une description du monstre. Dans les groupes de trois élèves, lisez (read) votre description pendant que (while) les autres font des dessins de votre monstre. Enfin, comparez votre monstre et les dessins.

11 ▶ Mes activités

*Écrivez un paragraphe sur vos activités. Utilisez le graphique suivant pour écrire (to write) cinq choses que vous **ne faites jamais**, cinq choses que vous **ne faites plus** et cinq choses que vous faites **toujours**. Utilisez les listes pour écrire votre paragraphe.*

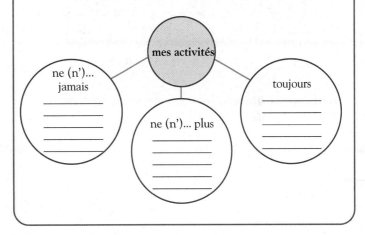

12 ▶ En partenaires

Avec un(e) partenaire, jouez les rôles d'une personne qui a mal aux dents et la réceptionniste du dentiste. La personne téléphone au cabinet du dentiste, explique son problème et demande si elle peut prendre rendez-vous avec le dentiste. La personne et la réceptionniste discutent les jours et les heures possibles. Enfin, la personne prend rendez-vous.

La santé

Like Americans, French people are increasingly conscious of physical fitness. By receiving adequate health care, watching their eating habits and exercising on a regular basis, **garder la ligne** (*keeping in shape*) has become a way of life for the French.

Mme Braure files a claim for health benefits at an office of *la sécu.*

The French system of national health care provides medical treatment for everyone who needs it. All taxpayers contribute to the social security system (**la Sécurité sociale,** or **"la sécu"**), which covers most of the costs of visits to doctors and dentists, as well as prescription medicines. To avoid serious illnesses, many people try to keep healthy by eating nutritious foods and exercising.

In recent years French cooking has changed to reflect a growing interest in healthy foods. In many French kitchens, products that are low in fat and high in fiber have replaced traditional heavy sauces and rich dairy products. Although a typical French meal normally consists of several courses, the portions tend to be quite small. Also, most French people snack very little between meals. When they do have **une petite faim** (*a little hunger*), they usually reach for a piece of fruit rather than for an artificially sweetened or salty snack.

Exercise is another way for the French to maintain physical well-being. Rather than relying on cars for transportation, many people choose to walk to their destinations. Health clubs provide aerobics and dance classes, as well as weight training equipment. Some people work out in their own homes with the help of exercise videos and TV programs. Many people exercise by taking advantage of inexpensive community facilities, such as public tennis courts and swimming pools. Soccer, cycling and martial arts clubs are popular with teenagers. Common family vacation activities offer other forms of exercise, such as mountain climbing (**l'alpinisme**), skiing, and windsurfing (**la planche à voile**). French people of all ages play **boules** (called **pétanque** in southern France), a form of lawn bowling.

A *boules* player tries to get his ball closer to the target ball than his two competitors. (Finistère)

Many French adults visit health spas to receive treatments for various ailments, such as liver, heart and digestive problems. During their stay, they rest, diet, drink mineral water and take thermal baths. The spas of Digne-les-Bains in the department of Alpes-de-Haute-Provence, open from March to November, are famous for treating rheumatism and respiratory illnesses.

Patients at a health spa relax on the terrace in between treatments. (Vichy)

Yet, with all their efforts to stay fit, the French face significant health-related issues. The increasing number of fast-food restaurants and their popularity with teenagers worry people who are concerned with nutrition. Smoking is also a serious problem for this age group. Strict laws have been passed limiting tobacco advertising and forbidding smoking in certain places. Strong anti-smoking campaigns have been launched to reduce the number of people who smoke.

Nutritionists are alarmed by the increasing demand for fast food because of its high fat content and "empty" calories.

At school or work and during their leisure hours, many French people spend both time and energy on maintaining good health. Regular medical and dental visits, participation in sports and a healthy diet all contribute to the goal of physical well-being.

13 ▸ La santé

Répondez aux questions.

1. How do French people keep in shape?
2. Who is covered under the French national health care system?
3. What health-related expenses are covered by the French social security system?
4. How big are the portions of food in a typical French meal?
5. Do the French often snack between meals?
6. Rather than relying on cars, how do many French people get to their destinations?
7. What are three sports in which the French participate to maintain physical well-being?
8. What is **boules**?
9. What are four things people do at a health spa?
10. What are two concerns about the health of French teenagers in general?

La Sécurité sociale covers most of the costs of visits to doctors and dentists.

14 ▸ Attention au cœur!

Regardez les dix suggestions pour maintenir un bon cœur (heart). Puis répondez aux questions.

Pour votre cœur...
dix conseils-santé.

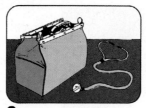

1 Mangez des fruits et des légumes pour les vitamines.

2 Voyez votre médecin une fois par an.

3 Contrôlez votre poids: l'excès fatigue le cœur.

4 Réduisez tabac et alcool.

5 Ménagez-vous chaque jour quelques pauses-détente.

6 Faites le plein d'air pur pendant le week-end.

7 Pratiquez tous les jours une demi-heure de marche.

8 Dormez au moins huit heures par nuit.

9 Ne consommez pas trop de sel.

10 Évitez l'excès de cholestérol.

1. Why should you eat a lot of fruits and vegetables?
2. How many times a year should you schedule a visit to your doctor?
3. What part of your body tires easily as a result of excess weight?
4. What two products should you avoid?
5. How long should you walk each day?
6. How many hours of sleep should you get each night?
7. Should you season your food with lots of salt?
8. How many of these suggestions do you follow?

Vocabulaire

Elle a mal au cœur.

Elle a mal à la tête.

Elle a mal aux dents.

Elle a mal au dos.

Elle a mal aux oreilles.

Elle a mal à la gorge.

Elle est malade.

Elle a la grippe.

Elle a de la fièvre.

Elle a un rhume.

Elle a des frissons.

Elle est fatiguée.

Elle a bonne mine.

Elle a mauvaise mine.

Elle est en bonne forme.

Elle est en mauvaise forme.

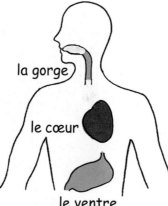

la gorge

le cœur

le ventre

Martine   Madame Bekhechi

Martine Bekhechi doesn't feel well, and her mother asks her what's wrong.

Je dois prendre
ta température.

Martine: **Atchoum!**
Mme Bekhechi: **À tes souhaits! Qu'est-ce que
                tu as?**
Martine: **Je ne suis pas en bonne forme.
                J'ai mal au cœur.**
Mme Bekhechi: **Tu as de la fièvre? Je dois
                prendre ta température.**
Martine: **J'ai des frissons aussi.**
Mme Bekhechi: **C'est peut-être la grippe. Tu
                dois rester au lit. Moi, je vais
                téléphoner au médecin.**

Le foie

Most stomachaches in France are blamed on the liver. When someone says that he or she has **une crise de foie** (literally, a liver attack), everyone understands that the person probably is experiencing indigestion rather than serious liver trouble.

Expressions de santé

The French use many colorful expressions to describe their health. Here are a few samples.

Il a les jambes en compote.	*His legs feel like jelly.*
Elle n'est pas dans son assiette.	*She's not feeling well.*
Elle a une fièvre de cheval.	*She has a very high temperature.*
Il a des fourmis dans les jambes.	*He has pins and needles in his legs.*
Elle est clouée au lit.	*She has to stay in bed.*
Il a un chat dans la gorge.	*He has a frog in his throat.*
Son estomac fait des nœuds.	*Her stomach is tied in knots.*

Les pharmacies

In French-speaking countries, a pharmacy (**une pharmacie**) has a bright green cross on the front of the building. When the cross is lit, the pharmacy is open.

Les herbes médicinales

Because many French people believe that certain plants can help relieve some aches and pains, most specialty stores and markets have herbal sections. Herbal teas are often given to people who don't feel well. Any tea made with natural herbs is called **une infusion**.

To find a pharmacy, look for the bright green cross.

L'homéopathie

The French sometimes use alternative medical treatments to complement traditional medicine. In one such treatment, **l'homéopathie** (*homeopathy*), a person takes small doses of a remedy which provokes the same symptoms as the sickness that the patient wants to fight. By taking these pills, the person eventually builds up a resistance to the illness. Although many people believe in this type of cure, others think that this form of medicine is largely psychosomatic. Stomach ailments, colds and headaches might all be treated by **l'homéopathie**. Sections of some pharmacies and entire specialty stores are devoted to this form of treatment.

Many pharmacies offer homeopathic treatments. (Angers)

1 ▶ Où a-t-elle mal?

Faites correspondre la lettre à la photo de la fille que vous entendez.

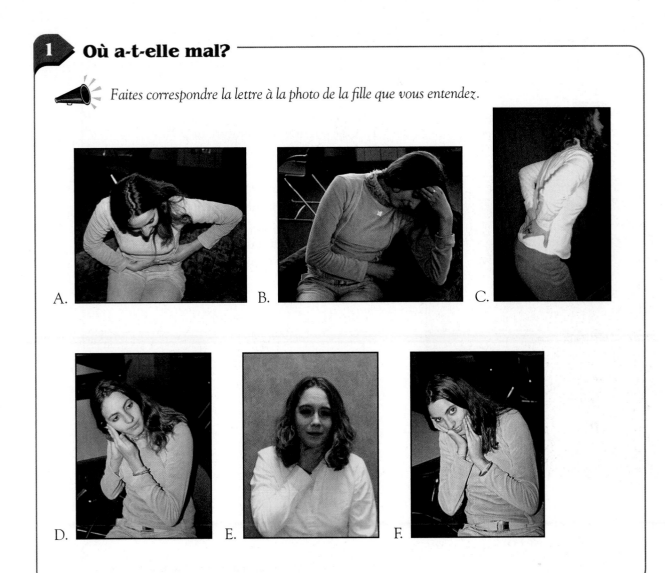

A.

B.

C.

D.

E.

F.

2 ▶ La maladie de Martine

Répondez aux questions.

1. Qui est malade?
2. Martine, qu'est-ce qu'elle a?
3. Où a-t-elle mal?
4. Qui va prendre la température de Martine?
5. Est-ce que Martine a des frissons?
6. Où est-ce que Martine va rester?
7. Mme Bekhechi va téléphoner à qui?

3 ▸ On est malade.

Les personnes suivantes, qu'est-ce qu'elles ont?

Modèle:

Le nez de Joël est très rouge.
Il a un rhume.

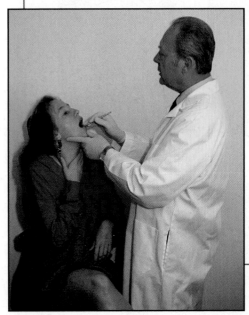

Mlle Chelon a mal à la gorge.

1. Chloé a une température de 39°.
2. Lance Armstrong finit le Tour de France.
3. Khaled mange trop de chocolat.
4. Sonia étudie beaucoup pour l'interro de maths.
5. Robert ne peut pas parler.
6. Mme Graedel prend rendez-vous avec le dentiste.

4 ▸ C'est à toi!

Questions personnelles.

1. Comment vas-tu aujourd'hui?
2. Tu es fatigué(e) aujourd'hui?
3. Tu as souvent mal à la tête?
4. Est-ce que tu as beaucoup de rhumes en hiver?
5. Quand tu as de la fièvre, qui prend ta température?
6. Ton médecin, il/elle s'appelle comment?
7. Quand tu es malade, est-ce que tu aimes regarder la télé?

Yves est fatigué aujourd'hui.

Present tense of the irregular verb *devoir*

The verb **devoir** (*to have to*) is irregular. It is often followed by an infinitive to express obligation.

devoir			
je	**dois**	nous	**devons**
tu	**dois**	vous	**devez**
il/elle/on	**doit**	ils/elles	**doivent**

Qu'est-ce que vous **devez** faire?   *What do you have to do?*

Je **dois** téléphoner au médecin.   *I have to call the doctor.*

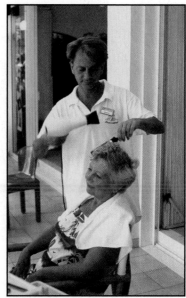

M. Villégier doit travailler.

Pratique

5 ▶ Chez le dentiste

On doit prendre rendez-vous avec le dentiste tous les (every) six mois. Basé sur la date de leur dernier (last) rendez-vous, dites si les personnes suivantes doivent prendre rendez-vous avec le dentiste.

Sophie et David Tulipe	deux ans
M. et Mme Chevalier	un mois
Benjamin Robillard	trois semaines
Mlle Parsy	dix mois
Nadia et Myriam Vernon	cinq jours
M. Vega	quatre ans
Normand et Robert Bouchard	une semaine
Mme Picot	sept mois
Philippe Nino	un an

Modèle:

Sophie et David Tulipe doivent prendre rendez-vous avec le dentiste.

6 ▶ Au marché aux puces

Qu'est-ce qu'on doit acheter pour dépenser tous (all) ses euros? Choisissez deux choses.

Modèle:

la prof (18 €)
La prof doit acheter la robe et le stylo.

1. nous (17 €)
2. tu (16 €)
3. les parents de Martine (22 €)
4. vous (12 €)

Communication

7 ▸ Une enquête

Posez des questions à cinq élèves pour déterminer leurs problèmes de santé. Posez sept questions à chaque élève. Notez les réponses. Puis dites à la classe combien d'élèves ont chaque problème de santé. Suivez le modèle.

Modèle:

Marie-Hélène: **Tu as mal à la tête?**
Abdou: **Oui, j'ai mal à la tête.**

. . . .

Marie-Hélène: **Deux élèves ont mal à la tête....**

mal à la tête	✔✔
mal au ventre	
mal à la gorge	
mal aux dents	
un rhume	
fatigué(e)	
malade	

8 ▸ Qu'est-ce qu'on doit faire?

Choisissez cinq problèmes de santé (de l'Activité 7). Pour chaque problème, écrivez deux phrases sur ce que vous devez faire ou ce que vous ne devez pas faire pour ne pas avoir ce problème.

Modèle:

mal aux dents
Je dois prendre rendez-vous avec le dentiste.
Je ne dois pas manger beaucoup de chocolat.

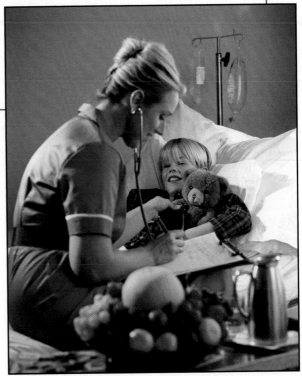

Tu dois rester au lit?

Illustrations

Take advantage of what you see in photos and illustrations in order to:

1) predict what you will be reading about, and

2) figure out the meaning of unknown words.

Before you read the magazine article that follows, use the illustrations to predict the main idea. Then, as you read the article, use the illustrations to figure out the meaning of words you don't know in order to understand the details.

La gym des kinés | **Atténuer les douleurs dorsales**

Le conseil de M. Lanne, kiné-ostéopathe. Pour soulager le haut du dos, appuyez-le contre le dossier de votre siège en avançant le bassin.

Assise, jambes jointes tendues, dos droit incliné vers l'arrière sans creuser les reins, mains posées à plat derrière vous. En inspirant, bombez la poitrine et rentrez le menton, puis relâchez. 20 fois.

Ces exercices sont indiqués pour soulager les tensions dans le haut du dos.

En tailleur, mains sur les genoux. En inspirant, tirez vos genoux vers vous tout en dégageant la poitrine et en étirant la nuque vers le ciel. Relâchez. 20 fois.

Sur le ventre, en appui sur les avant-bras parallèles. Sur l'inspiration, renversez la tête en arrière en serrant les omoplates. Sur l'expiration, descendez peu à peu la tête entre les bras. 10 fois.

9 ▸ Faisons des exercices!

Utilisez les illustrations pour répondre aux questions.

1. Which exercise requires you to . . .
    A. squat?
    B. sit down?
    C. lie on your stomach?
2. Which exercise requires you to . . .
    A. tip your head backward?
    B. tip your head forward?
    C. raise your head by stretching your neck?
3. How many times should you repeat each exercise?
4. When you drop your head between your arms during exercise 3, should you do it quickly or slowly?
5. What part of the body are the exercises for?
6. What do the exercises relieve?
7. You know that the French word for "arm" is **bras**. What is the French word for "forearm"?
8. People in what occupations could benefit most from doing these exercises?

Nathalie et Raoul

✓ Évaluation

✓ Évaluation culturelle

Decide if each statement is **vrai** or **faux**.

1. Chamonix is a winter sports resort located in **les Pyrénées** in southwestern France.
2. **Le Mont Blanc** got its name because it remains snow covered all year long.
3. Cross-country skiing is more popular with French teens than downhill skiing is.
4. Geneva, Switzerland, serves as the headquarters for many international organizations.
5. Everyone in Switzerland speaks French.
6. The French have a national health care system that provides medical treatment for everyone.
7. Many French people visit health spas to treat liver, heart and digestive ailments by resting, dieting and taking thermal baths.
8. Fortunately, French teens in general do not have a serious smoking problem.
9. When people have indigestion or a stomachache in France, they usually blame it on their liver.
10. **L'homéopathie** is an alternative medical treatment in which patients build up a resistance to the illness they are suffering from.

People taking the ferry on *le lac Léman* in Lausanne are among the 20 percent of Swiss people who speak French.

✓ Évaluation orale

With a partner, play the roles of an American student just arriving in France after a grueling European tour and a French tour guide.

Say you don't feel well.

Ask what the matter is.

Give your symptoms.

Tell what the student's problem must be and what he or she should or should not do to get better. Also say if it's necessary to make an appointment to see the doctor.

✓ Évaluation écrite

Imagine that you are the French tour guide who has just spoken with the sick American student. Write a report telling who is sick, how he or she is feeling, what the matter is, what symptoms he or she has, what problem he or she has, what he or she should or should not do to get better and whether or not the student needs to make an appointment to see a doctor.

✓ Évaluation visuelle

Write a dialogue based on the photos. In the first part of the dialogue, based on the first two photos, Éric calls to make an appointment to see a nurse. In the second part, based on the third photo, he complains to the nurse and points out his problems, and the nurse gives him advice. (You may want to refer to the *Révision de fonctions* on page 378 and the *Vocabulaire* on page 379.)

Révision de fonctions

Can you do all of the following tasks in French?

- I can express astonishment.
- I can express emotions.
- I can point out something.
- I can make a complaint.
- I can explain a health-related problem.
- I can express sympathy.
- I can express concern.
- I can say what needs to be done.
- I can give advice.
- I can reassure someone.
- I can make a prediction.
- I can make an appointment.
- I can state approximate time.
- I can give information about various topics, using negative expressions.

Il faut lire aux enfants.

To express astonishment, use:

Oh là là!   *Wow! Oh no! Oh dear!*

To express emotions, use:

J'ai peur.   *I'm afraid.*

To point out something, use:

Regarde!   *Look!*

To make a complaint, use:

Je ne suis pas en bonne forme.   *I'm not in good shape.*

To explain a problem, use:

J'ai mal aux dents.   *I have a toothache.*
J'ai mal au cœur.   *I feel nauseous.*

To commiserate, use:

Je regrette.   *I'm sorry.*

To express concern, use:

Qu'est-ce que tu as?   *What's the matter with you?*

To express need and necessity, use:

Il faut garder les jambes solides.   *You need (it is necessary) to keep your legs steady.*
Je dois prendre ta température.   *I need to take your temperature.*

To give advice, use:

Tu dois rester au lit.   *You have to stay in bed.*
Il faut baisser la tête.   *You must lower your head.*
Mais pas trop.   *But not too much.*

To express reassurance, use:

Mais non, c'est facile.   *(But) no, it's easy.*

To make a prediction, use:

C'est peut-être la grippe.   *Maybe it's the flu.*

To make an appointment, use:

Je voudrais prendre rendez-vous avec....   *I'd like to make an appointment with . . . .*

To state approximate time, use:

Aussitôt que possible.   *As soon as possible.*

To give information, use:

Nous **n'avons plus** de place ce matin.   *We don't have any more room this morning.*
Monsieur Odermatt **n'est jamais** ici le jeudi après-midi.   *Mr. Odermatt is never here on Thursday afternoon.*
Il **n'y a personne** ici.   *There's no one here.*
Je **ne** fais **rien.**   *I'm not doing anything.*

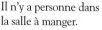

Il n'y a personne dans la salle à manger.

Vocabulaire

À tes souhaits! Bless you! C

l' après-midi (m.) afternoon B

Au secours! Help! A

aussitôt que as soon as B

avoir bonne/mauvaise mine to look well/sick C

avoir chaud to be warm, hot A

avoir froid to be cold A

avoir mal (à...) to hurt, to have a/an . . . ache, to have a sore . . . B

    avoir mal au cœur to feel nauseous C

avoir peur (de) to be afraid (of) A

baisser to lower A

un bâton ski pole A

une bouche mouth B

un bras arm A

un cabinet (doctor or dentist's) office B

chaud: avoir chaud to be warm, hot A

un cœur heart C

    avoir mal au cœur to feel nauseous C

un corps body A

un cou neck A

une dent tooth B

devoir to have to C

un docteur doctor B

un doigt finger A

    un doigt de pied toe A

un dos back A

une épaule shoulder A

facile easy A

falloir to be necessary, to have to A

fatigué(e) tired C

faut: il faut it is necessary, one has to/must, we/you have to/must A

la fièvre fever C

une figure face B

une forme: être en bonne/mauvaise forme to be in good/bad shape C

des frissons (m.) chills C

froid: avoir froid to be cold A

garder to keep A

un genou knee A

une gorge throat C

la grippe flu C

jamais: ne (n')... jamais never B

une jambe leg A

une main hand A

mal: avoir mal (à...) to hurt, to have a/an . . . ache, to have a sore . . . B

malade sick C

la mine: avoir bonne/mauvaise mine to look well/sick C

ne (n')... jamais never B

ne (n')... personne no one, nobody, not anyone B

ne (n')... plus no longer, not anymore B

ne (n')... rien nothing, not anything B

un nez nose B

un œil eye B

Oh là là! Wow! Oh no! Oh dear! A

une oreille ear B

une personne: ne (n')... personne no one, nobody, not anyone B

la peur: avoir peur (de) to be afraid (of) A

un pied foot A

    un doigt de pied toe A

la place room, space B

plus: ne (n')... plus no longer, not anymore B

prendre rendez-vous to make an appointment B

Qu'est-ce que tu as? What's the matter with you? C

quelqu'un someone, somebody B

un(e) réceptionniste receptionist B

regarder to look (at) A

regretter to be sorry B

un rendez-vous appointment B

    prendre rendez-vous to make an appointment B

rester to stay, to remain C

un rhume cold C

rien: ne (n')... rien nothing, not anything B

la santé health A

le secours: Au secours! Help! A

solide steady A

un souhait: À tes souhaits! Bless you! C

une température temperature C

une tête head A

trop too much A

un ventre stomach C

Unité

11

En vacances

In this unit you will be able to:
- write postcards
- describe past events
- sequence events
- ask for information
- inquire about details
- tell location
- give directions
- give addresses
- identify objects
- express likes and dislikes
- state a preference
- express emotions

www.emcp.com

Vocabulaire

l'Europe (f.)

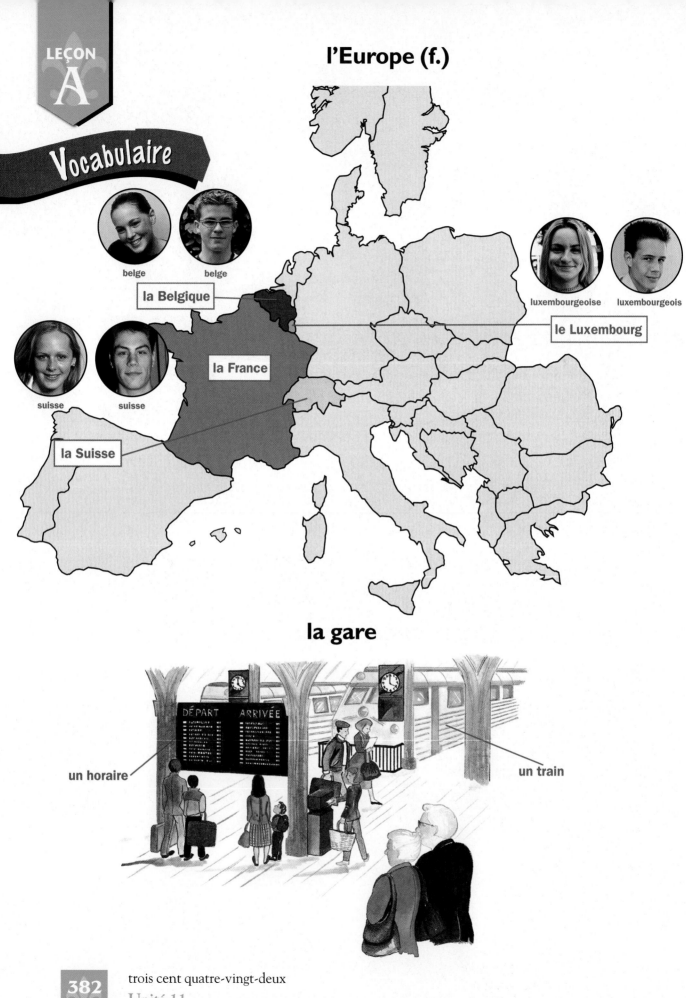

belge

belge

la Belgique

luxembourgeoise

luxembourgeois

le Luxembourg

la France

suisse

suisse

la Suisse

la gare

DÉPART   ARRIVÉE

un horaire

un train

Diane

Nicolas

Diane and Nicolas are talking about what they did during vacation.

Diane: Tiens, Nicolas! Quand est-ce que tu es rentré de vacances?

Nicolas: Ma famille et moi, nous sommes rentrés hier soir. Le train est arrivé à la gare à 22h05.

Diane: Vous êtes allés en Belgique, n'est-ce pas?

Nicolas: Oui, nous sommes partis pour Bruxelles le 29 octobre. C'est une belle ville. Et toi, tu es restée ici?

Diane: Oui, je suis sortie avec des amis la veille de la Toussaint. C'est tout.

Deux fêtes

Two French holidays begin the month of November: **la Toussaint** (*All Saints' Day*) on November 1 and **le jour des Morts** (*the Day of the Dead*) on November 2. On these two days the French remember their war dead as well as deceased relatives and loved ones. Flowers, especially chrysanthemums, are placed on the graves of family and friends. Students celebrate the holidays by taking a week of vacation.

Le train

Many French people travel by train. Some people who live in the suburbs of Paris take the train to work instead of drive a car. The **SNCF (Société nationale des chemins de fer français)**, a state-owned company, operates the French rail system, known for its trains that are

The *gare de Lyon* is one of six major train stations in Paris.

The *TGV* has a superior suspension system for a smooth ride.

on schedule, convenient and affordable. France has the most extensive network of tracks in Europe, and many people choose to travel by train when on vacation. France's modern **TGV (Train à grande vitesse)** runs 24 hours a day, covers all parts of France and extends into other European countries. It reaches speeds of up to 322 m.p.h., but usually goes about 186 m.p.h.

La Belgique

Belgium lies northeast of France on the North Sea. Belgians are divided primarily into two groups, according to which language they speak. The French-speaking Walloons live in the southern part of the country; the Dutch-speaking Flemings live in northern Belgium. Another country known for its good food, Belgium is the capital of French fries and **gaufres**, thick waffles covered with syrup, fresh fruit or cream. Belgian chocolates have a worldwide reputation.

Traditional *gaufres* are square, but these popular desserts may come in various shapes.

Bruxelles

Brussels, the capital of Belgium, houses the headquarters of organizations such as the European Union (EU) and the North Atlantic Treaty Organization (NATO). Ornate buildings that date from the 1500s, sidewalk cafés, and bird and flower markets decorate the city's main square (**la Grand-Place**). In 1815 Napoléon Bonaparte suffered his final defeat near Brussels in the city of Waterloo.

Flags representing nations in the European Union fly outside the European Parliament. (Bruxelles)

The historic buildings in Brussels' *Grand-Place*, which are in the Flemish Baroque style, overlook colorful flower markets. (Belgium)

1 Vrai ou faux?

*Écrivez "V" si la phrase est vraie;
écrivez "F" si la phrase est fausse.*

2 ▶ Complétez!

Trouvez dans la liste suivante l'expression qui complète correctement chaque phrase.

hier soir	français	22h05	Toussaint
le 29 octobre	Nicolas	Belgique	Diane

1. ... est rentré de vacances.
2. Nicolas et sa famille sont rentrés....
3. Le train est arrivé à....
4. Nicolas est allé en....
5. Nicolas est parti....
6. En Belgique on parle....
7. ... est sortie avec des amis.
8. La... est le premier novembre.

3 ▶ Quel pays est-ce?

Identifiez chaque pays (country).

Modèle:

C'est la France.

C'est à toi!

Questions personnelles.

1. Est-ce que tu préfères l'école ou les vacances?
2. Est-ce que tu prends souvent le train?
3. À quelle heure est-ce que tu vas rentrer après les cours aujourd'hui?
4. Est-ce que tu vas sortir avec tes amis ce vendredi soir?
5. Est-ce que tu restes à la maison la veille de la Toussaint?
6. Qu'est-ce que tu fais la veille de la Toussaint?

Nous prenons souvent le train.

Langue active

Passé composé with être

The **passé composé** is a verb tense used to tell what happened in the past. This tense is composed of two words: a helping verb and a past participle. To form the **passé composé** of certain verbs, use the appropriate present tense form of the helping verb **être** and the past participle of the main verb.

Vous **êtes allé** en Belgique.   *You went to Belgium.*

(helping verb)   (past participle of **aller**)

To form the past participle of **-er** verbs, drop the **-er** of the infinitive and add an é: **aller → allé**.

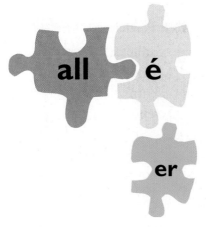

The past participle of the verb agrees in gender (masculine or feminine) and in number (singular or plural) with the subject. For a masculine singular subject, add nothing to the past participle; for a masculine plural subject, add an **s**. For a feminine singular subject, add an **e**; for a feminine plural subject, add an **es**.

aller					
je	suis	allé	nous	sommes	allés
je	suis	allée	nous	sommes	allées
tu	es	allé	vous	êtes	allé
tu	es	allée	vous	êtes	allée
			vous	êtes	allés
			vous	êtes	allées
il	est	allé	ils	sont	allés
elle	est	allée	elles	sont	allées
on	est	allé			

Nora, tu **es allée** au cinéma?   *Nora, did you go to the movies?*

Non, je **suis allée** chez moi.   *No, I went home.*

To form the past participle of most **-ir** verbs, drop the **-ir** and add an **i**: **partir → parti**. (For some verbs that end in **-ir,** add a **u**.)

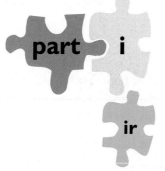

Most of the verbs that use **être** in the **passé composé** *express motion or movement* of the subject from one place to another.

Infinitive	Past Participle
aller	allé
arriver	arrivé
entrer	entré
rentrer	rentré
rester	resté
partir	parti
sortir	sorti
but: venir	venu

To make a negative sentence in the **passé composé**, put **ne (n')** before the form of **être** and **pas** after it.

Ma sœur **n'est pas** rentrée de vacances hier.   *My sister didn't come back from vacation yesterday.*

Le train **n'est pas** arrivé à la gare à 22h00.   *The train didn't arrive in the station at 10:00 P.M.*

To ask a question in the **passé composé** using inversion, put the subject pronoun after the form of **être**.

Thierry **est**-il déjà **parti**?   *Did Thierry leave already?*

Et toi, pourquoi n'**es**-tu pas **restée** à la boum?   *And why didn't you stay at the party?*

The **passé composé** has more than one meaning in English.

Ils **sont sortis**.   { *They have gone out.*
    They went out.

Sont-ils **sortis**?   *Did they go out?*

Le train est-il déjà arrivé?

Pratique

5 **En vacances**

Dites si les personnes suivantes sont parties pour la Belgique ou la Suisse.

Modèles:

Karine
Karine est partie pour la Belgique.

M. Dumont
M. Dumont est parti pour la Suisse.

1. Bruno

2. Mme Clerc

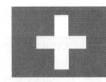
3. Amina

4. M. Vert

5. le prof de français

6. la prof d'allemand

Alexandre is sending his friend Marie-Claire a postcard from his trip to West Africa with his parents.

PAR AVION

Chère Marie-Claire,

Ce petit séjour est formidable! L'avion est parti de Roissy-Charles de Gaulle, et nous sommes arrivés à l'aéroport à Abidjan en Côte-d'Ivoire. Nous sommes restés chez ma grand-mère qui est ivoirienne. Quatre jours après nous sommes partis pour Dakar. Le premier jour au Sénégal on est allé à Cayar, un petit village. Le deuxième jour nous sommes revenus à Dakar. Hier on est allé à Saint-Louis pour faire le tour de la ville. L'Afrique me plaît beaucoup! Je n'ai pas envie de rentrer!

Grosses bises,
Alexandre

Les aéroports de Paris

Planes from all over the world use the international airports of Roissy-Charles de Gaulle and Orly. Both on the outskirts of Paris, Roissy is to the north and Orly is to the south of the city. Air France and Air Inter are the two French nationally owned airlines.

Escalators enclosed in glass tubes crisscross the center of the main terminal at Roissy-Charles de Gaulle.

Among its many destinations, Air France flies regularly to Guadeloupe, while Air Inter specializes in flights within the country.

La Côte-d'Ivoire

The Ivory Coast received its name from French sailors who traded for ivory in this West African country in the fifteenth century. It became independent from France in 1960 and has rapidly developed into one of the most prosperous and progressive countries in the region. Abidjan, called the "Pearl of Africa," is the Ivory Coast's largest city and the main seaport on the Atlantic Ocean. Tourists enjoy water sports on Abidjan's beautiful beaches.

Le Sénégal

Although Senegal also became independent from France, it keeps close cultural and economic ties with the country that governed it for 300 years. About the size of South Dakota, Senegal has a landscape that varies from dry land in the north near the Sahara Desert, to grassy plains in the center, to rain forests in the southwest. Its seven million people belong to a variety of ethnic groups. French is taught in schools and used in government, business and the media. However, most Senegalese also speak Wolof, the national language. From the modern capital of Dakar to the seventeenth century French settlement at Saint-Louis to the tiny fishing village of Cayar, from peanut farms to wildlife preserves, Senegal is a country full of contrasts.

In Senegal, commercial signs are often in French. (Dakar)

1 Les nombres ordinaux

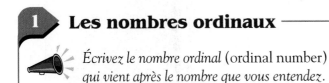

Écrivez le nombre ordinal (ordinal number) *qui vient après le nombre que vous entendez.*

2 En Afrique

Répondez aux questions.

1. Est-ce qu'Alexandre et ses parents sont allés en Afrique ou est-ce qu'ils sont allés en Europe?
2. De quel aéroport est-ce que l'avion est parti?
3. Où est-ce qu'Alexandre et sa famille sont arrivés?
4. Qui habite en Côte-d'Ivoire?
5. Où est-ce qu'Alexandre et ses parents sont allés après quatre jours en Côte-d'Ivoire?
6. Où est-ce que la famille d'Alexandre est allée le premier jour au Sénégal?
7. Est-ce qu'Alexandre aime l'Afrique?
8. Est-ce qu'Alexandre veut rentrer?

3 La nationalité

Selon d'où viennent certaines personnes, dites leur nationalité. Suivez le modèle.

Modèle:

Hanako vient du Japon.
Elle est japonaise.

Karim vient du Maroc.

Adja est sénégalaise.

1. Brigitte vient de Belgique.
2. Abdou vient de Côte-d'Ivoire.
3. Yasmine vient de Tunisie.
4. Bernard vient de Suisse.
5. Paul vient du Luxembourg.
6. Malika vient du Maroc.
7. Sonia vient de République Démocratique du Congo.
8. Salim vient d'Algérie.
9. Amina vient du Sénégal.

4 C'est à toi!

Questions personnelles.

1. Est-ce que tu as des amis sénégalais ou ivoiriens?
2. Est-ce que tu es allé(e) en Afrique?
3. Aimes-tu voyager en avion?
4. Est-ce que tu préfères voyager avec ta famille ou avec tes amis?
5. Vas-tu souvent chez ta grand-mère?
6. Ta grand-mère et ton grand-père, d'où viennent-ils?
7. Qu'est-ce que tu as envie de faire après les cours aujourd'hui?

Mlle Arié aime
voyager en avion.

Ordinal numbers

Numbers like "first," "second" and "third" are called ordinal numbers because they show the order in which things are placed. All ordinal numbers in French, except **premier** and **première**, end in **-ième**. To form most ordinal numbers, add **-ième** to the cardinal number. If a cardinal number ends in **-e**, drop this **e** before adding **-ième**. Note that "first," "fifth" and "ninth" are formed irregularly.

un, une	→	premier (m.), première (f.)
deux	→	deuxième
trois	→	troisième
quatre	→	quatrième
cinq	→	cinquième
six	→	sixième
sept	→	septième
huit	→	huitième
neuf	→	neuvième
dix	→	dixième

C'est mon **premier** voyage en Afrique.
Le **deuxième** jour nous sommes revenus à Dakar.

This is my first trip to Africa.
On the second day we came back to Dakar.

Le premier mai on donne du muguet (*lilies of the valley*).

Pratique

5 ▶ Quel jour est-ce?

Utilisez un nombre ordinal pour donner l'ordre de chaque jour de la semaine. (Attention: Lundi est le premier jour de la semaine en France.)

Modèle:

mardi
Mardi est le deuxième jour de la semaine.

1. vendredi
2. dimanche
3. mercredi
4. samedi
5. jeudi
6. lundi

Le monde francophone

During hundreds of years of colonial expansion, the French people spread their language and culture throughout the world. Today, more than 150,000,000 people are native French speakers; millions more use this international language in their daily lives.

Some French citizens, such as those in Corsica, live beyond France's borders. This Mediterranean island, near the west coast of Italy, is one of metropolitan France's 96 administrative divisions (**départements**). Outside of Europe, some French citizens live in France's overseas departments (**Départements d'Outre-Mer**): Martinique and Guadeloupe in the Caribbean, Réunion in the Indian Ocean and French Guiana in South America. Residents of these departments enjoy all the rights that mainland French citizens have.

People in France's overseas territories (**Territoires d'Outre-Mer**) also maintain close cultural and economic ties with France. Although they have no voice in French politics, the French government protects them in times of international crisis. Among these territories are French Polynesia, a group of islands in the South Pacific, and New Caledonia, an island near Australia.

French Polynesia counts 220,000 inhabitants, many of whom work in tourism.

In Europe, several countries bordering France have designated French as one of their official languages. People in parts of Belgium, Luxembourg and Switzerland speak French at home and when they travel or do business in neighboring countries. In the tiny principality of Monaco, near the Italian border but surrounded on three sides by France, the only official language is French.

The principality of Monaco includes Monaco, Monte-Carlo and the port.

In North America, many Canadians speak both French and English. Throughout the country, communication in government, business, schools and entertainment is usually bilingual. In the Province of Quebec, French is the native language of approximately 80 percent of the population and has been named the only official language.

In the Province of Quebec, all signs, like these in Montreal, are in French.

A Cajun band performs on Bourbon Street in the French Quarter of New Orleans, Louisiana.

French and French-Canadian settlers in New England brought the French language and culture to the United States. Both Creoles, descendants of the original French settlers, and Cajuns, whose French-Canadian ancestors were called "Acadians," now live in Louisiana. In fact, Louisiana was named after the French king Louis XIV. Names of cities such as Pierre (South Dakota), Des Moines (Iowa), Saint Louis (Missouri), Boise (Idaho) and Detroit (Michigan) reflect the French presence in America.

France once had the largest colonial empire in Africa. People in more than 20 African countries speak French, even though all these countries have gained their independence. Because these people represent various ethnic groups, French is often used as the common language of communication. Many people in **le Maghreb** and on the large island of Madagascar off the eastern coast of Africa communicate in French on a daily basis. In West Africa, the French influence still remains strong in the Ivory Coast, the Democratic Republic of the Congo and Senegal.

Senegal's president has lived in the presidential palace in Dakar since the country's independence from France in 1960.

France's former colonial empire extended far beyond the African continent. Today many people living in Haiti in the Caribbean and in Vietnam, Cambodia and Laos in Southeast Asia also speak French.

As the world continues to become smaller and smaller through faster means of communication and greater travel opportunities, the French language remains a key to understanding for vast numbers of people.

In Vietnam's Ho Chi Minh City, the former *Hôtel de Ville*, or city hall, was built during French colonial rule.

12 ▶ Le monde francophone

Répondez aux questions.

1. How did the French language and culture originally spread throughout the world?
2. What French department is located in the Mediterranean?
3. Which overseas department of France is in South America?
4. What are two of the French overseas territories?
5. What are the names of three European countries (other than France) where many people speak French?
6. In what Canadian province is French the only official language?
7. What are the two major areas of the United States settled by the French and French Canadians?
8. What cities do you know in the United States that have French names?
9. Why do various ethnic groups in some African countries still use French?
10. What are three former French colonies in Southeast Asia?

Along with Cambodia and Laos, Vietnam used to be a French colony.

13 ▸ Un horaire Air France

Regardez l'horaire des vols Air France entre Paris et cinq autres villes francophones. Pour répondre aux questions, notez que :

1 = lundi
2 = mardi
3 = mercredi
4 = jeudi
5 = vendredi
6 = samedi
7 = dimanche
G ou **A** après l'heure = Roissy-Charles de Gaulle
S après l'heure = Orly

ABIDJAN Côte d'Ivoire. Port-Bouet 16 km. taxi 2500 CFA / taxe 1000 CFA / UTA/AF 11 av. Anoma. / BP 1527 / ☎ 33 22 31. — ABJ GMT

Days	Dep		Arr			Flight
1-------	12 00G	X	18 50	D10	FY	RK 047
2-------	08 45G	R	15 35	D10	FJY	UT 803
2-------	23 59G	X	07 05a	D10	FY	RK 023
3-------	10 30G	X	17 40	D10	FY	RK 081
3-------	10 40G	R	19 10	747	FJY	UT 831
4-------	15 30G	R	22 05	D10	FJY	UT 807
4-------	23 45G	R	05 00a	747	FJY	UT 837
5-------	10 15G	X	18 05	D10	FY	RK 027
5-------	10 15G	X	17 30	D10	FY	RK 031
5-------	22 15G	T	05 00a	D10	FJY	UT 801
6-------	11 20G	R	18 15	D10	FJY	UT 805
6-------	22 15G	X	06 30a	AB3	FY	RK 021
7-------	13 00G	X	20 50	D10	FY	RK 041
7-------	22 40G	T	05 30a	747	FJY	UT 809

CASABLANCA Maroc / Mohammed V 35 km / car 20 dirhams / 15 av. de l'Armée Royale / ☎ 22 41 33 - R : 27 42 42 — CAS GMT

Days	Dep		Arr			Flight
-3---	09 15S	T	11 10	727	CY	AFAT2045
12-4---	09 15S	T	11 10	727	CY	AFAT2017
-5-7	09 15S	T	11 10	AB3	CY	AFAT2045
-7	09 15S	T	11 10	AB3	CY	AFAT2017
	15 00S	R	17 55	757	FY	ATAF781
-23-5-	15 00S	R	16 55	727	FY	ATAF703
	15 00S	R	17 55	727	Y	ATAF781
1234567	17 00S	R	22 00	737	FY	ATAF783
2----	18 30S	R	20 25	727	FY	ATAF751
1--4567	19 50S	R	22 55	727	CY	AFAT2035
-5--	19 50S	R	22 45	727	CY	AFAT2015
	20 00S	T	23 20	727	Y	ATAF723

〽 MERIDIEN ☎ 36 35 35 / Telex 24692

DAKAR Sénégal / Yoff 17 km / 47 av. A. Sarraut BP 142 / ☎ 22 29 41 - R : 22 49 49 — DKR GMT

Days	Dep		Arr			Flight
1	09 35A	X	14 20	AB3	FY	AF 301
1	10 00G	X	16 30	AB4	FY	RK 007
2	07 45A	R	14 10	AB3	FY	AF 303
2	11 00G	X	17 00	AB4	FY	RK 019
3	07 45A	T	13 55	AB3	FY	AF 305
3	12 00G	R	19 55	AB4	FY	RK 011
4	11 30G	X	18 10	AB4	FY	RK 001
4	15 30A	R	22 20	AB3	Y	AF 309
5	15 00G	X	20 50	D10	FY	RK 003
5	15 30A	R	21 55	AB3	FY	AF 315
6	23 59G	T	04 50a	AB4	FY	RK 017
6	15 00G	X	21 15	D10	FY	RKAF015
6	15 50A	R	22 20	AB3	FY	AF 317
7	23 59G	X	07 30a	DC8	FY	RK 035
7	08 00A	P	12 45	AB3	YM	AFRK321
7	13 40A	X	19 45	AB3	FY	AF 323
7	18 00G	X	23 59	AB4	FY	RK 009

MONTREAL Canada / Mirabel 53 km / car 8 dollars / 979 Ouest b. de Maisonneuve / ☎ (514) 284 2825 — YUL -5

Days	Dep		Arr			Flight
1234567	14 20G	P	15 45	747	FJY	AC 871
-23-56-	12 30A	X	14 05	74M	FJY	AF 033
-7	15 30A	X	17 05	74M	FJY	AF 033

PAPEETE Tahiti / Faaa 6 km / c/o Air Polynésie / BP 314 / ☎ 42 23 33 — PPT -10

Days	Dep		Arr			Flight
-3---	19 15G	X	05 45a	D10	FJY	UT 501
-5--	13 00A	X	22 55	747	FJY	AF 007
-6-	19 15G	X	05 45a	D10	FJY	UT 503

© 15790 F du 7/11 au 11/1

1. You can fly from Paris to four of these cities every day of the week. Which city does not have daily service?
2. At what time does a flight from Paris to Casablanca leave every day of the week? From which airport does this flight leave?
3. On what two days is there only one flight from Paris to Montreal?
4. If you want to fly to Montreal on Monday, from which airport would you leave?
5. At what time does the plane for Papeete leave Paris on Friday?
6. How many flights from Paris to Dakar leave on Saturday?
7. Does the 10:15 A.M. flight from Paris to Abidjan get in earlier or later than the flight leaving Paris at 10:45 A.M.?
8. If you want to fly to Dakar on Sunday and arrive there in the early afternoon, at what time would your flight leave?
9. If you want to fly to Abidjan on a 747 but don't want to fly at night, what day would you leave?
10. The 12:30 P.M. flight from Paris to Montreal arrives at 2:05 P.M. Why is there only about an hour and a half difference between departure and arrival times for this transatlantic flight?

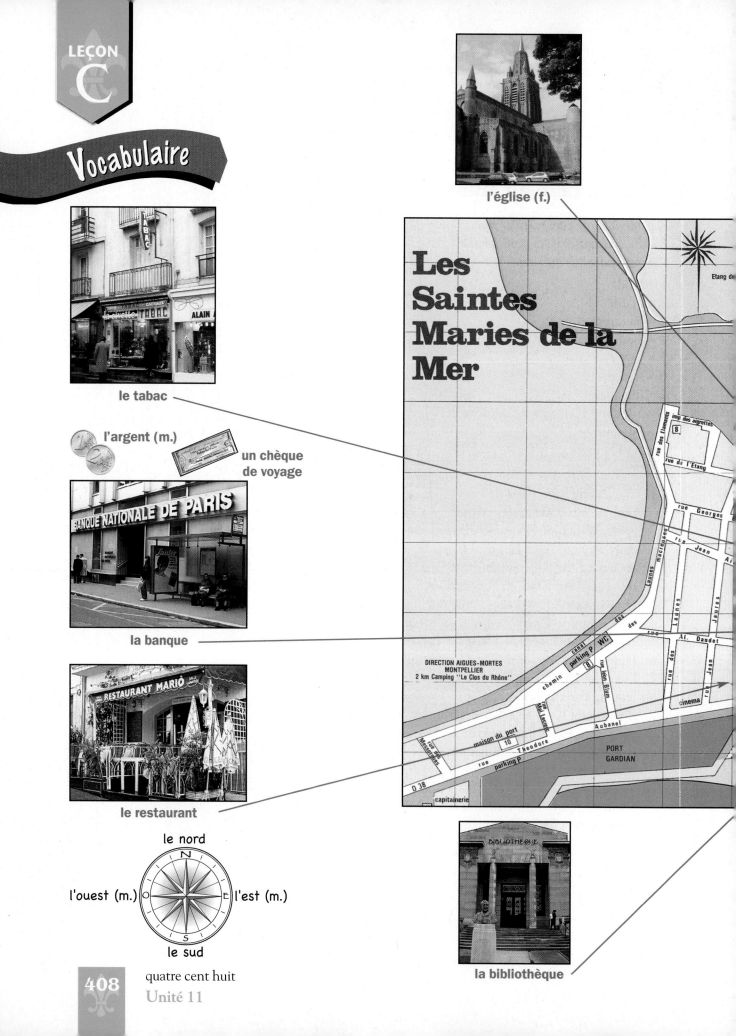

l'église (f.)

le tabac

l'argent (m.)

un chèque
de voyage

la banque

le restaurant

le nord

l'ouest (m.)   l'est (m.)

le sud

**Les
Saintes
Maries de la
Mer**

DIRECTION AIGUES-MORTES
MONTPELLIER
2 km Camping "Le Clos du Rhône"

PORT
GARDIAN

la bibliothèque

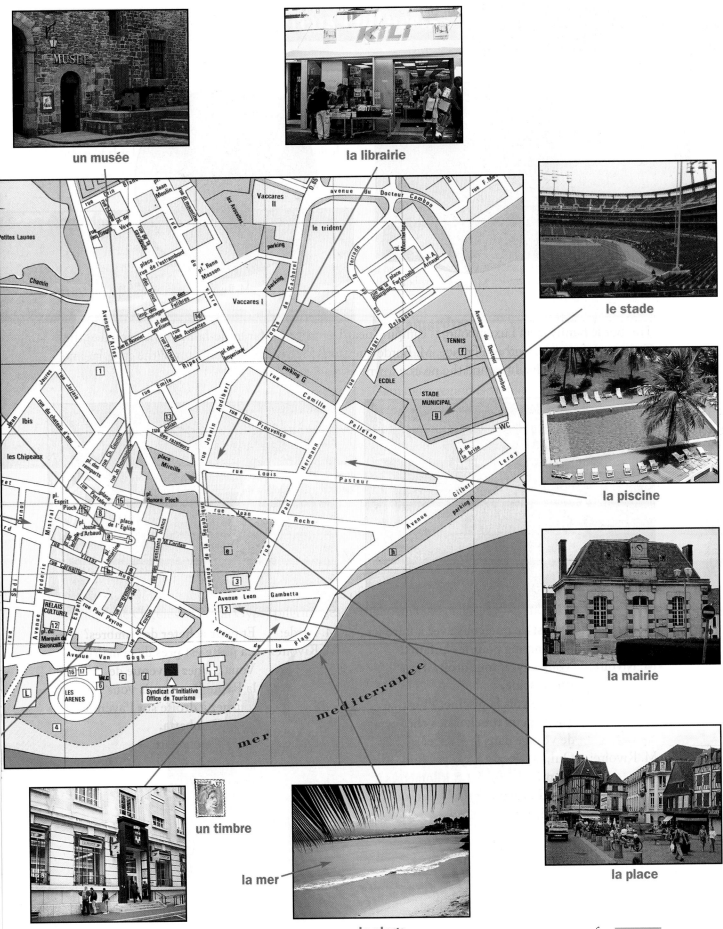

un musée

la librairie

le stade

la piscine

la mairie

la place

un timbre

la mer

la poste

la plage

Mistral

L'avenue Frédéric Mistral in Les Saintes-Maries-de-la-Mer honors a famous French poet who won the Nobel Prize in literature in 1904. Mistral wrote in Provençal, a French dialect spoken in southern France.

L'argent

You can change money and traveler's checks in France at **la banque** or **le bureau de change** (*money exchange*). Or, using a credit card, you can get money from an ATM (**un distributeur**) at a more favorable exchange rate.

An ATM is also called *un guichet automatique*.

This *tabac* also sells magazines, newspapers and postcards.

La poste

At a post office you can buy stamps, send letters and packages, use public telephones, buy **télécartes** (*phone cards to use in public phone booths*) and use the Minitel. Some French people even pay their gas and telephone bills at the post office.

Le tabac

Stamps and phone cards are also sold at **le tabac** (**le bureau de tabac**). A distinctive reddish-orange sign with the word **TABAC** on it makes these shops easy to recognize at a distance.

---

1 Où allez-vous?

Écrivez l'expression qui représente où vous allez pour faire les choses suivantes.

| la plage | le tabac | le restaurant | le musée | la librairie | le stade |

2 ▶ Qu'est-ce que c'est?

Identifiez!

Modèle:

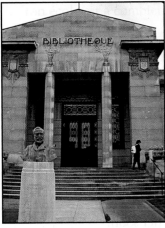

C'est une bibliothèque.

1.

2.

3.

4.

5.

6.

7.

8.

9.

6 **Qu'est-ce qu'on voit?**

Selon où sont certaines personnes, dites ce qu'elles voient.

des livres	beaucoup de timbres	la mer	des avions
la réceptionniste	des boutiques	une serveuse	des baguettes

Modèle:

Magali est au centre commercial.
Elle **voit des boutiques.**

1. Abdel-Cader est à la librairie. Il....
2. Vous êtes à la boulangerie. Vous....
3. M. et Mme Potvin sont au restaurant. Ils....
4. Je suis au cabinet du docteur Vaillancourt. Je....
5. Cécile est à la plage. Elle....
6. Les demi-sœurs de Catherine sont à la poste. Elles....
7. Tu es à l'aéroport. Tu....

Jean-Pierre est à la gare. Il voit des trains.

7 **En route**

Vous et vos amis allez vous retrouver au café. Dites ce que vous voyez en route.

Modèle:

Béatrice et son frère/mer
Béatrice et son frère voient la mer.

1. tu/piscine
2. les garçons/stade
3. Karima et moi/plage
4. Djamel et toi/poste
5. Clarence/église
6. je/bibliothèque
7. Sara et son cousin/musée
8. Véro/banque

Qui voit la poste et l'hôtel?

Communication

8 ▶ **Les directions**

Quelques amis vont venir chez vous cet après-midi après les cours.
Écrivez les directions détaillées entre l'école et votre maison.

9 ▶ **Pour aller aux Arènes?**

Imaginez que vous habitez aux Saintes-Maries-de-la-Mer. Vous avez un ami qui est au stade de tennis
*sur **l'Avenue du Docteur Cambon**. Il veut aller aux **Arènes** au centre de la ville. Utilisez la carte pour*
lui donner des directions détaillées.

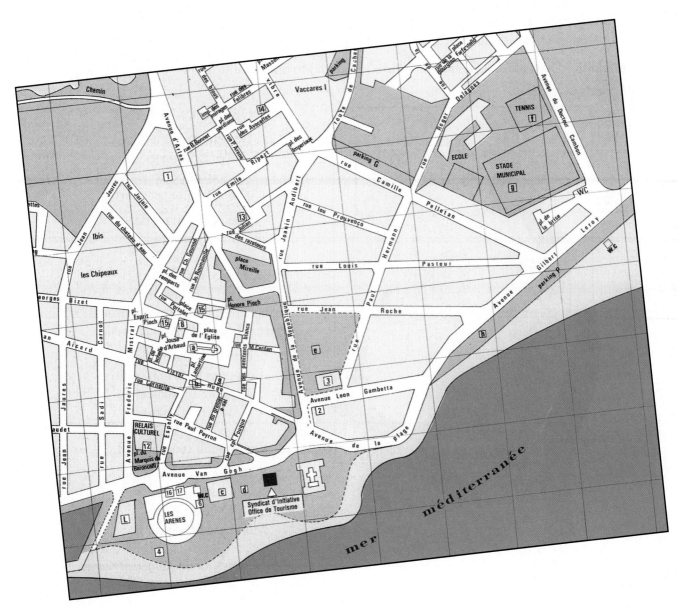

Review of Reading Strategies

Cameroon is a country in western equatorial Africa. Cameroonian author Elalongué Epanya Yondo wrote the poem that follows during the country's struggle for independence from France and England in the late 1950s and early 1960s.

Use the reading strategies that you have learned so far to help you understand what the poem means:

1. Use the cues provided by the *illustration* to predict what the poem is about and to guess the meaning of new words.
2. *Skim* the poem to figure out its context.
3. Note the *text organization*–see how the poem is divided into sections, called "stanzas."
4. Identify *cognates* to understand meaning.
5. Practice the technique of *inference*–use the context of words you know to unlock the meanings of these you don't know.
6. Take into account *cultural differences* between American life and that in the French-speaking setting.
7. Use *critical reading*–that is, evaluate the information the poem contains.
8. *Scan* the poem to hunt for answers to the questions that follow it.

In addition, look for *comparisons* using "like" (**comme**) to uncover the deeper meaning of the poem.

DORS MON ENFANT

Dors mon enfant dors
Quand tu dors
Tu es beau
Comme un oranger fleuri.

Dors mon enfant dors
Dors comme
La mer haute
Caressée par les clapotis
De la brise
Qui vient mourir en woua-woua
Au pied de la plage sablonneuse.

Dors mon enfant dors
Dors mon beau bébé noir
Comme la promesse
D'une nuit de lune
Au regard de l'Aube
Qui naît sur ton sommeil.

Dors mon enfant dors
Tu es si beau
Quand tu dors
Mon beau bébé noir dors.

Elalongué Epanya Yondo, *Kamerun! Kamerun!*
©Présence Africaine

10 ▸ "Dors mon enfant"

Répondez aux questions.

1. What does the illustration suggest that the poem is about? If the poem is a song, what kind of song do you think it is?
2. Try to "see" the illustration as it would be drawn if the poem were set in the United States. What cultural differences are there between your mental picture and the illustration? Are there any similarities?
3. Can you figure out what the word **dors** means in the title of the poem? Look for clues in the illustration and use the context of the other words you already know in the title to help you. (Hint: **dors** is a form of an infinitive you've seen before.)
4. What words in the poem are cognates?
5. The poem states that the child is beautiful. Is this a fact or an opinion? If it is an opinion, whose opinion is it?
6. In the poem the mother first compares the beauty of her son to a flowering orange tree, using the word **comme**. What two other comparisons does the mother make?
7. Cameroon is very close to the equator. What can you see in the illustration and find in the poem itself about the climate and location of the country?
8. The poem represents the hope of the mother for her son's future. Recalling the political conditions during which the author wrote the poem, do you see a relationship between the child and Cameroon? What is it?

Nathalie et Raoul

Évaluation

✓ Évaluation culturelle

Decide if each statement is **vrai** or **faux**.

1. The **SNCF**, the government-owned company that operates French trains, is well known for its prompt, affordable service.
2. Belgians are divided into four groups according to the languages they speak.
3. During the fifteenth century French sailors named the Ivory Coast for the ivory they traded there.
4. Senegal has close economic and cultural ties with France because it is one of the few African colonies still governed by France.
5. More than 150 million people speak French around the world.
6. France is divided into nearly 100 administrative divisions called **départements**.
7. Although French is spoken in many African countries, France is the only French-speaking country in Europe.
8. In North America, the French influence is especially strong in the Province of Quebec in Canada and in Louisiana.
9. Les Saintes-Maries-de-la-Mer is a town near the mouth of the Rhône River that hosts Gypsy pilgrimages.
10. You can buy **télécartes** at the post office and at **le tabac**.

Belgians speak French or Flemish. (Bruxelles)

✓ Évaluation orale

With a partner, play the roles of a person who has just returned from a French-speaking country in Europe and someone who has just returned from a French-speaking African country. Greet each other. Ask and tell where (in what country and city) you arrived. Next ask and tell where you went in that country. Then ask and tell when you returned home. Finally, ask and tell how much you like what you saw and did.

✓ Évaluation écrite

Write in French a description of the trip to the French-speaking country in Europe and the trip to the French-speaking country in Africa, based on the information you gave and heard in the previous activity. Also mention two other French-speaking countries you would like to see and tell why you would like to see them.

✓ Évaluation visuelle

For each highlighted country, first identify the person's nationality, then tell what country he or she lives in and finally say that he or she is from any city in that country. Follow the model. (You may want to refer to the *Révision de fonctions* on pages 421-22, the *Vocabulaire* on page 423 and the map of Africa on page 403.)

Modèle:

Caroline est française.
Elle habite en France.
Elle est de Fontainebleau.

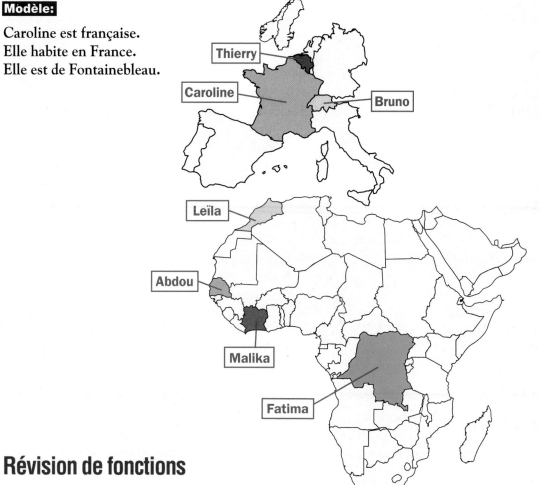

Révision de fonctions

Can you do all of the following tasks in French?
- I can write a postcard.
- I can talk about what happened in the past.
- I can talk about things sequentially.
- I can ask for detailed information.
- I can tell location.
- I can give directions.

- I can give addresses.
- I can identify objects.
- I can tell what I like.
- I can state my preference.
- I can express emotions.

To write postcards, use:

Cher (Chère)...,	*Dear . . . ,*
Grosses bises,	*Big kisses,*

To describe past events, use:

Je **suis sorti(e)** avec mes amis.	*I went out with my friends.*
Nous **sommes allés** au cinéma.	*We went to the movies.*
On **est revenu** à minuit.	*We came back at midnight.*
Vous **êtes rentrés** en Suisse.	*You returned to Switzerland.*
L'avion **est parti** de Roissy-Charles de Gaulle.	*The plane left Roissy-Charles de Gaulle.*

Nicole est sortie avec son ami Alexandre. (Bruxelles)

Il **est arrivé** à Genève à 20h00.	*It arrived in Geneva at 8:00 P.M.*
Chantal **est entrée** dans l'aéroport.	*Chantal entered the airport.*
Ses frères **sont venus** aussi.	*Her brothers came also.*
Pourquoi **es-tu resté** chez toi?	*Why did you stay home?*

To sequence events, use:

Le premier jour....	*The first day . . . .*
Après quatre **jours....**	*After four days . . . .*
Hier....	*Yesterday . . . .*
Aujourd'hui....	*Today . . . .*
Demain....	*Tomorrow . . . .*

To ask for information, use:

Et pour acheter des timbres?	*And (where do I go) to buy stamps?*

To inquire about details, use:

Qu'est-ce que vous avez **à faire** ici?	*What's there to do here?*

Hier Chloé est arrivée à la gare.

To tell location, use:

Mon père est parti **pour** Bruxelles, **en** Belgique.	*My father left for Brussels, in Belgium.*
Les Caron sont arrivés **à** Boston, **aux** États-Unis.	*The Carons arrived in Boston, in the United States.*
Après une semaine, ils sont allés à la plage **au** Mexique.	*After one week, they went to the beach in Mexico.*
Il y a une banque **près d'ici.**	*There's a bank near here.*
La banque n'est pas **loin.**	*The bank isn't far.*
Il/Elle est à 5 kilomètres.	*It's 5 kilometers.*
Il/Elle est au nord.	*It's (to the) north.*
Il/Elle est à l'est.	*It's (to the) east.*
Il/Elle est au sud.	*It's (to the) south.*
Il/Elle est à l'ouest.	*It's (to the) west.*
Il/Elle est à gauche.	*It's on the left.*
Il/Elle est à droite.	*It's on the right.*
Il/Elle est tout droit.	*It's straight ahead.*

Tu tournes à droite sur l'avenue Mistral.

To give directions, use:

Allez tout droit.	*Go straight ahead.*
Vous prenez l'avenue Foch.	*You take Foch Avenue.*
Vous tournez à droite/gauche sur l'avenue du Maine.	*You turn right/left on Maine Avenue.*

To give an address, use:

Il/Elle est sur l'avenue Victor Hugo.	*It's on Victor Hugo Avenue.*

To identify objects, use:

Il y a une piscine.	*There is a swimming pool.*

To say what you like, use:

L'Afrique **me plaît** beaucoup!	*I like Africa a lot!*

Cette crêpe me plaît beaucoup!

To state a preference, use:

J'ai envie de rentrer!	*I want to come home!*

To express emotions, use:

Ce séjour **est formidable!**	*This stay is terrific!*

Vocabulaire

un **aéroport** airport B
l' **Afrique (f.)** Africa B
l' **Algérie (f.)** Algeria B
algérien, algérienne Algerian B
l' **argent (m.)** money C
une **avenue** avenue C
un **avion** airplane B
avoir envie de to want, to feel like B

une **banque** bank C
belge Belgian A
la **Belgique** Belgium A
une **bibliothèque** library C
une **bise** kiss B

un **camping** campground C
un **chèque (de voyage)** (traveler's) check C
cher, chère dear B
chez at the house/home of B
cinquième fifth B
congolais, congolaise Congolese B
la **Côte-d'Ivoire** Ivory Coast B

deuxième second B
dixième tenth B

une **église** church C
l' **envie (f.): avoir envie de** to want, to feel like B
l' **est (m.)** east C
l' **Europe (f.)** Europe A

formidable great, terrific B

une **gare** train station A
gros, grosse big, large B

hier yesterday A
un **horaire** schedule, timetable A
huitième eighth B

ivoirien, ivoirienne Ivorian B

une **librairie** bookstore C
loin far C
le **Luxembourg** Luxembourg A
luxembourgeois(e) Luxembourger A

une **mairie** town hall C
le **Maroc** Morocco B
marocain(e) Moroccan B
me: ... me plaît. I like . . . . B
une **mer** sea C
un **musée** museum C

neuvième ninth B
le **nord** north C
l' **ouest (m.)** west C

partir to leave A
un **passeport** passport B
une **piscine** swimming pool C
une **place** (public) square C
une **plage** beach C
plaît: ... me plaît. I like . . . . B
une **poste** post office C
près (de) near C

quatrième fourth B

rentrer to come home, to return, to come back A
la **République Démocratique du Congo** Democratic Republic of the Congo B
un **restaurant** restaurant C
revenir to come back, to return B

un **séjour** stay B
le **Sénégal** Senegal B
sénégalais(e) Senegalese B
septième seventh B
sixième sixth B
un **stade** stadium C
le **sud** south C
suisse Swiss A
la **Suisse** Switzerland A

un **tabac** tobacco shop C
un **timbre** stamp C
toucher to cash C
tourner to turn C
la **Toussaint** All Saints' Day A
tout all, everything A
tout droit straight ahead C
un **train** train A
troisième third B
la **Tunisie** Tunisia B
tunisien, tunisienne Tunisian B

la **veille** night before A
un **village** village B
une **ville** city A
voir to see C

Unité 12

À Paris

In this unit you will be able to:
- write journal entries
- describe past events
- sequence events
- express need and necessity
- ask for information
- give opinions
- compare things

www.emcp.com

Vocabulaire

un bateau

un tableau

un monument

un jardin

une statue

un tombeau

un hôtel

un cimetière

une station de métro

un plan

un billet

un guichet

le métro

l'arc de triomphe

Karine

Notre-Dame

le Louvre

la tour Eiffel

Karine Couty, a student from Papeete, Tahiti, is spending the month of July in France. In her journal she describes some of her experiences in Paris.

le 5 juillet

Ce matin j'ai quitté l'hôtel à neuf heures. D'abord, j'ai marché sur l'avenue des Champs-Élysées de l'arc de triomphe au Drugstore. Là, j'ai mangé, puis, j'ai continué mon chemin jusqu'au Louvre où j'ai regardé de beaux tableaux. J'aime la Joconde de Léonard de Vinci. Puis, j'ai décidé de prendre le métro pour voir le tombeau de Jim Morrison au cimetière du Père-Lachaise, mais j'ai perdu mon plan de métro. Alors je suis allée au guichet du métro, et j'ai demandé un nouveau plan.

Paris est vraiment la "Ville lumière"! J'ai fini la journée en bateau sur la Seine d'où j'ai regardé beaucoup de beaux monuments: la tour Eiffel, Notre-Dame, les jardins des Tuileries, et même la petite statue de la Liberté. Quel paradis! D'après mon professeur de français, il faut venir à Paris au moins trois fois: une fois quand on est jeune, une fois quand on est amoureux et une fois quand on a de l'argent et qu'on peut vraiment vivre bien! Imagine, c'est seulement ma première fois ici....

Tahiti

Papeete, the largest city on the South Pacific island of Tahiti, is the capital of French Polynesia. Many Tahitians work in tourism, the island's major industry. Blessed with luxuriant vegetation and spectacular waterfalls, Tahiti has been portrayed as a tropical paradise by many painters and writers, including the French artist Paul Gauguin and the American author James Michener.

Wearing a floral crown of hibiscus blossoms braided with palm fronds is a tradition still alive in Tahiti.

Le Drugstore

As its name implies, **le Drugstore** in Paris sells some over-the-counter products, such as aspirin. However, this contemporary café primarily serves light meals and American-style ice cream specialties.

Most people who see the *Mona Lisa* are surprised at how small it is. (Paris)

La Joconde

The French name for the *Mona Lisa*, a painting by the Italian artist Leonardo da Vinci, is *la Joconde*. Probably the best-known painting in the **Louvre**, it became famous because of the woman's mysterious smile. The French king François I not only brought the painting back from Italy, but the artist as well. Da Vinci spent the last years of his life in France.

Le métro

The Paris subway system, called the **métro** (the shortened form of **métropolitain**), is known for its efficiency, speed, cleanliness and reasonable fares. The first **métro** line opened in 1900; to-day, over 300 stations dot the city. Most of them are named after streets, squares, monuments, famous people, historical places and the former gates (**portes**) to the

An "M," "*Métro*" or "*Métropolitain*" sign indicates the entrance to a *métro* station. (Paris)

city. Modern express lines, called **R.E.R.**, have recently been added to the **métro** system. They serve the suburbs and make fewer stops in the center of Paris than do the other lines. To ride the subway, you first buy a ticket or **un carnet** (a group of ten tickets). Although each **métro** line has a number, you refer to the line by the stations at each end of it. Follow the signs for the end point in the direction in which you are going. To transfer from one line to another, follow the **correspondance** signs. The **métro** runs from 5:00 A.M. to 1:00 A.M.

Le cimetière du Père-Lachaise

Le cimetière du Père-Lachaise is the largest cemetery in Paris. Here lie the remains of such famous people as the composer Frédéric Chopin and the playwright Molière. Many American tourists visit the tomb of Jim Morrison, a singer with the rock group the Doors. He died in Paris in 1971.

Jim Morrison's tomb, the most popular site in *Père-Lachaise*, is still frequently decorated by people who appreciate his music. (Paris)

A replica of Bartholdi's Statue of Liberty is on the *pont de Grenelle* in Paris.

La Liberté éclairant le monde

The French gave the United States the Statue of Liberty in 1886. A small copy of the statue stands in Paris as a continuing reminder of the friendship between the two countries.

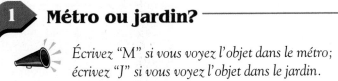

1 **Métro ou jardin?**

*Écrivez "M" si vous voyez l'objet dans le métro;
écrivez "J" si vous voyez l'objet dans le jardin.*

2 ▸ Le journal de Karine

Répondez par "vrai" ou "faux."

1. Karine est en vacances à Tahiti.
2. Karine a quitté l'hôtel à dix heures.
3. L'arc de triomphe est sur l'avenue des Champs-Élysées.
4. Karine aime *la Joconde* de Léonard de Vinci.
5. Le tombeau de Jim Morrison est au Louvre.
6. Karine a perdu son plan de métro.
7. Karine a fini la journée en bateau sur le Rhône.
8. C'est la troisième fois que Karine est à Paris.

Le bateau est devant le musée d'Orsay. (Paris)

3 ▸ Où va-t-on?

Selon ce qu'elles veulent faire, dites où vont les personnes suivantes.

1. François veut voir le tombeau de Molière.
2. Julien veut faire un tour en bateau.
3. Mathieu et ses parents veulent mettre leurs vêtements dans l'armoire.
4. Grégoire veut faire les magasins.
5. Marguerite veut regarder des tableaux.
6. M. Dupleix veut acheter un billet.
7. Les enfants veulent jouer.

A. la Seine
B. le musée
C. le guichet
D. l'avenue des Champs-Élysées
E. le cimetière
F. le jardin
G. l'hôtel

4 ▸ C'est à toi!

Questions personnelles.

1. Combien de fois est-ce que tu es allé(e) au cinéma ce mois?
2. Est-ce que tu préfères aller au musée ou au cinéma?
3. Quels tableaux aimes-tu?
4. Est-ce que tu préfères aller en vacances à Tahiti ou à Paris? Pourquoi?
5. Quel monument à Paris veux-tu voir?
6. L'avenue où tu habites s'appelle comment?
7. À quelle heure est-ce que tu quittes la maison pour aller à l'école?

Tu aimes les tableaux de Paul Gauguin?

Passé composé with avoir

You have learned that the **passé composé** is made up of a helping verb and the past participle of the main verb. You use the appropriate present tense form of the helping verb **être** with certain verbs. But the majority of verbs form their **passé composé** with the helping verb **avoir**.

J'**ai regardé** des monuments.   *I looked at some monuments.*

(helping verb)   (past participle of **regarder**)

Remember that to form the past participle of **-er** verbs, drop the **-er** of the infinitive and add an é: **regarder** → **regardé**.

The past participle of verbs that use **avoir** in the **passé composé** does not agree with the subject. Therefore, the past participle stays the same while the form of **avoir** changes according to the subject.

regarder					
j'	ai	regardé	nous	avons	regardé
tu	as	regardé	vous	avez	regardé
il/elle/on	a	regardé	ils/elles	ont	regardé

As-tu **regardé** la télé?   *Did you watch TV?*

Non, j'**ai regardé** mon plan.   *No, I looked at my map.*

Remember that to form the past participle of most **-ir** verbs, drop the **-ir** and add an **i**: **finir** → **fini**.

Most infinitives that end in **-re** form their past participles by dropping the **-re** and adding a **u**: **vendre** → **vendu**.

To make a negative sentence in the **passé composé**, put **n'** before the form of **avoir** and **pas** after it.

Les élèves **n'**ont **pas** fini le tour.   *The students didn't finish the tour.*

To ask a question in the **passé composé** using inversion, put the subject pronoun after the form of **avoir**.

Quand le prof **a**-t-il **perdu** son plan de Paris?   *When did the teacher lose his Paris map?*

5 ▸ Oh là là!

Dites ce que les touristes ont perdu en vacances.

Modèle:

Jean-François/un tee-shirt
Jean-François a perdu un tee-shirt.

1. Amina/des CDs
2. les parents d'Amina/de l'argent
3. je/mon sac à dos
4. M. Smith/son passeport
5. Fabrice et toi, vous/des chèques de voyage
6. tu/une chaussette
7. M. et Mme Orgeval/leur plan de la ville
8. ma famille et moi, nous/nos billets d'avion

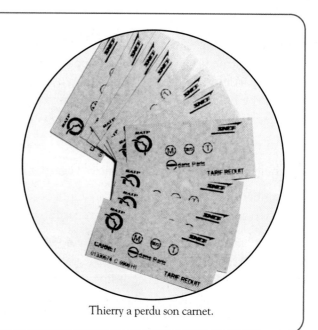

Thierry a perdu son carnet.

6 ▸ À pied ou en métro?

Quelques touristes ont décidé de voir la ville de Paris à pied. Les autres ont acheté des billets de métro. Dites qui a décidé de marcher. Suivez le modèle.

Modèle:

Jean-François
Jean-François n'a pas marché.

1. Amina

2. les parents d'Amina

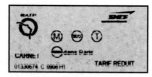

3. je

4. M. Smith

5. Fabrice et toi, vous

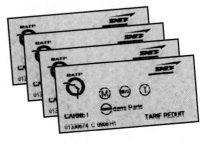

6. tu

7. M. et Mme Orgeval

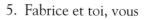

8. ma famille et moi, nous

7 ▶ **Qu'a-t-on fait?**

Selon où elles sont allées, choisissez une activité qui dit ce que certaines personnes ont fait vendredi.
Suivez le modèle.

Modèle:

Sophie est allée en boîte.
Elle a dansé.

finir les devoirs	nager
attendre le train	danser
acheter des timbres	manger un hamburger
toucher des chèques de voyage	regarder des tableaux

1. Khadim est allé au fast-food.
2. Les Dupont sont allés au Louvre.
3. Florence et sa sœur sont allées à la plage.
4. Mlle Wang est allée à la banque.
5. Luc et Patrick sont allés à la bibliothèque.
6. Mme Lannion et sa fille sont allées à la gare.
7. Marc est allé au tabac.

Mme Courtes est allée au café où elle a mangé un sandwich.

8 ▶ **Pendant le weekend**

Qu'est-ce que vous et vos amis avez fait pendant un long weekend?
Suivez le modèle.

Modèle:

Le premier jour Raoul a skié. Le deuxième jour il....

1. Raoul

2. Christine et Saleh

3. mes amis et moi, nous

Demandez à votre partenaire s'il ou elle a fait certaines choses hier. Répondez aux questions et puis alternez. Suivez le modèle.

Modèles:

étudier le français

A: **As-tu étudié le français hier?**

B: **Oui, j'ai étudié le français hier./**
   Non, je n'ai pas étudié le français hier.

aller au cinéma

B: **Es-tu allé(e) au cinéma hier?**

A: **Oui, je suis allé(e) au cinéma hier./**
   Non, je ne suis pas allé(e) au cinéma hier.

1. venir à l'école
2. finir tes devoirs
3. jouer au foot
4. aller au fast-food
5. rester à la maison
6. regarder la télé
7. travailler
8. sortir avec des amis

Communication

10 Mon voyage à Paris

Imaginez que vous avez passé une semaine à Paris avec des amis. Pendant le voyage vous avez écrit seulement des notes pour mettre dans votre journal. Maintenant changez ces notes en phrases complètes.

1ᵉʳ jour–12.7

banque-chèques de voyage

Louvre-la Joconde

librairie-plan de Paris

jardins des Tuileries-fleurs, enfants

restaurant-Le Petit Quinquin: poulet,
   frites, coca

2ᵉ jour–13.7

avenue des Champs-Élysées

magasin-Prisunic: tee-shirt,
   arc de triomphe

Drugstore-glace au chocolat

tabac-timbres

cinéma-film américain

11 ▸ Trouvez une personne qui....

Interviewez vos amis pour trouver qui a fait les activités suivantes pendant le weekend. Écrivez les nombres de 1 à 15. Puis posez les questions suivantes à chaque ami(e). Si un(e) ami(e) répond que oui, il/elle écrit son nom près du nombre. Trouvez un(e) ami(e) différent(e) pour chaque question.

1. jouer au basket
2. manger de la pizza
3. rester au lit samedi matin
4. acheter des vêtements
5. travailler
6. sortir avec des amis
7. aller au cinéma
8. regarder la télé
9. étudier le français
10. aller au centre commercial
11. dormir jusqu'à dix heures dimanche
12. perdre quelque chose
13. aller au fast-food
14. finir les devoirs
15. nager

Modèle:

Jean-Paul: **Tu as joué au basket?**
Clémence: **Oui, j'ai joué au basket.**
(Writes her name beside number 1.)

12 ▸ Un paragraphe

*Dans un paragraphe écrivez ce que vous avez fait le weekend passé. Pour chaque jour, dites où vous êtes allé(e), ce que vous avez fait et si vous avez travaillé. Vous pouvez utiliser les verbes **regarder, parler, jouer, manger, étudier, travailler, dormir, voyager, acheter, finir, aller, rentrer, rester** et **sortir**.*

Je suis sortie avec ma famille.

Prononciation

The sound [k]

The sound [k] is written as **c** (before **a**, **o** or **u**), **k** or **qu**. The sound [k] in French is different from the English sound "k." In producing the French sound, no air escapes from the mouth. To see if you pronounce the French [k] correctly, hold a sheet of paper about two inches in front of your mouth. Then say the following sentences without making the paper move.

De **qu**elle **c**ouleur est le **c**ostume?

Caroline et **C**olette prennent du **c**oca et du **k**etchup.

Les **c**arottes **c**oûtent un euro **qu**arante.

Combien de **C**anadiens ont des **c**oiffeurs américains?

À **qu**elle heure **c**ommence le **c**ours?

The paper should move only when you pronounce the English equivalent of each of these words:

café	Canada
cuisine	camembert
camping	cousin

Vocabulaire

une musicienne

un feu d'artifice

un musicien

un bal

un défilé

une rue

Karine

le musée d'Orsay

le Centre Pompidou

les Invalides

Karine continues to write in her journal, describing a busy week in Paris.

le 17 juillet

J'ai passé une bonne semaine. Lundi j'ai vu le Centre Pompidou où je suis montée jusqu'au cinquième étage pour bien voir Paris. Puis, j'ai pris un coca sur la place et j'ai regardé des musiciens. Mardi matin je suis allée à la Défense où j'ai visité l'arche et les magasins modernes. Mardi soir il y a eu un bal dans la rue. J'ai dansé jusqu'à trois heures du matin! Puis, j'ai été obligée de prendre un taxi pour rentrer à l'hôtel, parce qu'on a fermé le métro. Mercredi j'ai regardé le grand défilé du 14 juillet, la fête nationale de la France. On a fait beaucoup de bruit! Puis, le soir j'ai vu un beau feu d'artifice. Jeudi j'ai visité le musée d'Orsay pour voir les tableaux impressionnistes. Vendredi j'ai vu le tombeau de Napoléon aux Invalides et la statue du <u>Penseur</u> au musée Rodin. Une semaine bien chargée, n'est-ce pas?

La Défense

Several modern neighborhoods, such as **la Défense**, have been built on the outskirts of Paris. With its enormous **arche de la Défense**, skyscrapers, apartments, businesses and shops, **la Défense** has changed the skyline of contemporary Paris.

L'arche de la Défense was built directly in line with *l'arc de triomphe, la place de la Concorde* and *l'arc de triomphe du Carrousel.* (Paris)

La Bastille

On July 14 the French celebrate their national holiday. They honor the day in 1789 when the people of Paris captured the **Bastille**, the royal prison. Although only seven non-political prisoners were there at that time, the capture of the old fortress symbolized the beginning of the French Revolution and a spirit of freedom for everyone. The monarchy eventually fell, and the people established a more democratic form of government. Although the **Bastille** itself was demolished shortly after being stormed, a 170-foot column today stands on the **place de la Bastille**.

On *la place de la Bastille* stands the bronze *colonne de Juillet*, topped with a gilded spirit of liberty that commemorates those who died there in July, 1830. (Paris)

Le défilé du 14 juillet

On Bastille Day, Parisians line the parade route hours in advance to have the best possible view of the annual military parade. A flyover with jets trailing blue, white and red smoke starts the parade. Then the French president comes down the parade route, usually **l'avenue des Champs-Élysées**. Both male and female members of the

On July 14, French President Chirac goes down *les Champs-Élysées* as part of the parade marking the French national holiday. (Paris)

police, the Foreign Legion, **la garde républicaine** and other military units are presented for the inspection of the president and the French people, along with various military hardware. Smaller towns often hold military parades as well. In the evening fireworks explode across the sky. Street dances take place the nights of July 13 and 14. The firefighters of Paris, for example, sponsor dances which last well into the morning hours.

Students from the *École Polytechnique* dazzle the crowds during the Bastille Day parade. (Paris)

1 La fête nationale

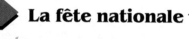

Écrivez "oui" si l'événement (event) est associé à la fête nationale de la France. Si non, écrivez "non."

2 Le journal de Karine

Répondez aux questions avec la lettre de l'expression qui convient (fits).

1. À quel étage du Centre Pompidou est-ce que Karine est montée?
2. Qui est-ce que Karine a regardé sur la place?
3. Où est-ce qu'il y a une arche moderne?
4. Où est-ce qu'il y a eu un bal?
5. Jusqu'à quelle heure est-ce que Karine a dansé?
6. Comment est-ce que Karine est rentrée?
7. Où sont les tableaux impressionnistes?
8. Où est le tombeau de Napoléon?
9. Où est la statue du *Penseur*?

A. aux Invalides
B. au cinquième
C. au musée d'Orsay
D. des musiciens
E. au musée Rodin
F. en taxi
G. à la Défense
H. dans la rue
I. jusqu'à trois heures du matin

Auguste Rodin a fait la statue du *Penseur*. (Paris)

3 ▸ À Paris

Identifiez!

Modèle:

C'est un taxi.

1.

2.

3.

4.

5.

6.

7.

8.

4 ▸ C'est à toi!

Questions personnelles.

1. Qu'est-ce que tu fais le 4 juillet?
2. Est-ce que tu préfères regarder un défilé ou un feu d'artifice?
3. Est-ce que tu aimes danser?
4. Quel musicien est-ce que tu préfères?
5. Est-ce que tu aimes les tableaux impressionnistes?
6. Dans ta famille, qui fait beaucoup de bruit?
7. Est-ce que tu as passé une bonne semaine? Pourquoi ou pourquoi pas?

quatre cent quarante et un

Leçon B

441

Irregular past participles

Some verbs that form their **passé composé** with **avoir** have irregular past participles.

Verb	Past Participle
avoir	eu
être	été
faire	fait
prendre	pris
voir	vu

As-tu **vu** le feu d'artifice?

Non, j'**ai été** obligé de rester à la maison.

Did you see the fireworks?

No, I had to (was obliged to) stay home.

As-tu vu le beau feu d'artifice à Paris?

Pratique

5 ▶ Hier

Dites ce qu'on a fait hier.

Modèle:

Karine/du roller
Karine a fait du roller hier.

1. M. Lefebvre/les courses
2. les étudiants/les devoirs
3. je/du sport
4. ta belle-sœur et toi, vous/ du shopping
5. mes cousins et moi, nous/du vélo
6. tu/un tour en bateau
7. Mme Boucher et son mari/ du footing

On a fait un tour en bateau sur la Seine.

6 ▶ La famille Troussard

Qu'est-ce que les Troussard ont fait pendant leur semaine à Paris? Écrivez le passé composé du verbe approprié.

> avoir   être   faire   prendre   voir

1. M. Troussard... obligé de passer une semaine à Paris. Donc, sa femme et ses fils sont venus à Paris aussi.
2. Ils... le métro pour aller à leur hôtel.
3. La famille Troussard... beaucoup de monuments à Paris.
4. Djamel Troussard... des photos de la tour Eiffel.
5. Le 14 juillet les Troussard sont allés aux Champs-Élysées où il y... un grand défilé.
6. Au défilé, les garçons... beaucoup de bruit!
7. Puis, le soir il y... un feu d'artifice.
8. Le 15 juillet les Troussard... un tour en bateau sur la Seine.

Les Troussard ont souvent pris le métro. (Paris)

7 ▶ La liste de Marie-Claude

Marie-Claude a fait une liste de choses à faire pendant le weekend. Dites si elle a fait toutes ces choses ou pas. Suivez le modèle.

> dormir jusqu'à dix heures du matin
> ✔ prendre rendez-vous avec le médecin
> faire les magasins
> voir le nouveau film au Gaumont
> ✔ finir les devoirs
> téléphoner à Cécile
> ✔ attendre Daniel à l'aéroport

Marie-Claude a fini les devoirs.

Modèle:

Elle n'a pas dormi jusqu'à dix heures du matin.

Communication

8 ▸ Le 4 juillet

Votre correspondant français est curieux. Qu'est-ce que les Américains font pour célébrer le 4 juillet? Alors, écrivez-lui une lettre qui décrit ce que font traditionnellement les Américains le 4 juillet. Dites aussi ce que vous, vos amis et votre famille avez fait le 4 juillet passé.

9 ▸ En partenaires

Avec un(e) partenaire, parlez de ce que vous avez fait le weekend passé. Apportez (Bring) en classe trois objets (ou photos) qui représentent vos activités.

Montrez votre objet (ou photo) et parlez d'une activité que vous avez faite.

Posez une question sur cette activité.

Répondez à la question et puis alternez.

Paris

"If you are lucky enough to have lived in Paris as a young man, then wherever you go for the rest of your life, it stays with you, for Paris is a moveable feast," wrote the American author Ernest Hemingway. Long considered to be the cultural capital of the world, Paris still attracts people interested in the arts. Visitors come from all over the globe to see the famous sights of this cosmopolitan city.

The origins of Paris go back many centuries. The city received its name from the **Parisii**, a Gallic tribe that settled on the **île de la Cité** over 2,000 years ago. The larger of the two islands in the Seine, the **île de la Cité** is called the "cradle" of Paris because the city's history began here. Tourists admire the quaint seventeenth century buildings on the smaller, more residential **île Saint-Louis**. Sightseers needing a break stop at Le Berthillon, a popular establishment known for its delicious ice cream.

Several monuments draw visitors to the **île de la Cité**. The cathedral of **Notre-Dame**, begun in the twelfth century, is a triumph of Gothic architecture with its ribbed vaulting and flying buttresses. These structures support the weight of the cathedral from the outside, allowing for thinner, higher walls filled with richly colored stained glass windows. Gargoyles, waterspouts sculpted in the form of long-necked creatures, and intricately carved statues decorate the church's façade.

The **Sainte-Chapelle**, a tiny church on the **île de la Cité**, was built in the thirteenth century to house relics from the religious Crusades. Another jewel of Gothic architecture, it contains enough stained glass windows to cover three basketball courts. Since most people

Notre-Dame sits on the site where a Gallo-Roman temple, a Christian basilica and a Romanesque church once stood. (Paris)

couldn't read during the Middle Ages, biblical stories were illustrated through the scenes on these windows, as well as on those of other Gothic churches.

Just a block away lies the **Conciergerie**, which was a state prison during the French Revolution. You can still visit cell number VI where Queen Marie-Antoinette, wife of King Louis XVI, spent her last days before being guillotined in 1793.

The Seine River divides Paris in half before it continues northwest to the English Channel. The Right Bank (**rive droite**) is north of the Seine; the Left Bank (**rive gauche**) is south of the Seine. More than 30 bridges, such as the **Pont-Neuf** (the oldest) and the **pont Alexandre-III** (the newest and most elaborate), join the two sides of the river. **Les bouquinistes** (*booksellers*) line the banks of the Seine with their stands full of secondhand books, posters, old prints and postcards.

On the Right Bank of the Seine is the **place Charles-de-Gaulle** where Napoléon had the **arc de triomphe** built to commemorate his military victories. Under the arch lies the Tomb of the Unknown Soldier. This square used to be called the **place de l'Étoile** because 12 avenues radiate from its center. The most famous of these streets, the **avenue des Champs-Élysées**, stretches to the **place de la Concorde**, where over one thousand French people were guillotined during the French Revolution. The largest square in western Europe, the **place de la Concorde** has an Egyptian obelisk and beautiful fountains at its center.

The **jardins des Tuileries**, the former gardens of French royalty, extend farther east along the river. Next to the gardens is the enormous **musée du Louvre** with its modern steel and glass pyramid designed by the American architect I. M. Pei. Formerly a royal palace, the **Louvre** houses one of the most extensive art collections in the world. Among its treasures are paintings, such as the

The square that had been known as the *place de la Révolution* was optimistically renamed the *place de la Concorde* ("Square of Peace") in 1794. (Paris)

Mona Lisa; sculptures, such as *Winged Victory*; period furniture; antiquities and the crown jewels of France. If you were to spend three minutes in front of each painting in the museum, it would take you over two and one-half months to view all of them.

The exterior of the *Louvre* combines classical and modern architecture. (Paris)

On the northern edge of the city, the basilica of **Sacré-Cœur** overlooks Paris from the hill of **Montmartre**, an artistic quarter of the city.

The white-domed basilica of *Sacré-Cœur* overlooks the *place du Tertre*, the artists' quarter. (Paris)

The Right Bank has contemporary buildings as well as historical landmarks. The **Centre national d'art et de culture Georges Pompidou**, familiarly called **Beaubourg**, was designed in a bold, functional style of architecture. The pipes, ducts, pillars and stairways of the glass structure are exposed; each is painted a different color according to its function (water, heating, air-conditioning, etc.). A "caterpillar" escalator brings visitors to the top of the building for a fabulous view of the city. The **Centre Pompidou** contains a computer music center, the city's biggest public library and a modern art museum. The square in front of the building remains a perpetual showcase, with street performers entertaining the public at all hours of the day and night.

Both the **musée d'Orsay** and the **musée Rodin** are on the Left Bank (**rive gauche**) of the Seine. Built in a former train station, the **musée d'Orsay** features artwork from the years 1848 to 1914. Paintings from such well-known artists as Claude Monet, Vincent Van Gogh, Pierre Auguste Renoir, Édouard Manet, Edgar Degas and Henri de Toulouse-Lautrec hang in this airy museum. The **musée Rodin** and its gardens contain some of the most famous pieces sculpted by Auguste Rodin, such as *The Thinker*, *The Burghers of Calais* and *The Gates of Hell*.

The tomb of Napoléon is located in the **hôtel des Invalides**, a former military hospital and now a military museum. Napoléon's remains are contained within six coffins, one inside the other.

Built by Gustave Eiffel for the World's Fair of 1889, the **tour Eiffel** is the symbol of Paris. Tourists take an elevator to the observation deck on the third level of the tower for a spectacular view of the city, or they may stop at the scenic restaurants on the first and second levels. For many years the tallest

Le musée d'Orsay opened in 1986 and quickly became one of Paris' most popular attractions.

structure in the world, the Eiffel Tower was originally scorned by many artists and writers who were offended by its geometric structure. Nevertheless, **la Grande Dame de Paris** has been used for a variety of purposes over the years, serving as a military observation station during World War I, a meteorological post, and a radio and television transmitting station. With new lights illuminating the tower from within, the Eiffel Tower sparkles in the night sky, reminding people that Paris is **la Ville lumière**.

An ancient yet beautiful and dynamic city, the Paris of today, including its suburbs, has over 10 million people and is the intellectual, economic, cultural and political center of France. As the German writer Goethe said, **Paris est la capitale du monde**.

The *tour Eiffel*, the tallest monument in Paris at 985 feet, is the symbol of the city.

10 ▸ Paris

Répondez aux questions.

1. What Gallic tribe settled on the **île de la Cité**?
2. Why is the **île de la Cité** called the "cradle" of Paris?
3. What is the name of the smaller of the two islands in the Seine?
4. What are two characteristics of Gothic architecture?
5. Why were biblical stories told in the stained glass windows of churches?
6. Where was Queen Marie-Antoinette imprisoned?
7. What is the oldest bridge in Paris?
8. Why did Napoléon have the **arc de triomphe** built?
9. Where were many people guillotined during the French Revolution?
10. What are two famous works of art in the **Louvre**?
11. Why do crowds gather outside the contemporary **Centre Pompidou**?
12. What are the names of two artists whose paintings are displayed at the **musée d'Orsay**?
13. Where is Napoléon's tomb?
14. Which monument is considered to be the symbol of Paris?
15. What did Ernest Hemingway mean when he said ". . . Paris is a moveable feast"?

11 ▸ Le métro

Regardez le plan de métro à la page 449 et répondez aux questions.

1. What station is at the opposite end of the line from Porte d'Orléans (on the Left Bank)?
2. How many **métro** lines serve Pasteur (on the Left Bank)?
3. Are there more or less than 15 stations on the line whose end points are Pont de Levallois-Bécon and Gallieni (line 3)?
4. The Voltaire station is on the Right Bank. What are the names of the stations at the end points of the line that passes through this station? What is the number of this line?
5. If you wanted to go from Concorde to Hôtel de Ville (both on the Right Bank), in what direction would you go? (Give the name of the station at the line's end point.)
6. If you were going from Rambuteau to Père-Lachaise (both on the Right Bank), in what direction would you go first? At what station would you transfer? In what direction would you finally go?
7. If you were going from Victor Hugo (on line 2 on the Right Bank) to Jacques Bonsergent (on line 5 on the Right Bank), in what direction would you go first? At what station would you transfer? In what direction would you finally go?

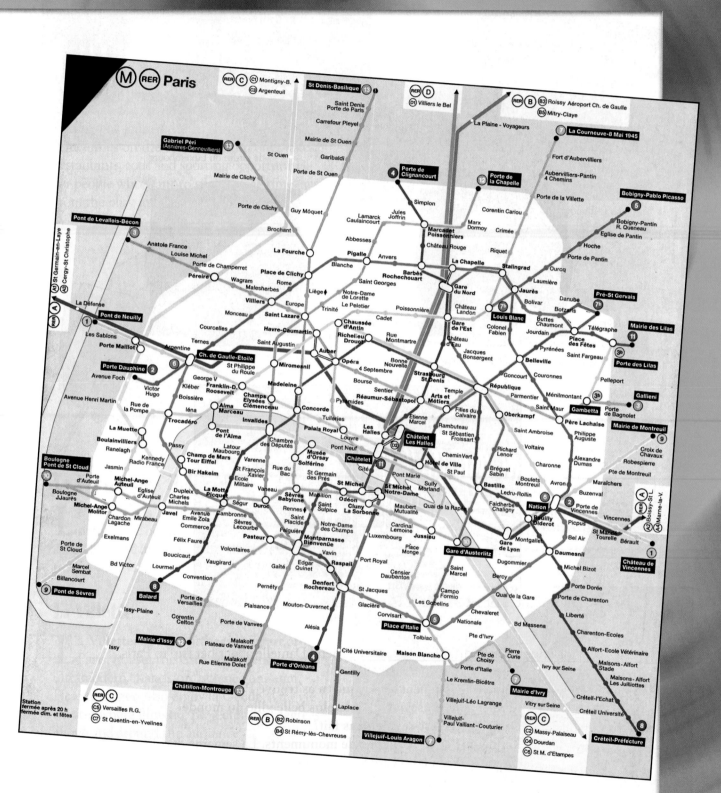

Dictionary Skills

If the reading skills that you have learned are not sufficient to help you understand a new word, you will need to use a French-English dictionary. The paragraph that follows is the beginning of a historical overview of the **Louvre**. After you read it, refer to the dictionary tips that will help you when you look up the three highlighted words.

> **XIIIᵉ siècle:**
> Le château royal du Louvre, fondé par Philippe-Auguste, est situé à Paris sur la rive droite de la Seine et **protège** la ville à l'ouest. La **grosse** tour centrale de cette forteresse **carrée** sert de prison, d'arsenal et de chambre au trésor.

Here are some tips on how to use a French-English dictionary:

1. *Before looking up a word, determine its part of speech (noun, verb, adjective, etc.).* The word's position in the sentence will help you. For example, **carrée** follows the noun meaning "fortress," so it must be an adjective. Look up **carrée** and read the definition for it as an adjective (it can also be a noun). It means "square."
2. *Look up verbs in their infinitive form.* Keep in mind that all French infinitives end in **-er**, **-ir** or **-re**. Which type of verb is **protège**? After mentally reviewing the endings of regular verbs, you can determine that this is an **-er** verb, making its infinitive **protéger**, which means "to protect."
3. *Realize that adjectives (and nouns) that have both masculine and feminine forms are listed in the dictionary in their masculine singular form.* Before you look up **grosse** in the dictionary, you must first determine its masculine singular form. Knowing that some feminine adjectives are formed by doubling the final consonant of a masculine adjective and adding an **e**, you can logically guess that the masculine form of **grosse** is **gros**.
4. *Be sure to check all the possible meanings of a word.* When you look up **gros** in the dictionary, you will find that it can mean "big," "large," "thick," "heavy" or "fat." Use the context of the sentence it appears in to figure out which meaning applies. Since **gros** modifies **la tour** ("tower"), it must mean "big" or "large."

Now read the rest of the historical description of the **Louvre**. Use cognates and context to figure out the meaning of words you don't know. Then answer the questions in Activity 10 to help you understand some other new words you encounter in the reading.

> **XIVᵉ siècle:**
> Charles V embellit le château et le transforme en demeure habitable.

> **XVIᵉ siècle:**
> François Iᵉʳ démolit la forteresse et commence le palais. Amateur d'art italien, il y installe ses tableaux préférés, *la Joconde* incluse. Pierre Lescot élève la partie sud-ouest de la Cour Carrée.

Fin du XVIe, début du XVIIe siècle:
Pour joindre le Louvre au Palais des Tuileries, la Petite Galerie et la Grande Galerie sont construites le long de la Seine.

XVIIe siècle:
Louis XIII et Louis XIV donnent à la Cour Carrée ses proportions actuelles. Claude Perrault est un des auteurs de la Colonade qui, à l'est, fait face à l'église Saint-Germain l'Auxerrois.

XVIIIe siècle:
Napoléon Ier achève la Cour Carrée et son décor. Il commence l'aile Richelieu qui longe la rue de Rivoli. Demeure des rois de France, siège des Académies, le Louvre devient musée pendant la Révolution en 1793.

XIXe siècle:
Napoléon III et ses architectes terminent les travaux à l'ouest. Les Tuileries brûlent en 1871 et l'unité de cet immense ensemble de palais est rompue.

XXe siècle:
Ieoh Ming Pei, architecte américain d'origine chinoise, construit une pyramide moderne de verre dans la cour du musée en 1989. Elle fonctionne comme entrée principale et librairie. En 1993 l'aile Richelieu est remise à neuf. Le Carrousel, centre commercial de luxe souterrain, est bâti.

Aujourd'hui:
Le musée devient un des plus riches du monde. Les collections justement célèbres ne font que croître.

le Louvre d'aujourd'hui

10 ▶ Le dictionnaire

Répondez aux questions.

1. Realizing that the word **embellit** is a verb form, what do you think its infinitive is?
2. The word **amateur** can mean either "amateur" or "lover (of something)." Which meaning applies here?
3. The word **élève** can function as a noun or as a verb. Which part of speech applies here?
4. The word **actuelles** is an adjective. What is its masculine singular form?
5. The word **ensemble** can function as an adverb or as a noun. Which part of speech applies here?
6. The word **neuf** can mean either "nine" or "new." Which meaning applies here?
7. The word **devient** looks similar to a verb form you have already learned. What is it? What do you think its infinitive is?
8. Choose three of the words you still don't understand from the list you made and answer the following questions about each word.
   A. What part of speech is the word?
   B. If it is a verb form, what is its infinitive?
   C. If it is an adjective, what is its masculine singular form?
   D. When you look it up in a French-English dictionary, how many different meanings does it have?
   E. Which meaning applies here?

Nathalie et Raoul

✓ Évaluation culturelle

Decide if each statement is **vrai** or **faux**.

1. *La Joconde*, the French name for Leonardo da Vinci's masterpiece, can be found in the **musée d'Orsay** in Paris.
2. The **R.E.R.**, an expansion of the Paris **métro** system, serves the suburbs with fewer stops in the center of the city.
3. France and the United States both have their national holiday on July 4.
4. The French celebrate Bastille Day with a military parade, fireworks and street dances.
5. **Notre-Dame**, the **Sainte-Chapelle** and the **Conciergerie** are all located on the **île de la Cité** in the Seine River.
6. Napoléon's **arc de triomphe** is the site where he had over one thousand people guillotined during the French Revolution.
7. The **Centre Pompidou** has a modern, functional style of architecture with its pipes, ducts, pillars and stairways on the outside of the building.
8. To view the paintings by such great French artists as Monet, Renoir and Toulouse Lautrec, visit the **Louvre**.
9. The **tour Eiffel** is best known because both the Tomb of the Unknown Soldier and the tomb of Jim Morrison lie underneath it.
10. Modern **quartiers** of Paris include **la Défense**, **la Villette** and **le Forum des Halles**.

A street performer prepares to entertain the crowd in front of the *Centre Pompidou*. (Paris)

✓ Évaluation orale

Imagine that you and your partner returned from separate one-week trips to Paris. One partner was part of a group of tourists specifically interested in seeing the sites; the other visited a former French exchange student and stayed with the student's family. First greet each other. Then ask and tell each other how you liked Paris. Next ask and tell when you arrived in Paris. Finally, ask and tell where you went and what you saw and did. Finish your conversation by asking and telling each other when you returned home.

✓ Évaluation écrite

Based on the previous activity, write a composition that describes the similarities and differences between your trip and your partner's trip to Paris. To organize your composition, make intersecting circles. In the first circle list only the things that you did and saw; in the second circle list only the things that your partner did and saw; in the section where the circles intersect list the things that both of you did and saw.

Moi — Mon ami(e) et moi — Mon ami(e)

✓ Évaluation visuelle

Imagine that you're visiting Paris for the first time. Use the four pictured highlights of your trip to write an entry in your journal about where you went, what you saw and what you did today. Also give your opinion on what you've just seen or done. (You may want to refer to the *Révision de fonctions* on pages 461-62 and the *Vocabulaire* on page 463.)

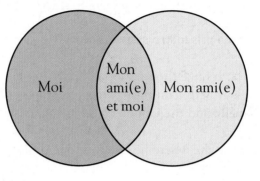

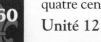

Révision de fonctions

Can you do all of the following tasks in French?

- I can write a journal entry.
- I can talk about what happened in the past.
- I can talk about things sequentially.
- I can say what needs to be done.
- I can ask for information.
- I can give my opinion by saying what I think.
- I can make comparisons by saying who or what has the most of a certain quality.

Le cimetière du Père-Lachaise est le plus grand cimetière de Paris.

To write journal entries, use:

le 5 juillet	*July 5*

To describe past events, use:

J'ai regardé de beaux tableaux.	*I looked at some beautiful paintings.*
J'ai fini la journée en bateau sur la Seine.	*I finished the day on a boat on the Seine.*
J'ai perdu mon plan de métro.	*I lost my subway map.*
J'ai vu le Centre Pompidou.	*I saw the **Centre Pompidou**.*
J'ai pris un café sur la place.	*I had coffee on the square.*
Il y a eu un bal dans la rue.	*There was a street dance.*
J'ai été obligé(e) de rentrer.	*I had to (was obliged to) come back.*
On a fait beaucoup de bruit.	*People made a lot of noise.*
Je suis monté(e) au cinquième étage.	*I went up to the fifth floor.*

Tu as vu le Louvre? (Paris)

To sequence events, use:

D'abord, j'ai marché sur l'avenue des Champs-Élysées.	*First I walked on the **Champs-Élysées**.*
Puis, j'ai continué mon chemin jusqu'au Louvre.	*Then I continued on my way (up) to the **Louvre**.*

Alors, je suis allée au guichet du métro.
Mardi matin je suis allé(e) à la Défense.
Mercredi j'ai regardé le défilé.
Le soir j'ai vu un beau feu d'artifice.
La semaine dernière j'ai aussi visité le
jardin du Luxembourg.

To express need and necessity, use:

J'ai été obligé(e) de prendre un taxi à l'hôtel.

Then I went to the subway ticket window.
*Tuesday morning I went to **la Défense**.*
Wednesday I watched the parade.
In the evening I saw some beautiful fireworks.
Last week I also visited the Luxembourg Gardens.

I had to (was obliged to) take a taxi to the hotel.

Robert et Fred ont été obligés de regarder
un plan de métro. (Paris)

To ask for information, use:

Comment est-ce que tu as trouvé Paris?

To give opinions, use:

Je pense que c'est la plus belle ville du monde.

To compare things, use:

Le Louvre est **le plus grand** musée de Paris.

How did you like Paris?

I think that it's the most beautiful city in the world.

*The **Louvre** is the largest museum in Paris.*

Nathalie et Raoul

Vocabulaire

amoureux, amoureuse in love *A*
un **arc** arch *A*
une **arche** arch *B*
au moins at least *A*

un **bal** dance *B*
un **bateau** boat *A*
un **billet** ticket *A*
un **bruit** noise *B*

un **centre** center *B*
chargé(e) full *B*
un **chemin** path, way *A*
un **cimetière** cemetery *A*
continuer to continue *A*

d'après according to *A*
de (d') by *A*; in *C*
décider (de) to decide *A*
un **défilé** parade *B*
demander to ask for *A*
dernier, dernière last *C*
du in (the) *B*

fermer to close *B*
une **fête** holiday, festival *B*
un **feu d'artifice** fireworks *B*
une **fois** time *A*

un **guichet** ticket window *A*

un **hôtel** hotel *A*

imaginer to imagine *A*
impressionniste Impressionist *B*

un **jardin** park *A*
jeune young *A*
une **journée** day *A*
jusqu'à up to, until *A*

la **liberté** liberty *A*
une **lumière** light *A*

marcher to walk *A*
un **métro** subway *A*
moderne modern *B*

moins: au moins at least *A*
le **monde** world *C*
monter to go up *B*
un **monument** monument *A*
un **musicien, une musicienne** musician *B*

national(e) national *B*

obligé(e): être obligé(e) de to be obliged to, to have to *B*

le **paradis** paradise *A*
passer to spend (time) *B*
penser (à) to think (of) *C*
perdre to lose *A*
un **plan** map *A*
plus: le/la/les plus (+ *adjective*) the most (+ adjective) *C*

un **quartier** quarter, neighborhood *C*
quitter to leave (a person or place) *A*

une **rue** street *B*

seulement only *A*
une **station** station *A*
une **statue** statue *A*

un **tableau** painting *A*
un **taxi** taxi *B*
un **tombeau** tomb *A*
une **tour** tower *A*
un **triomphe** triumph *A*

visiter to visit (a place) *B*
vivre to live *A*
vraiment really *A*

Grammar Summary

Subject Pronouns

Singular	Plural
je	nous
tu	vous
il/elle/on	ils/elles

Indefinite Articles

Singular		Plural
Masculine	Feminine	
un	une	des

Definite Articles

Singular			Plural
Before a Consonant Sound		Before a Vowel Sound	
Masculine	Feminine		
le	la	l'	les

À + Definite Articles

Singular			Plural
Before a Consonant Sound		Before a Vowel Sound	
Masculine	Feminine		
au	à la	à l'	aux

De + Definite Articles

Singular			Plural
Before a Consonant Sound		Before a Vowel Sound	
Masculine	Feminine		
du	de la	de l'	des

Partitive Articles

Before a Consonant Sound		Before a Vowel Sound
Masculine	Feminine	
du pain	**de la** glace	**de l'**eau

In negative sentences the partitive article becomes *de (d')*.

Expressions of Quantity

combien	how much, how many
assez	enough
beaucoup	a lot, many
(un) peu	(a) little, few
trop	too much, too many

These expressions are followed by *de (d')* before a noun.

Question Words

combien	how much, how many
comment	what, how
où	where
pourquoi	why
qu'est-ce que	what
quand	when
quel, quelle	what, which
qui	who, whom

Question Formation

1. By a rising tone of voice
   Vous travaillez beaucoup?
2. By beginning with *est-ce que*
   Est-ce que vous travaillez beaucoup?
3. By adding *n'est-ce pas?*
   Vous travaillez beaucoup, n'est-ce pas?
4. By inversion
   Travaillez-vous beaucoup?

Possessive Adjectives

Singular			Plural
Masculine	**Feminine before a Consonant Sound**	**Feminine before a Vowel Sound**	
mon	ma	mon	mes
ton	ta	ton	tes
son	sa	son	ses
notre	notre	notre	nos
votre	votre	votre	vos
leur	leur	leur	leurs

Demonstrative Adjectives

	Masculine before a Consonant Sound	**Masculine before a Vowel Sound**	**Feminine**
Singular	ce	cet	cette
Plural	ces	ces	ces

Quel

	Masculine	Feminine
Singular	quel	quelle
Plural	quels	quelles

Agreement of Adjectives

	Masculine	Feminine
add **e**	Il est bavard.	Elle est bavarde.
no change	Il est suisse.	Elle est suisse.
change **-er** to **-ère**	Il est cher.	Elle est chère.
change **-eux** to **-euse**	Il est paresseux.	Elle est paresseuse.
double consonant + **e**	Il est gros.	Elle est grosse.

Irregular Feminine Adjectives

Masculine before a Consonant Sound	Masculine before a Vowel Sound	Feminine
blanc		blanche
frais		fraîche
long		longue
beau	bel	belle
nouveau	nouvel	nouvelle
vieux	vieil	vieille

Position of Adjectives

Most adjectives usually follow their nouns. But adjectives expressing beauty, age, goodness and size precede their nouns. Some of these preceding adjectives are:

autre	joli
beau	mauvais
bon	nouveau
grand	petit
gros	vieux
jeune	

Comparative of Adjectives

plus	+	adjective	+	**que**
moins	+	adjective	+	**que**
aussi	+	adjective	+	**que**

Superlative of Adjectives

le/la/les	+	**plus**	+	adjective

Regular Verbs—Present Tense

-er parler			
je	parle	nous	parlons
tu	parles	vous	parlez
il/elle/on	parle	ils/elles	parlent

-ir finir			
je	finis	nous	finissons
tu	finis	vous	finissez
il/elle/on	finit	ils/elles	finissent

-re perdre			
je	perds	nous	perdons
tu	perds	vous	perdez
il/elle/on	perd	ils/elles	perdent

Irregular Verbs

acheter			
j'	achète	nous	achetons
tu	achètes	vous	achetez
il/elle/on	achète	ils/elles	achètent

aller			
je	vais	nous	allons
tu	vas	vous	allez
il/elle/on	va	ils/elles	vont

avoir			
j'	ai	nous	avons
tu	as	vous	avez
il/elle/on	a	ils/elles	ont

devoir			
je	dois	nous	devons
tu	dois	vous	devez
il/elle/on	doit	ils/elles	doivent

être			
je	suis	nous	sommes
tu	es	vous	êtes
il/elle/on	est	ils/elles	sont

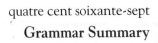

faire

je	fais		nous	faisons
tu	fais		vous	faites
il/elle/on	fait		ils/elles	font

falloir

il	faut

mettre

je	mets		nous	mettons
tu	mets		vous	mettez
il/elle/on	met		ils/elles	mettent

pleuvoir

il	pleut

pouvoir

je	peux		nous	pouvons
tu	peux		vous	pouvez
il/elle/on	peut		ils/elles	peuvent

préférer

je	préfère		nous	préférons
tu	préfères		vous	préférez
il/elle/on	préfère		ils/elles	préfèrent

prendre

je	prends		nous	prenons
tu	prends		vous	prenez
il/elle/on	prend		ils/elles	prennent

venir

je	viens		nous	venons
tu	viens		vous	venez
il/elle/on	vient		ils/elles	viennent

voir

je	vois		nous	voyons
tu	vois		vous	voyez
il/elle/on	voit		ils/elles	voient

vouloir			
je	veux	nous	voulons
tu	veux	vous	voulez
il/elle/on	veut	ils/elles	veulent

Regular Imperatives

-er parler	-ir finir	-re perdre
parle	finis	perds
parlez	finissez	perdez
parlons	finissons	perdons

Verbs + Infinitive

adorer	devoir	regarder
aimer	falloir	venir
aller	pouvoir	vouloir
désirer	préférer	

Negation in Present Tense

ne... jamais	Je **ne** vois **jamais** Hélène.
ne... pas	Vous **ne** mangez **pas**.
ne... personne	Il **n'y** a **personne** ici.
ne... plus	Tu **ne** fais **plus** de footing?
ne... rien	Nous **ne** faisons **rien**.

Numbers

0 = zéro	14 = quatorze	42 = quarante-deux	91 = quatre-vingt-onze
1 = un	15 = quinze	50 = cinquante	92 = quatre-vingt-douze
2 = deux	16 = seize	51 = cinquante et un	100 = cent
3 = trois	17 = dix-sept	52 = cinquante-deux	101 = cent un
4 = quatre	18 = dix-huit	60 = soixante	102 = cent deux
5 = cinq	19 = dix-neuf	61 = soixante et un	200 = deux cents
6 = six	20 = vingt	62 = soixante-deux	201 = deux cent un
7 = sept	21 = vingt et un	70 = soixante-dix	1.000 = mille
8 = huit	22 = vingt-deux	71 = soixante et onze	1.001 = mille un
9 = neuf	30 = trente	72 = soixante-douze	2.000 = deux mille
10 = dix	31 = trente et un	80 = quatre-vingts	1.000.000 = un million
11 = onze	32 = trente-deux	81 = quatre-vingt-un	2.000.000 = deux millions
12 = douze	40 = quarante	82 = quatre-vingt-deux	
13 = treize	41 = quarante et un	90 = quatre-vingt-dix	

Ordinal Numbers

1er = premier		6e = sixième	
2e = deuxième		7e = septième	
3e = troisième		8e = huitième	
4e = quatrième		9e = neuvième	
5e = cinquième		10e = dixième	

Passé Composé—Regular Past Participles

jouer			
j'ai	joué	nous avons	joué
tu	as joué	vous avez	joué
il/elle/on a	joué	ils/elles ont	joué

finir			
j'ai	fini	nous avons	fini
tu as	fini	vous avez	fini
il/elle/on a	fini	ils/elles ont	fini

attendre			
j'ai	attendu	nous avons	attendu
tu as	attendu	vous avez	attendu
il/elle/on a	attendu	ils/elles ont	attendu

Passé Composé—Irregular Past Participles

Infinitive	Past Participle
avoir	eu
être	été
faire	fait
prendre	pris
voir	vu

Passé Composé with **Être**

aller		
je	suis	allé
je	suis	allée
tu	es	allé
tu	es	allée
il	est	allé
elle	est	allée
on	est	allé
nous	sommes	allés
nous	sommes	allées
vous	êtes	allé
vous	êtes	allés
vous	êtes	allée
vous	êtes	allées
ils	sont	allés
elles	sont	allées

Some of the verbs that use *être* as the helping verb in the *passé composé* are:

Infinitive	Past Participle
aller	allé
arriver	arrivé
entrer	entré
partir	parti
rentrer	rentré
rester	resté
sortir	sorti
venir	venu

Vocabulaire

French/English

All words and expressions introduced as active vocabulary in *C'est à toi!* appear in this end vocabulary. The number following the meaning of each word or expression indicates the unit in which it appears for the first time. If there is more than one meaning for a word or expression and it has appeared in different units, the corresponding unit numbers are listed.

A

à to 2; at 4; in 6; *À bientôt.* See you soon. 1; *À demain.* See you tomorrow. 2; *à droite* to (on) the right 9; *à gauche* to (on) the left 9; *À tes souhaits!* Bless you! 10

acheter to buy 7

adorer to love 7

un **aéroport** airport 11

une **affiche** poster 4

l' **Afrique (f.)** Africa 11

l' **âge (m.)** age 5; *Tu as quel âge?* How old are you? 5

un **agent de police** police officer 6

ah oh 1

aimer to like, to love 2

l' **Algérie (f.)** Algeria 11

algérien, algérienne Algerian 11

l' **Allemagne (f.)** Germany 6

l' **allemand (m.)** German (language) 4

allemand(e) German 6

aller to go 2; *allons-y* let's go (there) 3

allô hello (on telephone) 1

alors (well) then 2

américain(e) American 6

un(e) **ami(e)** friend 6

amoureux, amoureuse in love 12

un **an** year 5; *J'ai... ans.* I'm ... years old. 5

l' **anglais (m.)** English (language) 4

anglais(e) English 6

l' **Angleterre (f.)** England 6

un **anniversaire** birthday 5

un **anorak** ski jacket 7

août August 5

un **appartement** apartment 9

après after 6

l' **après-midi (m.)** afternoon 10

un **arbre** tree 9

un **arc** arch 12

une **arche** arch 12

l' **argent (m.)** money 11

une **armoire** wardrobe 9

arriver to arrive 1

assez rather, quite 7; *assez de* enough 8

une **assiette** plate 9

attendre to wait (for) 8

au to (the), at (the) 2; in (the) 6; *au moins* at least 12; *au revoir* good-bye 1; *Au secours!* Help! 10; *au-dessus de* above 9

aujourd'hui today 6

aussi also, too 2; as 8

aussitôt que as soon as 10

l' **automne (m.)** autumn, fall 6

autre other 6; *un(e) autre* another 6

aux to (the), at (the), in (the) 7

avec with 4

une **avenue** avenue 11

un **avion** airplane 11

un(e) **avocat(e)** lawyer 6

avoir to have 4; *avoir besoin de* to need 4; *avoir bonne/mauvaise mine* to look well/sick 10; *avoir chaud* to be warm, hot 10; *avoir envie de* to want, to feel like 11; *avoir faim* to be hungry 4; *avoir froid* to be cold 10; *avoir mal (à...)* to hurt, to have a/an . . . ache, to have a sore . . . 10; *avoir mal au cœur* to feel nauseous 10; *avoir peur (de)* to be afraid (of) 10; *avoir quel âge* to be how old 5; *avoir soif* to be thirsty 4; *avoir... ans* to be . . . (years old) 5

avril April 5

B

une **baguette** long, thin loaf of bread 8

une **baignoire** bathtub 9

un **bain: une salle de bains** bathroom 9

baisser to lower 10

un **bal** dance 12

un **balcon** balcony 9

une **banane** banana 8

une **banque** bank 11

des **bas (m.)** (panty) hose 7

le **basket (basketball)** basketball 2

des **baskets (f.)** hightops 7

un **bateau** boat 12

un **bâton** ski pole 10

bavard(e) talkative 5

beau, bel, belle beautiful, handsome 5

beaucoup a lot, (very) much 2; *beaucoup de* a lot of, many 8

un **beau-frère** stepbrother, brother-in-law 5

un **beau-père** stepfather, father-in-law 5

beige beige 7

belge Belgian 11

la **Belgique** Belgium 11

une **belle-mère** stepmother, mother-in-law 5

une **belle-sœur** stepsister, sister-in-law 5

ben: bon ben well then 2

le **besoin: avoir besoin de** to need 4

bête stupid, dumb 5

Beurk! Yuk! 7

le **beurre** butter 8

une **bibliothèque** library 11

bien well 1; really 2; *bien sûr* of course 9

Bienvenue! Welcome! 9

un **billet** ticket 12

la **biologie** biology 4

une **bise** kiss 11

blanc, blanche white 7

bleu(e) blue 5

blond(e) blond 5

un **blouson** jacket (outdoor) 7

le **bœuf** beef 8

une **boisson** drink, beverage 3

une **boîte** dance club 2; can 8

un **bol** bowl 9

bon, bonne good 2; *bon ben* well then 2; *bon marché* cheap 7

bonjour hello 1

bonsoir good evening 9

une **botte** boot 7

une **bouche** mouth 10

une **boucherie** butcher shop 8

une **bouillabaisse** fish soup 8

une **boulangerie** bakery 8

une **boum** party 7

une **bouteille** bottle 8

une **boutique** shop, boutique 7

un **bras** arm 10

un **bruit** noise 12

brun(e) dark (hair), brown 5

un **bureau** desk 4

C

c'est this is, it's 1; he is, she is 5; that's 6

ça that, it 3; *Ça fait....* That's/It's . . . . 3; *Ça fait combien?* How much is it/that? 3; *Ça va?* How are things going? 1; *Ça va bien.* Things are going well. 1

un **cabinet** (doctor or dentist's) office 10

un **cadeau** gift, present 5

un **café** café; coffee 3

un **cahier** notebook 4

un **calendrier** calendar 4

le **camembert** Camembert cheese 8

le **camping** camping 2

un **camping** campground 11

le **Canada** Canada 6

canadien, canadienne Canadian 6

un **canapé** couch, sofa 9

une **cantine** cafeteria 4

une **carotte** carrot 8

une **carte** map 4

un **CD** CD 4

ce, cet, cette; ces this, that; these, those 8

ce sont they are, these are, those are 5

cent (one) hundred 3

un **centre** center 12; *un centre commercial* shopping center, mall 7

une **cerise** cherry 8

une **chaise** chair 4

une **chambre** bedroom 9

un **champignon** mushroom 8

la **chance** luck 6

un **chapeau** hat 7

une **charcuterie** delicatessen 8

chargé(e) full 12

un **chat** cat 5

chaud(e) warm, hot 6; *avoir chaud* to be warm, hot 10

une **chaussette** sock 7

une **chaussure** shoe 7

un **chemin** path, way 12

une **chemise** shirt 7

un **chèque de voyage** traveler's check 11

cher, chère expensive 7; dear 11

chercher to look for 7

un **cheval** horse 5

des **cheveux (m.)** hair 5

chez to the house/home of 2; at the house/home of 11; *chez moi* to my house 2

un **chien** dog 5

la **chimie** chemistry 4

la **Chine** China 6

chinois(e) Chinese 6

des **chips (m.)** snacks 9

le **chocolat** chocolate 3

une **chose** thing 7; *quelque chose* something 7

ciao bye 1

un **cimetière** cemetery 12

le **cinéma** movies 2

cinq five 1

cinquante fifty 3

cinquième fifth 11

un **coca** Coke 3

un **cœur** heart 10; *avoir mal au cœur* to feel nauseous 10

un **coiffeur, une coiffeuse** hairdresser 6

combien how much 3; *combien de* how much, how many 8

comme like, for 3; *comme ci, comme ça* so-so 3

commencer to begin 4

comment what 1; how 3; *Comment vas-tu?* How are you? 3

un(e) **comptable** accountant 6

la **confiture** jam 8

congolais(e) Congolese 11

continuer to continue 12

une **corbeille** wastebasket 4

un **corps** body 10

un **costume** man's suit 7

la **Côte-d'Ivoire** Ivory Coast 11

un **cou** neck 10

une **couleur** color 7

un **cours** course, class 4

les **courses: faire les courses** to go grocery shopping 8

court(e) short 7

le **couscous** couscous 9

un(e) **cousin(e)** cousin 5

un **couteau** knife 9

coûter to cost 3

un **couvert** table setting 9

un **crabe** crab 8

un crayon pencil 4
une crémerie dairy store 8
une crêpe crêpe 3
une crevette shrimp 8
un croissant croissant 8
une cuiller spoon 9
une cuisine kitchen 9
un cuisinier, une cuisinière
cook 6
une cuisinière stove 9

D

d'abord first 8
d'accord OK 1
d'après according to 12
dans in 4
danser to dance 2
une date date 5
de (d') of, from 4; a, an,
any 6; some 9; in, by 12
décembre December 5
décider (de) to decide 12
un défilé parade 12
déjà already 3
le déjeuner lunch 9; le petit
déjeuner breakfast 9
demain tomorrow 2
demander to ask for 12
demi(e) half 4; et demi(e)
thirty (minutes), half past 4
un demi-frère half-brother 5
une demi-sœur half-sister 5
une dent tooth 10
un(e) dentiste dentist 6
dernier, dernière last 12
derrière behind 4
des some 3; from (the), of
(the) 6; any 8
désirer to want 3; Vous
désirez? What would you
like? 3
un dessert dessert 3
le dessin drawing 4
dessus: au-dessus de above 9
deux two 1
deuxième second 11
devant in front of 4
devoir to have to 10
les devoirs (m.) homework 2
un dictionnaire dictionary 4

diligent(e) hardworking 5
dimanche (m.) Sunday 4
le dîner dinner, supper 9
dis say 2
une disquette diskette 4
dix ten 1
dix-huit eighteen 1
dixième tenth 11
dix-neuf nineteen 1
dix-sept seventeen 1
un docteur doctor 10
un doigt finger 10; un doigt de
pied toe 10
un dollar dollar 7
donc so, then 9
donner to give 3; Donnez-
moi.... Give me 3
dormir to sleep 2
un dos back 10
une douche shower 9
douze twelve 1
la droite: à droite to (on) the
right 9
du from (the), of (the) 6;
some, any 8; in (the) 12
un DVD DVD 4

E

l' eau (f.) water 3; l'eau minérale
(f.) mineral water 3
une école school 4
écoute listen 1
écouter to listen (to) 2;
écouter de la musique to
listen to music 2
une église church 11
égoïste selfish 5
Eh! Hey! 1
un(e) élève student 4
elle she, it 2
elles they (f.) 2
un emploi du temps schedule 4
en to (the) 2; on 5; in 6; en
solde on sale 7
enchanté(e) delighted 9
encore still 9
un(e) enfant child 5
ensemble together 4
un ensemble outfit 7
une entrée entrance 9

entrer to enter, to come in 9
l' envie (f.): avoir envie de to
want, to feel like 11
une épaule shoulder 10
un escalier stairs, staircase 9
l' Espagne (f.) Spain 6
l' espagnol (m.) Spanish
(language) 4
espagnol(e) Spanish 6
est is 3
l' est (m.) east 11
est-ce que? (phrase
introducing a question) 6
et and 2
un étage floor, story 9
les États-Unis (m.) United
States 6
l' été (m.) summer 6
être to be 5; Nous sommes le
(+ date). It's the (+ date). 5
un(e) étudiant(e) student 4
étudier to study 2; Étudions....
Let's study 4
euh uhm 8
un euro euro 3
l' Europe (f.) Europe 11
un évier sink 9
excusez-moi excuse me 7

F

facile easy 10
la faim: J'ai faim. I'm hungry. 3
faire to do, to make 2; faire du
(+ number) to wear size (+
number) 7; faire du footing to
go running 2; faire du roller
to go in-line skating 2; faire
du shopping to go shopping 2;
faire du sport to play sports 2;
faire du vélo to go biking 2;
faire le tour to take a tour 9;
faire les courses to go grocery
shopping 8; faire les devoirs
to do homework 2; faire les
magasins to go shopping 7;
faire un tour to go for a ride 6
fait: Ça fait.... That's/It's 3;
Quel temps fait-il? What's
the weather like? How's the
weather? 6; Il fait beau. It's
(The weather's) beautiful/
nice. 6; Il fait chaud. It's
(The weather's) hot/warm. 6;

Il fait du soleil. It's sunny. 6;
Il fait du vent. It's windy. 6;
Il fait frais. It's (The weather's) cool. 6; *Il fait froid.* It's (The weather's) cold. 6; *Il fait mauvais.* It's (The weather's) bad. 6

falloir to be necessary, to have to 10

une **famille** family 5

un **fast-food** fast-food restaurant 3

fatigué(e) tired 10

faut: il faut it is necessary, one has to/must, we/you have to/must 10

un **fauteuil** armchair 9

une **femme** wife; woman 5; *une femme au foyer* housewife 6; *une femme d'affaires* businesswoman 6

une **fenêtre** window 4

fermer to close 12

un **fermier, une fermière** farmer 6

une **fête** holiday, festival 12

un **feu d'artifice** fireworks 12

une **feuille de papier** sheet of paper 4

février February 5

la **fièvre** fever 10

une **figure** face 10

une **fille** girl 4; daughter 5

un **film** movie 2

un **fils** son 5

finir to finish 4

une **fleur** flower 9

une **fois** time 12

le **foot (football)** soccer 2

le **footing** running 2

une **forme: être en bonne/ mauvaise forme** to be in good/bad shape 10

formidable great, terrific 11

un **four** oven 9

une **fourchette** fork 9

frais, fraîche cool, fresh 6

une **fraise** strawberry 8

le **français** French (language) 4

français(e) French 6

la **France** France 6

un **frère** brother 5

un **frigo** refrigerator 9

des **frissons (m.)** chills 10

des **frites (f.)** French fries 3

froid(e) cold 6; *avoir froid* to be cold 10

le **fromage** cheese 3

un **fruit** fruit 8

G

un **garage** garage 9

un **garçon** boy 4

garder to keep 10

une **gare** train station 11

un **gâteau** cake 8

la **gauche: à gauche** to (on) the left 9

généreux, généreuse generous 5

un **genou** knee 10

gentil, gentille nice 9

la **géographie** geography 4

une **glace** ice cream 3; *une glace à la vanille* vanilla ice cream 3; *une glace au chocolat* chocolate ice cream 3

une **gorge** throat 10

le **goûter** afternoon snack 9

grand(e) tall, big, large 7

une **grand-mère** grandmother 5

un **grand-père** grandfather 5

un **grenier** attic 9

la **grippe** flu 10

gris(e) gray 5

gros, grosse big, fat, large 11

la **Guadeloupe** Guadeloupe 5

un **guichet** ticket window 12

H

habiter to live 9

un **hamburger** hamburger 3

des **haricots verts (m.)** green beans 8

l' **heure (f.)** hour, time, o'clock 3; *Quelle heure est-il?* What time is it? 3

hier yesterday 11

l' **histoire (f.)** history 4

l' **hiver (m.)** winter 6

un **homme** man 6; *un homme au foyer* househusband 6; *un homme d'affaires* businessman 6

un **horaire** schedule, timetable 11

un **hot-dog** hot dog 3

un **hôtel** hotel 12

huit eight 1

huitième eighth 11

I

ici here 6

il he, it 2

il y a there is, there are 7

ils they (m.) 2

imaginer to imagine 12

un **immeuble** apartment building 9

impressionniste Impressionist 12

un **infirmier, une infirmière** nurse 6

un **informaticien, une informaticienne** computer specialist 6

l' **informatique (f.)** computer science 4

un **ingénieur** engineer 6

intelligent(e) intelligent 5

une **interro (interrogation)** quiz, test 2

inviter to invite 2

l' **Italie (f.)** Italy 6

italien, italienne Italian 6

ivoirien, ivoirienne from the Ivory Coast 11

J

j' I 1

jamais: ne (n')... jamais never 10

une **jambe** leg 10

le **jambon** ham 3

janvier January 5

le **Japon** Japan 6

japonais(e) Japanese 6

un **jardin** garden, lawn 9; park 12

jaune yellow 7

le **jazz** jazz 2

je I 1

un **jean** (pair of) jeans 7

jeudi (m.) Thursday 4

jeune young 12

des **jeux vidéo (m.)** video games 2

joli(e) pretty 7

jouer to play 2; *jouer au basket*

to play basketball 2; *jouer au foot* to play soccer 2; *jouer au tennis* to play tennis 2; *jouer au volley* to play volleyball 2; *jouer aux jeux vidéo* to play video games 2

un **jour** day 4

un(e) **journaliste** journalist 6

une **journée** day 12

juillet July 5

juin June 5

une **jupe** skirt 7

le **jus d'orange** orange juice 3; *le jus de fruit* fruit juice 9; *le jus de pomme* apple juice 3; *le jus de raisin* grape juice 3

jusqu'à up to, until 12

juste just, only 4

K

le **ketchup** ketchup 8

un **kilogramme (kilo)** kilogram 8

un **kilomètre** kilometer 5

L

là there, here 4

là-bas over there 7

le **lait** milk 8

une **lampe** lamp 9

le **latin** Latin (language) 4

le, la, l' the 2; *le* (+ **day of the week**) on (+ day of the week) 4; *le* (+ **number**) on the (+ ordinal number) 1

un **lecteur de DVD** DVD player 4

un **légume** vegetable 8

les the 2

leur their 5

la **liberté** liberty 12

une **librairie** bookstore 11

une **limonade** lemon-lime soda 3

lire to read 2

un **lit** bed 9

un **livre** book 4

loin far 11

long, longue long 7

une **lumière** light 12

lundi (m.) Monday 4

le **Luxembourg** Luxembourg 11

luxembourgeois(e) from Luxembourg 11

M

m'appelle: je m'appelle my name is 1

Madame (Mme) Mrs., Ma'am 1

Mademoiselle (Mlle) Miss 1

un **magasin** store 7; *un grand magasin* department store 7

mai May 5

un **maillot de bain** swimsuit 7

une **main** hand 10

maintenant now 8

une **mairie** town hall 11

mais but 2

une **maison** house 9

mal bad, badly 3; *avoir mal (à...)* to hurt, to have a/an ... ache, to have a sore ... 10

malade sick 10

maman (f.) Mom 8

manger to eat 2; *manger de la pizza* to eat pizza 2; *une salle à manger* dining room 9

un **manteau** coat 7

un(e) **marchand(e)** merchant 8

un **marché** market 8

marcher to walk 12

mardi (m.) Tuesday 4

un **mari** husband 5

le **Maroc** Morocco 11

marocain(e) Moroccan 11

marre: J'en ai marre! I'm sick of it! I've had it! 4

marron brown 7

mars March 5

la **Martinique** Martinique 5

les **maths (f.)** math 4

un **matin** morning 8; *le matin* in the morning 8

mauvais(e) bad 6

la **mayonnaise** mayonnaise 8

me (to) me 11

méchant(e) mean 5

un **médecin** doctor 6

un **melon** melon 8

un **membre** member 5

même even 9

une **mer** sea 11

merci thanks 1

mercredi (m.) Wednesday 4

une **mère** mother 5

Messieurs-Dames ladies and gentlemen 3

un **métro** subway 12

mettre to put (on), to set 9

mexicain(e) Mexican 6

le **Mexique** Mexico 6

un **micro-onde** microwave 9

midi noon 3

mille (one) thousand 4

un **million** million 5

la **mine: avoir bonne/mauvaise mine** to look well/sick 10

minuit midnight 3

une **minute** minute 4

moche ugly 7

moderne modern 12

moi me, I 2

moins minus 4; less 8; *au moins* at least 12; *moins le quart* quarter to 4

un **mois** month 5

mon, ma; mes my 5

le **monde** world 12

Monsieur Mr., Sir 1

monter to go up 12

montrer to show 4; *Montrez-moi....* Show me 4

un **monument** monument 12

un **morceau** piece 8

la **moutarde** mustard 8

mûr(e) ripe 8

un **musée** museum 11

un **musicien, une musicienne** musician 12

la **musique** music 2

N

n'est-ce pas? isn't that so? 5

nager to swim 2

une **nappe** tablecloth 9

national(e) national 12

ne (n')... jamais never 10

ne (n')... pas not 2

ne (n')... personne no one, nobody, not anyone 10

ne (n')... plus no longer, not anymore 10

ne (n')... rien nothing, not anything 10

neiger: Il neige. It's snowing. 6

neuf nine 1

neuvième ninth 11

un **nez** nose 10

noir(e) black 5

non no 1

le **nord** north 11

notre; nos our 5

nous we 2; us 5

nouveau, nouvel, nouvelle new 7

novembre November 5

O

obligé(e): être obligé(e) de to be obliged to, to have to 12

octobre October 5

un **œil** eye 10

un **œuf** egg 8

oh oh 4; *Oh là là!* Wow! Oh no! Oh dear! 10

un **oignon** onion 8

un **oiseau** bird 5

OK OK 8

une **omelette** omelette 3

on they, we, one 2; *On y va?* Shall we go (there)? 2

un **oncle** uncle 5

onze eleven 1

orange orange 7

une **orange** orange 3

un **ordinateur** computer 4

une **oreille** ear 10

ou or 3

où where 4

ouais yeah 8

l' **ouest (m.)** west 11

oui yes 1

P

le **pain** bread 8

un **pantalon** (pair of) pants 7

par per 4

le **paradis** paradise 12

parce que because 5

pardon excuse me 1

un **parent** parent; relative 5

paresseux, paresseuse lazy 5

parler to speak, to talk 6

partir to leave 11

pas not 1

un **passeport** passport 11

passer to show (a movie) 2; to spend (time) 12

une **pastèque** watermelon 8

le **pâté** pâté 8

une **pâtisserie** pastry store 8

une **pêche** peach 8

une **pendule** clock 4

penser (à) to think (of) 12

perdre to lose 12

un **père** father 5

une **personne: ne (n')... personne** no one, nobody, not anyone 10

petit(e) short, little, small 7; *le petit déjeuner* breakfast 9

des **petits pois (m.)** peas 8

(un) **peu** (a) little 2; *(un) peu de* (a) little, few 8

la **peur: avoir peur (de)** to be afraid (of) 10

peut-être maybe 7

la **philosophie** philosophy 4

une **photo** photo, picture 5

la **physique** physics 4

une **pièce** room 9

un **pied** foot 10; *un doigt de pied* toe 10

une **piscine** swimming pool 11

une **pizza** pizza 2

un **placard** cupboard 9

la **place** room, space 10; *une place* (public) square 11

une **plage** beach 11

plaît: ... me plaît. I like 11

un **plan** map 12

pleuvoir: Il pleut. It's raining. 6

plus more 8; *le/la/les plus* (+ adjective) the most (+ adjective) 12; *ne (n')... plus* no longer, not anymore 10

une **poire** pear 8

les **pois (m.): des petits pois (m.)** peas 8

un **poisson** fish 5; *un poisson rouge* goldfish 5

le **poivre** pepper 9

une **pomme** apple 3; *une pomme de terre* potato 8

le **porc** pork 8

une **porte** door 4

porter to wear 7

possible possible 2

une **poste** post office 11

un **pot** jar 8

un **poulet** chicken 8

pour for 2; (in order) to 7

pourquoi why 2

pouvoir to be able to 8

préférer to prefer 2

premier, première first 5

prendre to take, to have (food or drink) 9; *prendre rendez-vous* to make an appointment 10

près (de) near 11

présenter to introduce 1

prie: Je vous en prie. You're welcome. 3

le **printemps** spring 6

un(e) **prof** teacher 4

un **professeur** teacher 4

une **profession** occupation 6

puis then 8

un **pull** sweater 7

Q

qu'est-ce que what 2; *Qu'est-ce que c'est?* What is it/this? 4; *Qu'est-ce que tu as?* What's the matter with you? 10

quand when 6

quarante forty 3

un **quart** quarter 4; *et quart* fifteen (minutes after), quarter after 4; *moins le quart* quarter to 4

un **quartier** quarter, neighborhood 12

quatorze fourteen 1

quatre four 1

quatre-vingt-dix ninety 3

quatre-vingts eighty 3

quatrième fourth 11

que how 5; than, as, that 8; *Que je suis bête!* How dumb I am! 5; *Que vous êtes gentils!* How nice you are! 9

quel, quelle what, which 3

quelqu'un someone, somebody 10

quelque chose something 7

quelques some 9

qui who, whom 2

une **quiche** quiche 3

quinze fifteen 1

quitter to leave (a person or place) 12

quoi what 4

R

un **raisin** grape 3

un(e) **réceptionniste** receptionist 10

regarder to watch 2; to look (at) 10

le **reggae** reggae 2

regretter to be sorry 10

un **rendez-vous** appointment 10; *prendre rendez-vous* to make an appointment 10

rentrer to come home, to return, to come back 11

un **repas** meal 8

la **République Démocratique du Congo** Democratic Republic of the Congo 11

ressembler à to look like, to resemble 5

un **restaurant** restaurant 11

rester to stay, to remain 10

revenir to come back, to return 11

le **rez-de-chaussée** ground floor 9

un **rhume** cold 10

rien: ne (n')... rien nothing, not anything 10

une **robe** dress 7

le **rock** rock (music) 2

le **roller** in-line skating 2

rose pink 7

rouge red 5

roux, rousse red (hair) 5

une **rue** street 12

S

s'appelle: elle s'appelle her name is 1; *il s'appelle* his name is 1

s'il te plaît please 9; *s'il vous plaît* please 3

un **sac à dos** backpack 4

une **salade** salad 3

une **salle à manger** dining room 9

une **salle de bains** bathroom 9

une **salle de classe** classroom 4

un **salon** living room 9

salut hi; good-bye 1

samedi (m.) Saturday 4

un **sandwich** sandwich 3; *un sandwich au fromage* cheese sandwich 3; *un sandwich au jambon* ham sandwich 3

la **santé** health 10

le **saucisson** salami 8

les **sciences (f.)** science 4

le **secours: Au secours!** Help! 10

seize sixteen 1

un **séjour** family room 9; stay 11

le **sel** salt 9

une **semaine** week 4

le **Sénégal** Senegal 11

sénégalais(e) Senegalese 11

sept seven 1

septembre September 5

septième seventh 11

un **serveur, une serveuse** server 3

une **serviette** napkin 9

seulement only 12

le **shopping** shopping 2

un **short** (pair of) shorts 7

si yes (on the contrary) 4; so 6

six six 1

sixième sixth 11

skier to ski 2

une **sœur** sister 5

la **soif: J'ai soif.** I'm thirsty. 3

un **soir** evening 7; *ce soir* tonight 8

soixante sixty 3

soixante-dix seventy 3

des **soldes (f.)** sale(s) 7

le **soleil** sun 6

solide steady 10

son, sa; ses his, her, one's, its 5

sortir to go out 2

un **souhait: À tes souhaits!** Bless you! 10

la **soupe** soup 8

sous under 4

un **sous-sol** basement 9

souvent often 6

un **sport** sport 2

un **stade** stadium 11

une **station** station 12

une **statue** statue 12

un **steak** steak 3; *un steak-frites* steak with French fries 3

une **stéréo** stereo 4

un **stylo** pen 4

le **sucre** sugar 9

le **sud** south 11

suisse Swiss 11

la **Suisse** Switzerland 11

super super, terrific, great 2

un **supermarché** supermarket 8

sur on 4; in 6

sûr: bien sûr of course 9

un **sweat** sweatshirt 7

sympa (sympathique) nice 5

T

t'appelles: tu t'appelles your name is 1

un **tabac** tobacco shop 11

une **table** table 9

un **tableau** (chalk)board 4; painting 12

une **taille** size 7

un **taille-crayon** pencil sharpener 4

un **tailleur** woman's suit 7

Tant mieux. That's great. 4

une **tante** aunt 5

un **tapis** rug 9

une **tarte (aux fraises)** (strawberry) pie 8

une **tasse** cup 9

un **taxi** taxi 12

te to you 1

un **tee-shirt** T-shirt 7

la **télé (télévision)** TV, television 2

téléphoner to phone (someone), to make a call 2

une **température** temperature 10

le **temps** weather 6; *Quel temps fait-il?* What's the weather like? How's the weather? 6

des **tennis (m.)** tennis shoes 7

le **tennis** tennis 2

la **terre: une pomme de terre** potato 8

une **tête** head 10

Tiens! Hey! 1

un **timbre** stamp 11

timide timid, shy 5

toi you 3

les **toilettes (f.)** toilet 9

une **tomate** tomato 8

un **tombeau** tomb 12

ton, ta; tes your 5

toucher to cash 11

toujours always 8; still 9

un **tour** trip 6; *le tour* tour 9

une **tour** tower 12

tourner to turn 11

tous les deux both 5

la **Toussaint** All Saints' Day 11

tout all, everything 11; *tout droit* straight ahead 11; *tout le monde* everybody 2

un **train** train 11

une **tranche** slice 8

travailler to work 6

treize thirteen 1

trente thirty 3

très very 3

un **triomphe** triumph 12

trois three 1

troisième third 11

trop too 8; too much 10; *trop de* too much, too many 8

une **trousse** pencil case 4

trouver to find 7

tu you 2

la **Tunisie** Tunisia 11

tunisien, tunisienne Tunisian 11

U

un **one** 1; a, an 2

une **a, an, one** 3

V

les **vacances (f.)** vacation 5

un **vase** vase 9

la **veille** night before 11

un **vélo** bicycle, bike 2

un **vendeur, une vendeuse** salesperson 7

vendre to sell 7

vendredi (m.) Friday 4

venir to come 6

le **vent** wind 6

un **ventre** stomach 10

un **verre** glass 9

vert(e) green 5

une **veste** (sport) jacket 7

des **vêtements (m.)** clothes 7

le **Vietnam** Vietnam 6

vietnamien, vietnamienne Vietnamese 6

vieux, vieil, vieille old 7

un **village** village 11

une **ville** city 11

vingt twenty 1

violet, violette purple 7

visiter to visit (a place) 12

vivre to live 12

voici here is/are 7

voilà here is/are, there is/are 3

voir to see 11

une **voiture** car 9

le **volley (volleyball)** volleyball 2

votre; vos your 5

voudrais would like 3

vouloir to want 8; *vouloir bien* to be willing 9

vous you 2; to you 9

un **voyage** trip 9

voyager to travel 6

voyons let's see 3

vrai(e) true 7

vraiment really 12

W

les **W.-C. (m.)** toilet 9

Y

le **yaourt** yogurt 8

des **yeux (m.)** eyes 5

Z

zéro zero 1

Zut! Darn! 4

Vocabulaire

English/French

All words and expressions introduced as active vocabulary in *C'est à toi!* appear in this end vocabulary. The number following the meaning of each word or expression indicates the unit in which it appears for the first time. If there is more than one meaning for a word or expression and it has appeared in different units, the corresponding unit numbers are listed.

A

a un 2; une 3; de (d') 6; *a lot* beaucoup 2; *a lot of* beaucoup de 2

to be **able to** pouvoir 8

above au-dessus de 9

according to d'après 12

accountant un(e) comptable 6

ache: to have a/an . . . ache avoir mal (à...) 10

to be **afraid (of)** avoir peur (de) 10

Africa l'Afrique (f.) 11

after après 6

afternoon l'après-midi (m.) 10

age l'âge (m.) 5

ahead: straight ahead tout droit 11

airplane un avion 11

airport un aéroport 11

Algeria l'Algérie (f.) 11

Algerian algérien, algérienne 11

all tout 11; *All Saints' Day* la Toussaint 11

already déjà 3

also aussi 2

always toujours 8

American américain(e) 6

an un 2; une 3; de (d') 6

and et 2

another un(e) autre 6

any de (d') 6; des, du 8

anymore: not anymore ne (n')... plus 10

anyone: not anyone ne (n')... personne 10

anything: not anything ne (n')... rien 10

apartment un appartement 9; *apartment building* un immeuble 9

apple une pomme 3; *apple juice* le jus de pomme 3

appointment un rendez-vous 10; *to make an appointment* prendre rendez-vous 10

April avril 5

arch un arc, une arche 12

arm un bras 10

armchair un fauteuil 9

to **arrive** arriver 1

as aussi, que 8; *as soon as* aussitôt que 10

to **ask for** demander 12

at à 4; *at (the)* au 2, aux 7; *at least* au moins 12

attic un grenier 9

August août 5

aunt une tante 5

autumn l'automne (m.) 6

avenue une avenue 11

B

back un dos 10; *to come back* rentrer, revenir 11

backpack un sac à dos 4

bad mal 3; mauvais(e) 6; *It's bad.* Il fait mauvais. 6

badly mal 3

bakery une boulangerie 8

balcony un balcon 9

banana une banane 8

bank une banque 11

basement un sous-sol 9

basketball le basket (basketball) 2; *to play basketball* jouer au basket 2

bathroom une salle de bains 9

bathtub une baignoire 9

to **be** être 5; *to be . . . (years old)* avoir... ans 5; *to be able to* pouvoir 8; *to be afraid (of)* avoir peur (de) 10; *to be cold* avoir froid 10; *to be how old* avoir quel âge 5; *to be hungry* avoir faim 4; *to be in good/bad shape* être en bonne/mauvaise forme 10; *to be necessary* falloir 10; *to be obliged to* être obligé(e) de 12; *to be sorry* regretter 10; *to be thirsty* avoir soif 4; *to be warm/hot* avoir chaud 10; *to be willing* vouloir bien 9

beach une plage 11

beans: green beans des haricots verts (m.) 8

beautiful beau, bel, belle 5; *It's beautiful.* Il fait beau. 6

because parce que 5

bed un lit 9

bedroom une chambre 9

beef le bœuf 8

to **begin** commencer 4

behind derrière 4

beige beige 7

Belgian belge 11

Belgium la Belgique 11

beverage une boisson 3

bicycle un vélo 2

big grand(e) 7; gros, grosse 11

bike un vélo 2

biking: to go biking faire du vélo 2

biology la biologie 4

bird un oiseau 5

birthday un anniversaire 5

black noir(e) 5
Bless you! À tes souhaits! 10
blond blond(e) 5
blue bleu(e) 5
board un tableau 4
boat un bateau 12
body un corps 10
book un livre 4
bookstore une librairie 11
boot une botte 7
both tous les deux 5
bottle une bouteille 8
boutique une boutique 7
bowl un bol 9
boy un garçon 4
bread le pain 8; *long, thin loaf of bread* une baguette 8
breakfast le petit déjeuner 9
brother un frère 5
brother-in-law un beau-frère 5
brown brun(e) 5; marron 7
building: apartment building un immeuble 9
businessman un homme d'affaires 6
businesswoman une femme d'affaires 6
but mais 2
butcher shop une boucherie 8
butter le beurre 8
to **buy** acheter 7
by de (d') 12
bye ciao 1

C

café un café 3
cafeteria une cantine 4
cake un gâteau 8
calendar un calendrier 4
call: to make a call téléphoner 2
Camembert cheese le camembert 8
campground un camping 11
camping le camping 2
can une boîte 8
Canada le Canada 6
Canadian canadien, canadienne 6
car une voiture 9
carrot une carotte 8

to **cash** toucher 11
cat un chat 5
CD un CD 4
cemetery un cimetière 12
center un centre 12; *shopping center* un centre commercial 7
chair une chaise 4
chalkboard un tableau 4
cheap bon marché 7
check: traveler's check un chèque de voyage 11
cheese le fromage 3; *Camembert cheese* le camembert 8; *cheese sandwich* un sandwich au fromage 3
chemistry la chimie 4
cherry une cerise 8
chicken un poulet 8
child un(e) enfant 5
chills des frissons (m.) 10
China la Chine 6
Chinese chinois(e) 6
chocolate le chocolat 3; *chocolate ice cream* une glace au chocolat 3
church une église 11
city une ville 11
class un cours 4
classroom une salle de classe 4
clock une pendule 4
to **close** fermer 12
clothes des vêtements (m.) 7
club: dance club une boîte 2
coat un manteau 7
coffee un café 3
Coke un coca 3
cold froid(e) 6; *It's cold.* Il fait froid. 6; *to be cold* avoir froid 10
cold un rhume 10
color une couleur 7
to **come** venir 6; *to come back* rentrer, revenir 11; *to come home* rentrer 11; *to come in* entrer 9
computer un ordinateur 4; *computer science* l'informatique (f.) 4; *computer specialist* un informaticien, une

informaticienne 6
Congolese congolais(e) 11
to **continue** continuer 12
cook un cuisinier, une cuisinière 6
cool frais, fraîche 6; *It's cool.* Il fait frais. 6
to **cost** coûter 3
couch un canapé 9
course un cours 4
couscous le couscous 9
cousin un(e) cousin(e) 5
crab un crabe 8
crêpe une crêpe 3
croissant un croissant 8
cup une tasse 9
cupboard un placard 9

D

dairy store une crémerie 8
dance un bal 12; *dance club* une boîte 2
to **dance** danser 2
dark (hair) brun(e) 5
Darn! Zut! 4
date une date 5
daughter une fille 5
day un jour 4; une journée 12
dear cher, chère 11
December décembre 5
to **decide** décider (de) 12
delicatessen une charcuterie 8
delighted enchanté(e) 9
Democratic Republic of the Congo la République Démocratique du Congo 11
dentist un(e) dentiste 6
department store un grand magasin 7
desk un bureau 4
dessert un dessert 3
dictionary un dictionnaire 4
dining room une salle à manger 9
dinner le dîner 9
diskette une disquette 4
to **do** faire 2; *to do homework* faire les devoirs 2
doctor un médecin 6; un docteur 10
dog un chien 5

dollar un dollar 7

door une porte 4

drawing le dessin 4

dress une robe 7

drink une boisson 3

dumb bête 5; *How dumb I am!* Que je suis bête! 5

DVD un DVD 4; *DVD player* un lecteur de DVD 4

E

ear une oreille 10

east l'est (m.) 11

easy facile 10

to **eat** manger 2; *to eat pizza* manger de la pizza 2

egg un œuf 8

eight huit 1

eighteen dix-huit 1

eighth huitième 11

eighty quatre-vingts 3

eleven onze 1

engineer un ingénieur 6

England l'Angleterre (f.) 6

English anglais(e) 6; *English (language)* l'anglais (m.) 4

enough assez de 8

to **enter** entrer 9

entrance une entrée 9

euro un euro 3

Europe l'Europe (f.) 11

even même 9

evening un soir 7

everybody tout le monde 2

everything tout 11

excuse me pardon 1; excusez-moi 7

expensive cher, chère 7

eye un œil 10; *eyes* des yeux (m.) 5

F

face une figure 10

fall l'automne (m.) 6

family une famille 5; *family room* un séjour 9

far loin 11

farmer un fermier, une fermière 6

fast-food restaurant un fast-food 3

fat gros, grosse 11

father un père 5

father-in-law un beau-père 5

February février 5

to **feel: to feel like** avoir envie de 11; *to feel nauseous* avoir mal au cœur 10

festival une fête 12

fever la fièvre 10

few (un) peu de 8

fifteen quinze 1; *fifteen (minutes after)* et quart 4

fifth cinquième 11

fifty cinquante 3

to **find** trouver 7

finger un doigt 10

to **finish** finir 4

fireworks un feu d'artifice 12

first premier, première 5; d'abord 8

fish un poisson 5; *fish soup* une bouillabaisse 8

five cinq 1

floor un étage 9; *ground floor* le rez-de-chaussée 9

flower une fleur 9

flu la grippe 10

foot un pied 10

for pour 2; comme 3

fork une fourchette 9

forty quarante 3

four quatre 1

fourteen quatorze 1

fourth quatrième 11

France la France 6

French français(e) 6; *French (language)* le français 4; *French fries* des frites (f.) 3

fresh frais, fraîche 6

Friday vendredi (m.) 4

friend un(e) ami(e) 6

fries: French fries des frites (f.) 3; *steak with French fries* un steak-frites 3

from de (d') 4; *from (the)* des 3, du 6

front: in front of devant 4

fruit un fruit 8; *fruit juice* le jus de fruit 9

full chargé(e) 12

G

games: to play video games jouer aux jeux vidéo 2; *video games* des jeux vidéo (m.) 2

garage un garage 9

garden un jardin 9

generous généreux, généreuse 5

geography la géographie 4

German allemand(e) 6; *German (language)* l'allemand (m.) 4

Germany l'Allemagne (f.) 6

gift un cadeau 5

girl une fille 4

to **give** donner 3; *Give me . . . .* Donnez-moi.... 3

glass un verre 9

to **go** aller 2; *let's go (there)* allons-y 3; *Shall we go (there)?* On y va? 2; *to go biking* faire du vélo 2; *to go for a ride* faire un tour 6; *to go grocery shopping* faire les courses 8; *to go in-line skating* faire du roller 2; *to go out* sortir 2; *to go running* faire du footing 2; *to go shopping* faire du shopping 2, faire les magasins 7; *to go up* monter 12

goldfish un poisson rouge 5

good bon, bonne 2; *good evening* bonsoir 9; *good-bye* au revoir, salut 1

grandfather un grand-père 5

grandmother une grand-mère 5

grape un raisin 3; *grape juice* le jus de raisin 3

gray gris(e) 5

great super 2; formidable 11; *That's great.* Tant mieux. 4

green vert(e) 5; *green beans* des haricots verts (m.) 8

ground floor le rez-de-chaussée 9

Guadeloupe la Guadeloupe 5

H

hair des cheveux (m.) 5

hairdresser un coiffeur, une coiffeuse 6

half demi(e) 4; *half past* et demi(e) 4

half-brother un demi-frère 5

half-sister une demi-sœur 5

ham le jambon 3; *ham sandwich* un sandwich au jambon 3

hamburger un hamburger 3

hand une main 10

handsome beau, bel, belle 5

hardworking diligent(e) 5

hat un chapeau 7

to **have** avoir 4; *I've had it!* J'en ai marre! 4; *one has to, we/you have to* il faut 10; *to have (food or drink)* prendre 9; *to have a/an . . . ache, to have a sore . . .* avoir mal 10; *to have to* devoir, falloir 10; être obligé(e) de 12

he il 2; *he is* c'est 5

head une tête 10

health la santé 10

heart un cœur 10

hello bonjour 1; *hello (on telephone)* allô 1

Help! Au secours! 10

her son, sa; ses 5; *her name is* elle s'appelle 1

here là 4; ici 6; *here are* voilà 3, voici 7; *here is* voilà 3, voici 7

Hey! Eh!, Tiens! 1

hi salut 1

hightops des baskets (f.) 7

his son, sa; ses 5; *his name is* il s'appelle 1

history l'histoire (f.) 4

holiday une fête 12

home: at the home of chez 11; *to come home* rentrer 11; *to the home of* chez 2

homework les devoirs (m.) 2; *to do homework* faire les devoirs 2

horse un cheval 5

hot chaud(e) 6; *It's hot.* Il fait chaud. 6; *to be hot* avoir chaud 10

hot dog un hot-dog 3

hotel un hôtel 12

hour l'heure (f.) 3

house une maison 9; *at the*

house of chez 11; *to my house* chez moi 2; *to the house of* chez 2

househusband un homme au foyer 6

housewife une femme au foyer 6

how comment 3; que 5; *How are things going?* Ça va? 1; *How are you?* Comment vas-tu? 3; *How dumb I am!* Que je suis bête! 5; *how many* combien de 8; *how much* combien 3, combien de 8; *How much is it/that?* Ça fait combien? 3; *How nice you are!* Que vous êtes gentils! 9; *How old are you?* Tu as quel âge? 5; *How's the weather?* Quel temps fait-il? 6

hundred: (one) hundred cent 3

hungry: I'm hungry. J'ai faim. 3; *to be hungry* avoir faim 4

to **hurt** avoir mal (à...) 10

husband un mari 5

I

I j', je 1; moi 2

ice cream une glace 3; *chocolate ice cream* une glace au chocolat 3; *vanilla ice cream* une glace à la vanille 3

to **imagine** imaginer 12

Impressionist impressionniste 12

in dans 4; à, en, sur 6; de (d') 12; *in (the)* au 6, aux 7, du 12; *in front of* devant 4; *in order to* pour 7; *in the morning* le matin 8

in-line skating le roller 2; *to go in-line skating* faire du roller 2

intelligent intelligent(e) 5

to **introduce** présenter 1

to **invite** inviter 2

is est 3; *isn't that so?* n'est-ce pas? 5

it elle, il 2; ça 3; *it is necessary* il faut 10; *it's* c'est 1; *It's . . . .* Ça fait.... 3; *It's bad.* Il fait mauvais. 6; *It's beautiful.* Il

fait beau. 6; *It's cold.* Il fait froid. 6; *It's cool.* Il fait frais. 6; *It's hot.* Il fait chaud. 6; *It's nice.* Il fait beau. 6; *It's raining.* Il pleut. 6; *It's snowing.* Il neige. 6; *It's sunny.* Il fait du soleil. 6; *It's the (+ date).* Nous sommes le (+ date). 5; *It's warm.* Il fait chaud. 6; *It's windy.* Il fait du vent. 6

Italian italien, italienne 6

Italy l'Italie (f.) 6

its son, sa; ses 5

Ivory Coast la Côte-d'Ivoire 11; *from the Ivory Coast* ivoirien, ivoirienne 11

J

jacket (outdoor) un blouson 7; *ski jacket* un anorak 7; *sport jacket* une veste 7

jam la confiture 8

January janvier 5

Japan le Japon 6

Japanese japonais(e) 6

jar un pot 8

jazz le jazz 2

jeans: (pair of) jeans un jean 7

journalist un(e) journaliste 6

juice: apple juice le jus de pomme 3; *fruit juice* le jus de fruit 9; *grape juice* le jus de raisin 3; *orange juice* le jus d'orange 3

July juillet 5

June juin 5

just juste 4

K

to **keep** garder 10

ketchup le ketchup 8

kilogram un kilogramme (kilo) 8

kilometer un kilomètre 5

kiss une bise 11

kitchen une cuisine 9

knee un genou 10

knife un couteau 9

L

ladies and gentlemen
Messieurs-Dames 3
lamp une lampe 9
large grand(e) 7; gros,
grosse 11
last dernier, dernière 12
Latin (language) le latin 4
lawn un jardin 9
lawyer un(e) avocat(e) 6
lazy paresseux, paresseuse 5
least: at least au moins 12
to **leave** partir 11; *to leave (a person or place)* quitter 12
left: to (on) the left à gauche 9
leg une jambe 10
lemon-lime soda une limonade 3
less moins 8
liberty la liberté 12
library une bibliothèque 11
light une lumière 12
like comme 3
to **like** aimer 2; *I like . . . .* me plaît. 11; *What would you like?* Vous désirez? 3; *would like* voudrais 3
to **listen (to)** écouter 2; *listen* écoute 1; *to listen to music* écouter de la musique 2
little petit(e) 7; *a little* (un) peu 2, (un) peu de 8
to **live** habiter 9; vivre 12
living room un salon 9
long long, longue 7
longer: no longer ne (n')... plus 10
to **look (at)** regarder 10; *to look for* chercher 7; *to look like* ressembler à 5; *to look well/sick* avoir bonne/ mauvaise mine 10
to **lose** perdre 12
lot: a lot beaucoup 2; *a lot of* beaucoup de 2
love: in love amoureux, amoureuse 12
to **love** aimer 2; adorer 7
to **lower** baisser 10
luck la chance 6

lunch le déjeuner 9
Luxembourg le Luxembourg 11; *from Luxembourg* luxembourgeois(e) 11

M

Ma'am Madame (Mme) 1
to **make** faire 2; *to make a call* téléphoner 2; *to make an appointment* prendre rendez-vous 10
mall un centre commercial 7
man un homme 6
many beaucoup 8; *how many* combien de 8; *too many* trop de 8
map une carte 4; un plan 12
March mars 5
market un marché 8
Martinique la Martinique 5
math les maths (f.) 4
matter: What's the matter with you? Qu'est-ce que tu as? 10
May mai 5
maybe peut-être 7
mayonnaise la mayonnaise 8
me moi 2; me 11; *to me* me 11
meal un repas 8
mean méchant(e) 5
melon un melon 8
member un membre 5
merchant un(e) marchand(e) 8
Mexican mexicain(e) 6
Mexico le Mexique 6
microwave un micro-onde 9
midnight minuit 3
milk le lait 8
million un million 5
mineral water l'eau minérale (f.) 3
minus moins 4
minute une minute 4
Miss Mademoiselle (Mlle) 1
modern moderne 12
Mom maman (f.) 8
Monday lundi (m.) 4
money l'argent (m.) 11
month un mois 5
monument un monument 12

more plus 8
morning un matin 8; *in the morning* le matin 8
Moroccan marocain(e) 11
Morocco le Maroc 11
most: the most (+ adjective) le/la/les plus (+ *adjective*) 12
mother une mère 5
mother-in-law une belle-mère 5
mouth une bouche 10
movie un film 2; *movies* le cinéma 2
Mr. Monsieur 1
Mrs. Madame (Mme) 1
much: how much combien 3; combien de 8; *How much is it/that?* Ça fait combien? 3; *too much* trop de 8, trop 10; *very much* beaucoup 2
museum un musée 11
mushroom un champignon 8
music la musique 2
musician un musicien, une musicienne 12
must: one/we/you must il faut 10
mustard la moutarde 8
my mon, ma; mes 5; *my name is* je m'appelle 1

N

name: her name is elle s'appelle 1; *his name is* il s'appelle 1; *my name is* je m'appelle 1; *your name is* tu t'appelles 1
napkin une serviette 9
national national(e) 12
nauseous: to feel nauseous avoir mal au cœur 10
near près (de) 11
to **be necessary** falloir 10; *it is necessary* il faut 10
neck un cou 10
to **need** avoir besoin de 4
neighborhood un quartier 12
never ne (n')... jamais 10
new nouveau, nouvel, nouvelle 7
nice sympa (sympathique) 5; gentil, gentille 9; *How nice*

you are! Que vous êtes gentils! 9; *It's nice.* Il fait beau. 6

night before la veille 11

nine neuf 1

nineteen dix-neuf 1

ninety quatre-vingt-dix 3

ninth neuvième 11

no non 1; *no longer* ne (n')... plus 10; *no one* ne (n')... personne 10

nobody ne (n')... personne 10

noise un bruit 12

noon midi 3

north le nord 11

nose un nez 10

not pas 1; ne (n')... pas 2; *not anymore* ne (n')... plus 10; *not anyone* ne (n')... personne 10; *not anything* ne (n')... rien 10

notebook un cahier 4

nothing ne (n')... rien 10

November novembre 5

now maintenant 8

nurse un infirmier, une infirmière 6

O

o'clock l'heure (f.) 3

to be obliged to être obligé(e) de 12

occupation une profession 6

October octobre 5

of de (d') 4; *of (the)* des, du 6; *of course* bien sûr 9

office (doctor or dentist's) un cabinet 10

often souvent 6

oh ah 1; oh 4; *Oh no! Oh dear!* Oh là là! 10

OK d'accord 1; OK 8

old vieux, vieil, vieille 7; *How old are you?* Tu as quel âge? 5; *I'm . . . years old.* J'ai... ans. 5; *to be . . . (years old)* avoir... ans 5; *to be how old* avoir quel âge 5

omelette une omelette 3

on sur 4; en 5; *on (+ day of the week)* le (+ day of the week) 4; *on sale* en solde 7; *on the (+ ordinal number)*

le (+ number) 1

one un 1; on 2; une 3; *no one* ne (n')... personne 10

one's son, sa; ses 5

onion un oignon 8

only juste 4; seulement 12

or ou 3

orange une orange 3; orange 7; *orange juice* le jus d'orange 3

other autre 6

our notre; nos 5

outfit un ensemble 7

oven un four 9

over there là-bas 7

P

painting un tableau 12

pants: (pair of) pants un pantalon 7

panty hose des bas (m.) 7

paper: sheet of paper une feuille de papier 4

parade un défilé 12

paradise le paradis 12

parent un parent 5

park un jardin 12

party une boum 7

passport un passeport 11

pastry store une pâtisserie 8

pâté le pâté 8

path un chemin 12

peach une pêche 8

pear une poire 8

peas des petits pois (m.) 8

pen un stylo 4

pencil un crayon 4; *pencil case* une trousse 4; *pencil sharpener* un taille-crayon 4

pepper le poivre 9

per par 4

philosophy la philosophie 4

to phone (someone) téléphoner 2

photo une photo 5

physics la physique 4

picture une photo 5

pie une tarte 8; *strawberry pie* une tarte aux fraises 8

piece un morceau 8

pink rose 7

pizza une pizza 2; *to eat pizza* manger de la pizza 2

plate une assiette 9

to play jouer 2; *to play basketball* jouer au basket 2; *to play soccer* jouer au foot 2; *to play sports* faire du sport 2; *to play tennis* jouer au tennis 2; *to play video games* jouer aux jeux vidéo 2; *to play volleyball* jouer au volley 2

please s'il vous plaît 3; s'il te plaît 9

pole: ski pole un bâton 10

police officer un agent de police 6

pool: swimming pool une piscine 11

pork le porc 8

possible possible 2

post office une poste 11

poster une affiche 4

potato une pomme de terre 8

to prefer préférer 2

present un cadeau 5

pretty joli(e) 7

purple violet, violette 7

to put (on) mettre 9

Q

quarter un quart 4; un quartier 12; *quarter after* et quart 4; *quarter to* moins le quart 4

quiche une quiche 3

quite assez 7

quiz une interro (interrogation) 2

R

to rain: It's raining. Il pleut. 6

rather assez 7

to read lire 2

really bien 2; vraiment 12

receptionist un(e) réceptionniste 10

red rouge 5; *red (hair)* roux, rousse 5

refrigerator un frigo 9

reggae le reggae 2

relative un parent 5

to remain rester 10

to **resemble** ressembler à 5

restaurant un restaurant 11;
fast-food restaurant un fast-
food 3

to **return** rentrer, revenir 11

ride: to go for a ride faire un
tour 6

right: to (on) the right à
droite 9

ripe mûr(e) 8

rock (music) le rock 2

room une pièce 9; la place 10;
dining room une salle à
manger 9; *family room* un
séjour 9; *living room* un
salon 9

rug un tapis 9

running le footing 2; *to go
running* faire du footing 2

S

saint: All Saints' Day la
Toussaint 11

salad une salade 3

salami le saucisson 8

sale(s) des soldes (f.) 7; *on sale*
en solde 7

salesperson un vendeur, une
vendeuse 7

salt le sel 9

sandwich un sandwich 3;
cheese sandwich un sandwich
au fromage 3; *ham sandwich*
un sandwich au jambon 3

Saturday samedi (m.) 4

say dis 2

schedule un emploi du
temps 4; un horaire 11

school une école 4

science les sciences (f.) 4

sea une mer 11

second deuxième 11

to **see** voir 11; *let's see* voyons 3;
See you soon. À bientôt. 1;
See you tomorrow. À
demain. 2

selfish égoïste 5

to **sell** vendre 7

Senegal le Sénégal 11

Senegalese sénégalais(e) 11

September septembre 5

server un serveur, une

serveuse 3

to **set** mettre 9

setting: table setting un
couvert 9

seven sept 1

seventeen dix-sept 1

seventh septième 11

seventy soixante-dix 3

**shape: to be in good/bad
shape** être en bonne/
mauvaise forme 10

sharpener: pencil sharpener
un taille-crayon 4

she elle 2; *she is* c'est 5

shirt une chemise 7

shoe une chaussure 7; *tennis
shoes* des tennis (m.) 7

shop une boutique 7

shopping le shopping 2;
shopping center un centre
commercial 7; *to go grocery
shopping* faire les courses 8;
to go shopping faire du
shopping 2, faire les
magasins 7

short court(e), petit(e) 7

shorts: (pair of) shorts un
short 7

shoulder une épaule 10

to **show** montrer 4; *Show me . . . .*
Montrez-moi.... 4; *to show (a
movie)* passer 2

shower une douche 9

shrimp une crevette 8

shy timide 5

sick malade 10; *I'm sick of it!*
J'en ai marre! 4

sink un évier 9

Sir Monsieur 1

sister une sœur 5

sister-in-law une belle-sœur 5

six six 1

sixteen seize 1

sixth sixième 11

sixty soixante 3

size une taille 7

skating: in-line skating le
roller 2; *to go in-line skating*
faire du roller 2

ski: ski jacket un anorak 7;
ski pole un bâton 10

to **ski** skier 2

skirt une jupe 7

to **sleep** dormir 2

slice une tranche 8

small petit(e) 7

snacks des chips (m.) 9;
afternoon snack le goûter 9

snow: It's snowing. Il
neige. 6

so si 6; donc 9; *so-so* comme
ci, comme ça 3

soccer le foot (football) 2; *to
play soccer* jouer au foot 2

sock une chaussette 7

soda: lemon-lime soda une
limonade 3

sofa un canapé 9

some des 3; du 8; de (d'),
quelques 9

somebody quelqu'un 10

someone quelqu'un 10

something quelque chose 7

son un fils 5

soon: as soon as aussitôt
que 10

sore: to have a sore . . . avoir
mal (à...) 10

to be **sorry** regretter 10

soup la soupe 8; *fish soup* une
bouillabaisse 8

south le sud 11

space la place 10

Spain l'Espagne (f.) 6

Spanish espagnol(e) 6;
Spanish (language) l'espagnol
(m.) 4

to **speak** parler 6

to **spend (time)** passer 12

spoon une cuiller 9

sport un sport 2; *sport jacket*
une veste 7; *to play sports*
faire du sport 2

spring le printemps 6

square: public square une
place 11

stadium un stade 11

staircase, stairs un escalier 9

stamp un timbre 11

station une station 12; *train
station* une gare 11

statue une statue 12

stay un séjour 11

to **stay** rester 10

steady solide 10

steak un steak 3; *steak with French fries* un steak-frites 3

stepbrother un beau-frère 5

stepfather un beau-père 5

stepmother une belle-mère 5

stepsister une belle-sœur 5

stereo une stéréo 4

still encore, toujours 9

stomach un ventre 10

store un magasin 7; *department store* un grand magasin 7

story un étage 9

stove une cuisinière 9

straight ahead tout droit 11

strawberry une fraise 8; *strawberry pie* une tarte aux fraises 8

street une rue 12

student un(e) élève, un(e) étudiant(e) 4

to **study** étudier 2; *Let's study . . . .* Étudions.... 4

stupid bête 5

subway un métro 12

sugar le sucre 9

suit: man's suit un costume 7; *woman's suit* un tailleur 7

summer l'été (m.) 6

sun le soleil 6

Sunday dimanche (m.) 4

sunny: It's sunny. Il fait du soleil. 6

super super 2

supermarket un supermarché 8

supper le dîner 9

sweater un pull 7

sweatshirt un sweat 7

to **swim** nager 2

swimming pool une piscine 11

swimsuit un maillot de bain 7

Swiss suisse 11

Switzerland la Suisse 11

T

table une table 9; *table setting* un couvert 9

tablecloth une nappe 9

to **take** prendre 9; *to take a tour* faire le tour 9

to **talk** parler 6

talkative bavard(e) 5

tall grand(e) 7

taxi un taxi 12

teacher un(e) prof, un professeur 4

television la télé (télévision) 2

temperature une température 10

ten dix 1

tennis le tennis 2; *tennis shoes* des tennis (m.) 7; *to play tennis* jouer au tennis 2

tenth dixième 11

terrific super 2; formidable 11

test une interro (interrogation) 2

than que 8

thanks merci 1

that ça 3; ce, cet, cette, que 8; *that's* c'est 6; *That's . . . .* Ça fait.... 3; *That's great.* Tant mieux. 4

the le, la, l', les 2

their leur 5

then puis 8; donc 9; *(well) then* alors 2

there là 4; *there are* voilà 3, il y a 7; *there is* voilà 3, il y a 7; *over there* là-bas 7

these ces 8; *these are* ce sont 5

they on 2; *they (f.)* elles 2; *they (m.)* ils 2; *they are* ce sont 5

thing une chose 7; *How are things going?* Ça va? 1; *Things are going well.* Ça va bien. 1

to **think (of)** penser (à) 12

third troisième 11

thirsty: I'm thirsty. J'ai soif. 3; *to be thirsty* avoir soif 4

thirteen treize 1

thirty trente 3; *thirty (minutes)* et demi(e) 4

this ce, cet, cette 8; *this is* c'est 1

those ces 8; *those are* ce sont 5

thousand: one thousand mille 4

three trois 1

throat une gorge 10

Thursday jeudi (m.) 4

ticket un billet 12; *ticket window* un guichet 12

time l'heure (f.) 3; une fois 12; *What time is it?* Quelle heure est-il? 3

timetable un horaire 11

timid timide 5

tired fatigué(e) 10

to à 2; *in order to* pour 7; *to (the)* au, en 2, aux 7

tobacco shop un tabac 11

today aujourd'hui 6

toe un doigt de pied 10

together ensemble 4

toilet les toilettes (f.), les W.-C. (m.) 9

tomato une tomate 8

tomb un tombeau 12

tomorrow demain 2

tonight ce soir 8

too aussi 2; trop 8; *too many* trop de 8; *too much* trop de 8, trop 10

tooth une dent 10

tour le tour 9; *to take a tour* faire le tour 9

tower une tour 12

town hall une mairie 11

train un train 11; *train station* une gare 11

to **travel** voyager 6

traveler's check un chèque de voyage 11

tree un arbre 9

trip un tour 6; un voyage 9

triumph un triomphe 12

true vrai(e) 7

T-shirt un tee-shirt 7

Tuesday mardi (m.) 4

Tunisia la Tunisie 11

Tunisian tunisien, tunisienne 11

to **turn** tourner 11

TV la télé (télévision) 2

twelve douze 1

twenty vingt 1

two deux 1

U

ugly moche 7
uhm euh 8
uncle un oncle 5
under sous 4
United States les États-Unis (m.) 6
until jusqu'à 12
up to jusqu'à 12
us nous 5

V

vacation les vacances (f.) 5
vanilla ice cream une glace à la vanille 3
vase un vase 9
vegetable un légume 8
very très 3; *very much* beaucoup 2
video games des jeux vidéo (m.) 2; *to play video games* jouer aux jeux vidéo 2
Vietnam le Vietnam 6
Vietnamese vietnamien, vietnamienne 6
village un village 11
to **visit (a place)** visiter 12
volleyball le volley (volleyball) 2; *to play volleyball* jouer au volley 2

W

to **wait (for)** attendre 8
to **walk** marcher 12
to **want** désirer 3; vouloir 8; avoir envie de 11
wardrobe une armoire 9
warm chaud(e) 6; *It's warm.* Il fait chaud. 6; *to be warm* avoir chaud 10
wastebasket une corbeille 4
to **watch** regarder 2
water l'eau (f.) 3; *mineral water* l'eau minérale (f.) 3
watermelon une pastèque 8
way un chemin 12
we nous, on 2
to **wear** porter 7; *to wear size (+ number)* faire du (+ number) 7
weather le temps 6; *The weather's bad.* Il fait mauvais. 6; *The weather's beautiful/nice.* Il fait beau. 6; *The weather's cold.* Il fait froid. 6; *The weather's cool.* Il fait frais. 6; *The weather's hot/warm.* Il fait chaud. 6; *What's the weather like? How's the weather?* Quel temps fait-il? 6
Wednesday mercredi (m.) 4
week une semaine 4
Welcome! Bienvenue! 9; *You're welcome.* Je vous en prie. 3
well bien 1; *well then* alors, bon ben 2
west l'ouest (m.) 11
what comment 1; qu'est-ce que 2; quel, quelle 3; quoi 4; *What is it/this?* Qu'est-ce que c'est? 4; *What time is it?* Quelle heure est-il? 3; *What would you like?* Vous désirez? 3; *What's the matter with you?* Qu'est-ce que tu as? 10; *What's the weather like?* Quel temps fait-il? 6
when quand 6
where où 4

which quel, quelle 3
white blanc, blanche 7
who, whom qui 2
why pourquoi 2
wife une femme 5
to be **willing** vouloir bien 9
wind le vent 6
window une fenêtre 4; *ticket window* un guichet 12
windy: It's windy. Il fait du vent. 6
winter l'hiver (m.) 6
with avec 4
woman une femme 5
to **work** travailler 6
world le monde 12
would like voudrais 3
Wow! Oh là là! 10

Y

yeah ouais 8
year un an 5; *I'm . . . years old.* J'ai... ans. 5; *to be . . . (years old)* avoir... ans 5
yellow jaune 7
yes oui 1; *yes (on the contrary)* si 4
yesterday hier 11
yogurt le yaourt 8
you tu, vous 2; toi 3; *to you* te 1, vous 9; *You're welcome.* Je vous en prie. 3
young jeune 12
your ton, ta, tes, votre, vos 5; *your name is* tu t'appelles 1
Yuk! Beurk! 7

Z

zero zéro 1

Grammar Index

Photo Credits

Cover: Ted Dahmen, Stealth Moose Designs and Duomo/CORBIS.

Abbreviations: top (t), bottom (b), left (l), right (r), center (c)

Adisa/Istock: 22 (bl), 27 (br)

Amorphis/Istock: 349 (tl)

Anderson, Leslie: 84 (b), 106 (pencils, pens), 123 (l), 141 (notebook, pens), 365 (cr, br), 369 (tr, bc)

Andy445/Istock: 14 (t), 22 (br), 27 (cl)

Armstrong, Rick: 430 (t)

B.S.P.I./CORBIS: 428 (c), 460 (tr)

Berndt, Eric R./Unicorn Stock Photos: 86 (t)

Bertoncelj, Dan/Istock: 191 (br)

Bibikow/Megapress: 256

Black, Ruth/Istock: 349 (br)

Bognar/Megapress: 234 (c)

Breloer, Gero/EPA/SIPA Press: 18-19

Brittany Ferries: 378 (b)

Burgess, Michele: 440 (b), 442 (b), 446 (b)

CandyBoxPhoto/Istock: 53 (tl), 53 (tr)

Cardinale, Stephane/CORBIS: 40 (t)

Carroll, Jamie/Istock: 4 (br)

Chew, Mike/CORBIS: 344-45

Chirol/French Government Tourist Office: 442 (t)

Comnet/Leo de Wys Inc.: 6 (cr)

Condé Nast Archive/CORBIS: 75

D'Angelo, J. J./La Documentation française: 200 (r)

Daniel, Julien/L'Œil Public/La Documentation française: 106

De Vries, Michel/Renault Communications: 322 (t)

Desprez, Bertrand/La Documentation française: 34 (b)

Dex Images/CORBIS: 42 (Annie....)

Dolemieux, Pascal/Métis/La Documentation française: 244 (r)

Dumas, Dominique/Renault Communications: 321 (tl), 323 (Modèle t, #1, #3, #6)

Eliandrick/Istock: 39 (br)

Englebert, Victor: viii, 78 (br), 150 (t), 179 (t), 202 (t), 209 (b), 224 (b), 243 (t), 286 (b), 321 (b), 333 (t), 339 (t), 362 (b), 385 (br), 395 (marocaine, marocain), 401 (t), 404 (t), 413 (#9)

Evirgen/Istock: 27 (cr), 317 (cm)

Faris, Randy/CORBIS: 176 (chinoise), 243 (t), 266 (t), 277 (t)

Felinda/Istock: 349 (br)

Florent, Flipper/Unicorn Stock Photos: 440 (t)

French Government Tourist Office: 397 (tr), 429 (b)

Fridkin, Stanislav/Istock: 46 (cr)

Fried, Robert: iv (b), v (b), vi, x, xiv, 2 (t), 4 (b), 15 (bl), 26, 27 (tr), 30, 38, 54 (br), 60 (c, b), 61 (t), 73, 74 (t), 76 (c, bl), 78 (t), 80, 85, 89 (b), 96 (b), 100 (cl), 114, 115 (b), 123 (r), 132 (b), 140, 142 (b), 144 (tl, bl), 149 (t, b), 150 (b), 157 (t, b), 158 (t), 165, 170, 178 (t, c), 180 (b), 181, 193 (t), 196 (t), 201 (b), 202 (b), 212, 217, 218 (c), 224 (c), 226 (t), 230, 247 (b), 249 (b), 250 (l), 252 (br), 253, 264 (t), 268 (b), 270 (b), 280, 282, 285 (r), 287 (b), 291 (tl, tr), 292, 293 (b), 297 (r), 300, 301 (r), 304, 320 (b), 325 (b), 368 (t), 370 (t), 377 (b), 384 (t), 385 (t), 390, 395 (algérienne), 397 (tl), 398 (tl), 401 (b), 405 (t, c), 408 (bibliothèque), 409 (piscine, mer/plage), 411 (c), 413 (bibliothèque), 416 (t), 420, 421, 426 (b), 427 (c, br), 428 (t, b), 434, 438 (bl, br), 439 (c), 441 (#1, #3), 443 (t), 445, 446 (t), 447 (t, b), 450 (t, b), 452, 453 (b), 457, 461 (t), 462

Garry, Jean-Marc: 158 (b)

gblue.com/Istock: 349 (bl)

Gibson, Keith: 22 (t, CD, dictionary), 23 (t), 27 (tl), 43 (bl, br), 46 (Modèle), 52 (l), 56-57, 71 (b), 72 (Modèle, #3, #7, #8), 87 (#2, #5, #8, #10), 104 (A., F.), 113 (l), 176 (anglaise, anglais), 188 (agent de police), 189 (tr), 191 (bc), 193 (b), 195 (t), 196 (b), 207 (t), 210 (#2, #3), 211 (b), 222 (tr, c, br), 224 (t), 227 (#3, #5, #6), 236, 250 (r), 252 (#2, #4, #7), 260-61, 264 (b), 266 (b), 267 (t, café), 275 (tl, tr, bl, br), 277 (c, b), 279 (b), 283, 286 (t), 287 (t), 293 (t), 302 (t, b), 303, 304 (t), 308, 320 (t), 321 (tc, cr), 322 (b), 323 (#2, #5), 325 (t), 331 (bl), 350 (c), 351, 357 (b), 358 (b), 371, 380-81, 382 (belge m. & f., luxembourgeoise, suisse m. & f.), 408 (église, tabac, banque, restaurant), 409 (musée, librairie, mairie, poste), 412 (t, b), 413 (#2, #3, #4, #5, #6, #7), 414 (t, b), 415 (t), 416 (b), 427 (tl, tr, bl), 438 (tl), 450 (cl), 461 (b)t

Glumack, Ben: 2 (c), 20 (Françoise…., Louis….), 22 (skis), 27 (cr, bl, br), 39 (tl, cc), 46 (#1, #2, #4, #5) 76 (tl, tc, tr, br), 87 (Modèle t, #7, #9), 104 (D.), 141 (family photo), 147 (br), 162 (cr), 176 (canadienne, canadien, américaine, américain, italienne, italien), 177 (tl, tc, tr, bl, br), 190 (tl, tc, tr, b), 206 (tl, tc, tr, b), 210 (#1, #5, #6), 227 (Modèle, #4), 233 (tl, tr, bl, br), 240 (Modèle, #1, #2, #3, #4, #5, #6), 252 (Modèle, #1, #3, #5, #6, #8), 331 (t, cl, cr, br), 336 (Modèle, #1, #2, #3, #4, #5, #6, #7), 346 (t), 353, 354 (tl, tr, bl, br), 377 (tl, tc, tr), 395 (sénégalaise, ivoirienne, ivoirien, congolaise, congolais), 409 (stade), 413 (#1)

Hill, Justine: 25 (bl), 333 (b)

Hodge, Joshua/Istock: 24 (tr)

Hodges, Walter/CORBIS: 176 (chinois)

Jitalia17/Istock: 225 (tr), 349 (bl)

Juno, Ray/CORBIS: 174-75

Kalina, Alex/Istock: 225 (tl), 225 (tc), 225 (br)

Karnow, Catherine/CORBIS: 176 (vietnamienne)

Kotlov, Alex/Istock: 22 (cr)

Kraft, Wolf: 13 (l, r), 48, 67 (l, r), 100 (bl), 124, 184 (t), 228, 365 (tr, cl, cc, bl), 369 (tl, tc, bl, br)

Landau, Robert/CORBIS: 424-25

Larson, June: 2 (br), 25 (#3), 109

Last, Victor: 203, 312 (t, b), 384 (c), 429 (t)

List, Richard/La Documentation française: 451 (b)

Magnum, Mike/Frozen Images: 45 (l)

McCarthy, Tom and Dee Ann/CORBIS: 204 (b)

Megapress: 234 (t)